Academic Administration

Sang M. Lee and
James C. Van Horn

Academic Administration
Planning, Budgeting, and Decision
Making with Multiple Objectives

Foreword by Ronald W. Roskins

University of Nebraska Press   Lincoln and London

Copyright 1983 by the University of Nebraska Press

Manufactured in the United States of America

The paper in this book meets the guidelines for permanence
and durability of the Committee on Production Guidelines for
Book Longevity of the Council on Library Resources.

Library of Congress Cataloging in Publication Data

Lee, Sang M., 1939-
Academic administration.

Includes index.
1. Universities and colleges – United States –
Administration.   2. Education, Higher – United
States – Planning.   3. System analysis.   I. Van Horn,
James C., 1945-   .   II. Title.
LB2341.L277   378.73   81-24061
ISBN 0-8032-2856-2   AACR2

To our families

Laura, Tosca, and Amy Lee

Nancy, Kristi, and Sarah Van Horn

Contents

Foreword

Today one of the most important elements of the American dream—providing quality educational opportunities for all of our citizens—has nearly been achieved. Of course there is still much more that should be done, but we as a nation can and should take pride in what we have accomplished. The numbers alone are staggering. During the 1981–82 academic year, more than $199.8 billion was spent on education in the United States, an increase of 240 percent over the amount spent just a decade ago. Adult citizens in this country now average 12.4 years of schooling. Over one-half of all Americans between the ages of three and thirty-four are currently enrolled in some sort of formal coursework. Slightly more than 31 percent of the individuals in this country over the age of eighteen have attended college or university classes for some period of time. Clearly this nation has extended meaningful educational opportunities to its citizens. As a direct result, we have helped these people improve their lives and have enriched the quality of our society.

Supporting educational programs is, however, only a first step. It is now, more than ever before, important for us to examine how effectively and efficiently our resources are being used. In a social and political climate which increasingly emphasizes accountability, a major evaluation of public support for education that places achievements and expenditures within a proper context is clearly in order. There is, in particular, a critical need for the development and application of appropriate analytical techniques for understanding and improving the administration of institutions of higher education.

In the midst of all of this, there is a strong need for the development and presentation of a systematic approach that both reflects the state of the art in administrative practice and accounts for the unique nature of institutions of higher education. The current work by professors Lee and Van Horn is, in my estimation, a giant step in that direction. In this work the authors have creatively integrated a planning-based management approach, referred to as ABO (Administration By Objectives), and a modern management science approach of goal programming that is capable of reflecting administrators' judgments in decision making. In my view this book represents one of the most important contributions to the field of systematic management of higher education in recent years.

This is a work which should be read by all who have an interest in higher education, and in particular by those who have an active role in the planning and administrative functions of this nation's colleges and universities. Properly understood and applied, the perspectives and techniques that are outlined will do much to enhance the quality and impact of all of our efforts.

Ronald W. Roskens
President
University of Nebraska

Preface

Until quite recently, colleges and universities could have been "well managed" by qualified and conscientious administrators acting on the basis of their best judgment. However, the environment in which higher education now finds itself requires that administrators receive assistance from more thorough and more analytical management techniques—ones that are capable of recognizing the importance of such things as faculty and student input, the role of tradition, the absence of measurable "output" products, and the special interests of constituents, along with the impact of a host of other factors on academic planning and decision making.

The administration of institutions of higher education is an extremely complex process. During the past decade, the increasing sophistication and cost of academic programs, coupled with double-digit rates of inflation and decreased financial support from government sources, have further complicated the planning and decision-making processes. These factors have led to a much stronger demand for greater attention to operational efficiency.

In our opinion, nearly all of the models currently available for application to issues in higher education are either too restrictive or too prescriptive. Most of them are "driven" by too much quantitative data and leave virtually no room for judgmental values. Not surprisingly, most of these models have been rejected by academic administrators. Our desire, both in the development of the methodology and in the writing of this book, was to select the best of what is currently available from the field of modern management and to synthesize it into an approach that is tailored for use by the academic community.

Our book describes a systematic approach to the management of institutions of higher education. The methodology couples administration by objectives (ABO), a management technique that helps academic administrators structure decisions in a systematic manner, with goal programming (GP), a decision-science tool that is ideally suited to the analysis of decisions involving multiple conflicting goals. The combination of ABO and GP provides a powerful new approach to planning and decision making in higher education.

It is clearly very important for all educational institutions in the United States, and particularly for colleges and universities, to concentrate increasingly on the formulation of long-term goals and objectives. Much of the tremendous productivity increase experienced by the Japanese economy over the past twenty years has been attributed to that country's concentration on future returns, even when attained at the expense of present gains. Dr. W. Edwards Deming, an eminent American whose lectures helped launch quality control in Japan during the 1950s, stresses that efforts, to be effective, require a longer-term direction. Furthermore, the preference for long-term growth over short-term gains naturally brings forth innovations. The procedure for higher education should thus be obvious: resources should be allocated to fulfill the long-term goals of a university and its constituencies. The next semester or the next year is not as important as the state of the institution five, ten, or twenty years from now. The factors that are required for innovation are knowledge about where the organization is headed and faith that it will get there in the future. Once long-term goals have been established, short-term objectives and action plans can be developed. These principles are the foundations on which the models in this book were developed, and they have been consistently incorporated into the managerial methods we are recommending.

The text begins in Part 1 with an overview of planning and budgeting in higher education and emphasizes the need to integrate those two processes. Also included is a review of the many modeling approaches aimed at effective resource allocation in higher education. Part 2 introduces ABO to the planning and management functions of colleges and universities and discusses the importance and benefits of using this approach. It also presents a chapter that covers the fundamentals of goal programming. Part 3 contains two chapters that provide an in-depth explanation of the goal programming application to academic administration. The first consists of five specific examples of the application of goal programming to actual problems in university decision making. An additional chapter details an extensive application of goal programming to the analysis of resource allocations in a large midwestern state university. This analysis clearly demonstrates the tremendous potential of the use of this tool in planning and decision making in colleges and universities. A discussion of decision-support systems is also included. The final chapter looks toward the future and outlines some of the many challenges academic administrators will face during the next decade.

The techniques detailed in this book can provide genuine insight into the important relationships among values and variables affecting institutions of higher education. As such, the book should be of interest to a wide range of people concerned with planning and budgeting in colleges and universities, including academic administrators at all levels, institutional research officers, planning commissions and governing boards, legislative fiscal analysts, and others. The book would also be appropriate for use in a college course on educational administration or public finance.

During the course of writing this book, we have enjoyed the assistance of a number of individuals. Special thanks go to Dr. Lori Sharp Franz of the University of South Carolina for her contributions to Chapter 7. We would also like to express appreciation to Dean Max D. Larsen of the College of Arts and Sciences and to Dean Gary Schwendiman of the College of Business Administration, both at the University of Nebraska–Lincoln, for their support of our efforts. Finally, Joyce Anderson, Joyce Thompson, Jane Chrastil, Cindy LeGrande, and Margaret Cullinane are gratefully acknowledged for their typing and editorial assistance.

Part One

Planning and Analysis for Academic Administration

Chapter 1 discusses the importance of planning and details the appropriate phases of the planning and budgeting processes for an institution of higher education. Particular attention is given to the differences between governance planning, leadership planning, and management planning. The conflicts that often exist between the developmental priorities of an institution and the ranking of resource allocation priorities in any given year are also examined. The section on budgeting outlines the many purposes served by budgets and also reviews several key issues such as the information burden of budgets, centralization of budgetary control, standard costing, and participatory decision making. Most important, the need for a systematic integration of the budgeting and planning processes is examined.

Chapter 2 provides a review of past and current applications of systems analysis in higher education. Decision models for higher education are viewed on a continuum ranging from the politically based incremental models to those encompassing economic rationality. Several models are discussed and analyzed, including NCHEM's RRPM 1.6, Stanford University's TRADES, and EDUCOM's EFPM.

Chapter 1

Educational Planning and Decision Making

Disputes over the best methods for academic management have existed since the turn of the century. In a 1910 report to the Carnegie Foundation for the Advancement of Teaching, faculty committees were criticized for demanding too large a role in university administration; university administrators were criticized for yielding too much autonomy to the departmental level, thus weakening the "essentials of real authority" (Cooke, 1910, p. 12). A 1972 Carnegie report echoed a similar theme and seemed to predict quite accurately the consequences which many institutions now face as a result of tighter resources:

> It will cause conflicts—of department versus department, of faculty against administration, of administration versus state authorities. Costs will confront quality; the new will challenge the old; the welfare of the total institution will battle against the status quo of its component parts. [Carnegie Commission on Higher Education, 1972, p. 21]

These findings are still of major concern to academic administrators. In a 1978 progress report based on its advisory planning conference comprised of twenty-three executives in higher education, the National Center for Higher Education Management Systems (NCHEMS) concluded that the key problem facing administrators was the lack of adequate research and development support for their efforts to make higher education more productive—more effective as well as more efficient (NCHEMS, 1978, p. 1). At the beginning of the decade of the 1980s, the most pressing issue for academic administrators, according to Shirley Hufstedler, the first secretary of education of the United States, was determining how to achieve financial solidity (Interview, 1980, p. 7).

The nature of the environment in which higher education functions is undergoing drastic changes: public bodies are demanding increased accountability; the traditional pool of potential college students is projected to decrease substantially; inflation, having already severely damaged many academic programs, is continuing at catastrophically high levels; mandatory retirement laws have been revised; and there is increased emphasis on issues of equity and protection. Even knowledge, the very commodity that higher education is in pursuit of, is expanding so rapidly that the resources needed to keep faculty and equipment up-to-date are placing a tremendous strain on some institutions. In addition, funding, particularly from state legislatures, is actually decreasing in some cases; and there are many other equally high priorities demanding additional tax funding at every level of government.

Figures 1.1, 1.2, and 1.3 depict vividly the trends that affected costs in education throughout the 1970s. During the early 1980s the trends changed some but actually became more perplexing—overall inflation was reduced, at least temporarily, to nearly one-half its previous pace but tax-based support decreased by an even higher percentage. The following framework projects the extent of financial pressure on higher education:

Forecast of Cost	*Budget Cost*	*Annual Rate of Increase*
Controllable Costs	70%	
Staff Salaries		6–7%
Benefits		8–9%
Noncontrollable Costs	30%	12–14%
Overall Rate of Cost Increase	100%	9–10%
Forecast of Revenues		
Tuition		
Gross		7%
Net		6–7%
Nontuition Revenues		8%
Overall Rate of Revenue Increase		7%
Net Difference/Shortfall in Revenues		2–3%

The obvious conclusion is that costs are expected to go up more quickly than revenues, by something in the range of 2–3 percent per year. Even if the nontuition sources of revenue increase as quickly as inflation, there will still be a financial squeeze on colleges and universities. And historically, in periods of rapid inflation nontuition revenues have never gone up enough to compensate for cost increases. Consequently the consensus is that, even if enrollment remains strong, the financial pressures of the 1980s will be much worse than those weathered in recent years.

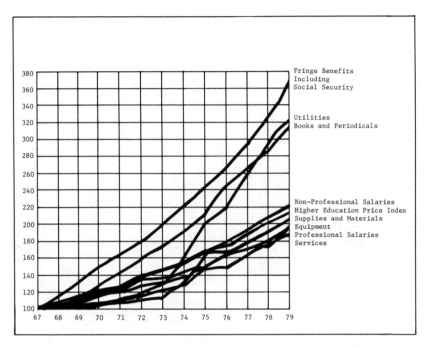

Figure 1.1
Historical Trends in Cost Components of Higher Education
SOURCE: D. Kent Halstead, Higher Education Prices and Price Indexes, HEW, GPO: 1975, p. 31, and Supplement (1978), p. 19.

Although executives in higher education have had close to a decade of experience in coping with high rates of inflation, they will still need an increasing level of sophistication and more creative approaches to the management of all of the resources of their institutions, including the human as well as the physical and financial resources.

The human resources—faculty and staff—are the most valuable assets of higher education institutions; yet, as depicted in figure 1.2, they have borne the greatest burden of inflation, losing purchasing power at a greater rate than workers generally since the early 1970s. Not much more can reasonably be taken from them to fight inflation in higher education.

On the physical capital side, higher education has likewise increased the intensity of its use of facilities, partially because new construction has declined while enrollments have continued to increase. In addition, deferred maintenance is probably accumulating to the point that some repairs can no longer be postponed without incurring actual physical risk to the people on campuses.

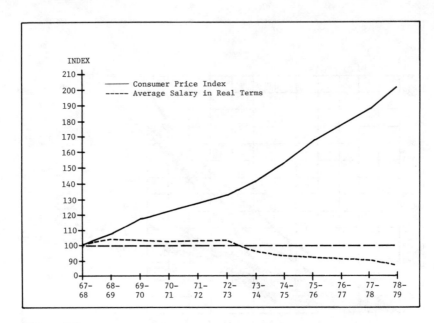

Figure 1.2
Index of Average Faculty Salary in Real Terms
and the Consumer Price Index
SOURCE: American Association of University Professors, "An Era of Continuing Decline:
Annual Report on the Economic Status of the Profession, 1978–1979." *Academe: Bulletin of
the AAUP*, September, 1979, p. 6.

These are some of the factors which, along with increasing pressures from
changing market conditions, are requiring educational institutions to develop
keener and more critical methods for use in supporting their planning and
decision-making processes. As economic conditions in general have become
more restrictive, scholars, planners, and management specialists have turned
their attention to higher education. In part, this is an indication of the per-
ceived importance of education to the continued development of this society.
It also represents concern about increasing the effectiveness of the leadership
functions of administrators in higher education. However, confusion continues to exist in both management and higher education over the best way to
arrive at the most appropriate use of resources available from public and private sources.

The purpose of this book is to present a framework for improving the planning, budgeting, and decision-making processes in higher education through
an integrated approach to administration by multiple objectives. The book has
the following three specific objectives:

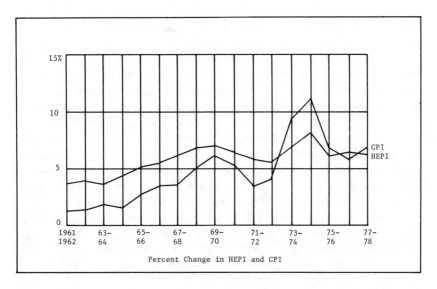

Figure 1.3
Comparison of Historical Cost Increases: Higher Education Index
and Consumer Price Index
SOURCE: D. Kent Halstead, Higher Education Prices and Price Indexes, HEW, GPO: 1975
pp. 9 and 31; and Supplement, pp. 10 and 19.

1. To bring together those concepts from the fields of management, management science, economics, educational administration, and systems analysis that are most useful for systematic planning, budgeting, and decision making in colleges and universities.
2. To incorporate these concepts into the *goal programming* framework and describe an administrative process which is capable of treating multiple objectives in an integrated manner.
3. To illustrate the application of the concepts and techniques of goal programming to real-world examples of problems faced by educational institutions.

Planning

The key to more effective leadership in the management of institutions of higher education is the wise application of improved principles of planning. Through planning, institutions can better understand the future toward which they are moving and can anticipate the nature and level of resources that will be necessary if their goals are to be achieved.

The importance of collegiate planning has been stressed for many years. In the mid-1950s, the Ford Foundation, under the leadership of Sidney Tickton, urged each college and university to prepare a ten-year long-range plan in anticipation of the enrollment bulge to come a decade later. The Ford Foundation tried in a variety of ways to stimulate institutions to formulate master plans, and that stimulation did produce some very successful ones. Most notably, Stanford University's $100 million development campaign was undertaken as part of that institution's plan for expansion, a project which had its beginnings in the Ford Foundation program. Since the 1950s, agreement on the need for and importance of planning to the viability and vitality of institutions has been well-documented. However, considerable confusion still remains about the intricacies of the planning process and how it should be carried out within the complexities of today's educational institutions.

Principles of Planning

Planning as a process cuts across the structures of governance, management, and leadership in higher education. Confusion over this fact has created difficulty for many institutions in their efforts to develop and sustain effective planning practices (Millett, 1977). To circumvent these problems it is important to have a clear understanding of governance planning, management planning, and leadership planning within a college or university.

Governance is the authority and responsibility for making the *major* decisions affecting the mission, programs, enrollment size, standards of quality, personnel policies, and budget of an institution. This authority is usually vested by law or by charter in a governing board. The general pattern is that board decisions are influenced by recommendations from campus leaders.

Campus-wide governance, as opposed to institutional governance, usually includes formalized structures such as the student senate, faculty senate, campus counsels, and a campus executive committee. Generally these groups are used to articulate the concerns and desires of their constituents to the campus president so that they may be incorporated into the president's recommendations to the governing board.

Management, on the other hand, can be viewed as work planning and work performance. For most academic institutions, work performance for the major output programs (instruction, research, creative activity, and public service) is handled by academic departments. For example, the basic decisions about course content and class offerings as well as the actual delivery of these services are provided by faculty members; initial faculty personnel decisions are made at the departmental level; even proposals for new areas of academic inquiry originate from departmental units. Program, budgeting, and personnel coordination are generally undertaken through college and campus-wide management structures. Support programs such as the library, student services, plant services, and administrative support are most commonly organized on a centralized basis to serve the institution as a whole.

Usually a governing board delegates a considerable amount of discretion to a president and to a faculty to interpret its policies and to make decisions on management matters. Likewise the chief executive officer usually is assisted by several principal associates (vice presidents) who have both line and staff responsibilities. Normally, the president and his associates will be instrumental in developing and recommending the institution's budget, and will also have input into most decisions made by the governing board. It is expected that these decisions and recommendations will be based on consultation with faculty, student, and alumni groups.

Leadership is the essential tie between governance and the management of an institution, providing guidance and direction for the entire enterprise. Leadership refers to directing behavior into channels that promote the achievement of the organization's goals. The role of leadership is vested in the president but is operationally defined in terms of the totality of functions performed by executives as individuals or as a group. The role of the president as leader is critical, but the functions of leadership are becoming more and more collegial in nature (Millett, 1977, p. 23).

As mentioned earlier, planning as a process cuts across all three of the structures of governance, management, and leadership. For the planning process to be successful, it is essential that institutions have a clear definition of governance planning, management planning, and leadership planning. The interrelationships of these three types of planning must be well understood in order to be carried out appropriately.

Planning Factors

A simplified view of the major factors that must be considered when establishing campus priorities and program profiles for an institution is depicted in figure 1.4. Each of these factors will be discussed briefly below.

Before any institution can address an issue such as program offerings or campus priorities, it must have in hand a statement of its mission: its educational philosophy, role and scope, and goals and objectives. "Educational philosophy" refers to the basic values held by the institution concerning the role of education in society, the role of basic and applied research, the purposes of a liberal education, the meaning of academic freedom, and similar educa-

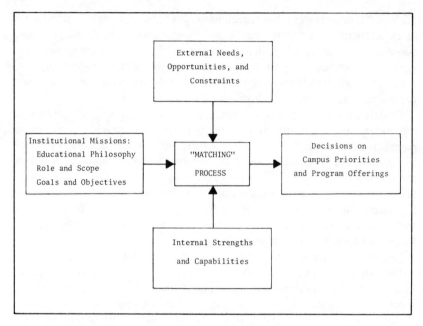

Figure 1.4
Major Inputs to Decisions on Campus Priorities and
Program Offerings

tional premises (Shirley and Volkwein, 1978, p. 475). The "role-and-scope" statement serves to focus the attention of the institution, not by identifying specific priorities or areas of emphasis, but rather by identifying general institutional boundaries.

The development of the role-and-scope statement falls in the area of governance planning. The types of things which must be considered under governance planning including changing social expectations, changing economic circumstances, changing concerns in governmental planning, and changing resources. The general boundaries developed by such mission statements should relate to the relative emphasis on graduate and undergraduate education, major constituencies to be served, relative emphasis on teaching, research, and service, and, in the instance of a multicampus system, governance planning must include decisions about the relationships of one campus to the other components of the system. These and other boundary dimensions must be clearly stated in order to provide the basic framework for subsequent decisions on campus priorities.

It is important, of course, that governing boards consider the views of the governance agencies of internal constituent groups. Such internal governance agencies generally wish to offer advice about alternative solutions to critical issues. These internal governance groups should have the privilege of being kept informed, of being asked for advice, and of being invited to help determine solutions. But internal governance agencies cannot be the decisive voice in institutional affairs. The final word in governance planning clearly belongs to governing boards. To reiterate, then, governance planning develops boundaries that delineate *what* the institution hopes to accomplish, rather than *how*.

Leadership planning involves the development of a planning structure, the establishment of planning guidelines (including pertinent data), and an insistence that management units prepare operating plans with care and precision. The factors that must be considered under leadership planning are shown in figure 1.4 as external needs, opportunities, and constraints, and should be recognized as the second major influence on program offerings and priorities. Examples of the focus of leadership planning would include the following:

The social/demographic characteristics of the geographical area
Location in the area of unique institutions or organizations
The types of industry located in the area
The existence of other area educational institutions, their missions, and
    the opportunities for collaboration
Other distinguishing characteristics or resources of a geographical area
    that may present unique opportunities
Distinguishing characteristics of the area that constrain the institution's
    ability to develop certain areas of knowledge.

These types of major areas must be assessed in terms of the educational philosophy and role and scope of the campus, to determine if particular needs or resources in the environment promise to reinforce the institution's educational mission. In general, the purpose of the environmental assessment is to identify key external factors, assess them in relation to campus mission, and finally to identify opportunities and constraints for particular types of programs (Shirley and Volkwein, 1977, p. 476). This assessment of external phenomena reveals what the campus *might do* or, in some instances, what it *should do*.

The third set of factors from figure 1.4, relating to the assessment of internal strengths and capabilities, relates to the process of management planning. This factor provides an indication of what the university *can do* or conversely what it *cannot do* (in quality fashion). As mentioned earlier, management planning evolves primarily from the work units of a department or college; management planning involves projecting the objectives of these units, their work loads, and their resource requirements over a future time span. While management planning is performed by output units (academic departments, research centers, and so forth), it must be guided by a general set of expectations developed by governance and leadership planning.

As indicated in figure 1.4, decisions on campus priorities and program offerings result from a proper "match" of (1) mission, (2) external factors, and (3) internal strengths and capabilities. This matching process is the decision-making part of the academic-administrative management process, and it is the responsibility of the campus leadership and management sectors. The improvement of this matching process is the subject of the remainder of this book.

Types of Planning

Most institutions have traditionally divided the planning process into three types: (1) academic planning, (2) facilities planning, and (3) financial planning. Academic planning is most frequently addressed at the college, school, and department levels. Faculty recruitment priorities are addressed, along with other departmental needs, in one-to-one interactions at successively higher managerial levels. Most universities then have a campus-wide review body which is responsible for assessing the quality and developmental needs of all programs. Campus-wide academic planning committees usually couch their deliberations under some assumptions about the future availability of financial resources. In other words, their planning is based on a set of givens regarding the future availability of resources.

Facilities planning, also usually carried out by a campus-wide division or committee, assumes the responsibility for insuring that decisions on space reflect the academic priorities of the campus. Facilities planning responsibilities include setting priorities on new capital construction requests, the assignment of classrooms, offices, and other academic program space. When a committee structure is used, these committees are the primary avenue for satisfying the space needs of high-growth programs through reallocation of existing facilities. These committees also function on the basis of some assumptions about the availability of new capital construction funding, or the possibility of renovating and improving existing space.

Financial planning itself is usually broken down into two major types of financial plans: capital and operating. Capital financial planning is generally undertaken by the facilities planning committee and then submitted as a part of the institution's total budget request. The operating budget plan is generally more complex than the capital budget, of course, and is nearly always prepared in a one- or two-year context. Moreover, the budgeting philosophy in most institutions is an incremental one. Although many institutions have attempted "planning-programming-budgeting systems" or "zero-based" budgeting, the one-year focus in financial planning is by far more prevalent. To a large extent, this is the result of the one-year time horizons of external bodies, including legislatures.

In general, few institutions attempt a systematic approach to forecasting long-range financial needs and resources, tying these to academic and facilities planning efforts. The goal of this book is to provide a mechanism for systematically integrating these major planning efforts.

Program Objectives

Second in importance only to the need for a clear statement of the institution's mission, structured with an awareness of the external environment, is the need for detailed planning for specific programs. This level of planning, described earlier as management planning, provides the essential building blocks for the total institutional plan. The typical programs in a college or university which are normally expected to develop their own statements of objectives and plans for achieving them are: (1) output programs (instruction, research, public service, and independent operations); (2) support, or overhead programs (academic support, student services, institutional support, and plant operation and maintenance); and (3) auxiliary operations.

John Millett (1977, p. 23) argues that good planning requires that the management of each of the above-mentioned types of programs be asked to develop clear statements of program objectives and to candidly provide their own self-assessment. To some extent, this concept of program planning within subordinate units can be the most difficult to put into effect. The nature of the little planning that did take place in collegiate institutions during the 1950s and 1960s was that it was presidentially originated and presidentially centered. Even today in many major institutions the involvement of all constituencies in the planning process is somewhat superficial and incomplete. Given the expected future of educational institutions and the complexities of the current and anticipated future externalities, it will be increasingly important for schools, departments, institutes, offices and their chairs, directors, deans, and the like, to not only participate in management planning but also to be ready to accept the results.

Program plans may be organized in various ways. Under the decentralized approach, each program or subordinate unit is expected to develop plans which, when reviewed, and as decisions are made and consolidations occur (the matching process) at higher levels, dovetail into the campus plan. While program plans can and do vary considerably with respect to complexity and sophistication, there are some elements which should be common to all plans. The following is an example of the type of information that should be developed for each program or unit:

1. Programmatic Information
    Broad rationale for the program and an indication of how the various elements should interact
    Behavioral objectives in the program
    Statements of degree requirements, actual courses to be offered, etc.
2. Evaluative Criteria
    A. Quality
        Quality of faculty
        Quality of students
        Quality of library holdings
        Quality of facilities and equipment
    B. Need
        Centrality of mission
        Present student demand
        Projected student demand
        Demand for graduates
        Comparative advantage
        Vocational advantage
    C. Costs
        Cost/revenue relationships
        Required expenditures by category
        Projected need for income
        Detailed budget changes expected within two to five years, with increases arranged according to priority
        Facilities requirements
3. Organizational Structure
    Duties and responsibilities of the various administrative officers
    Statements on the relationship between the program and higher, lower, or lateral programs and activities
4. Program Review
    Statements on evaluation techniques to be used for full program review

The evaluative criteria listed in item number 2 above are essentially those outlined by Shirley and Volkwein (1978) in their article on establishing academic program priorities. These authors have further provided "rating categories" for these criteria and an explanation of what impact the evaluation of individual programs might have on "program clusters." They also provide an example of the sample results of a program evaluation process for three programs, A, B, and C, as outlined in table 1.1.

Table 1.1

Sample Results of a Program-Evaluation Process*

Evaluative Criteria	Program		
	A	B	C
Quality			
Faculty	Strong	Excellent	Weak
Student	High	High	Low
Library	Adequate	Excellent	Adequate
Facility	Adequate	Excellent	Adequate
Need			
Centrality to mission	Yes	No	No
Present student demand	Declining	Stable	Stable
Projected student demand	Declining	Stable	Stable
Demand for graduates	Low	High	Low
Locational advantage	No	Yes	No
Comparative advantage	No	Yes	No
Cost/Revenue Relationship	Adequate	Adequate	Poor

*SOURCE: Robert C. Shirley and Frederick J. Volkwein, "Establishing Academic Program Priorities," *Journal of Higher Education*, 49, no. 5 (1978).

Clearly, evaluative criteria (listed under item number 2) are the most crucial for use by academic administrators in the decision-making process about campus priorities. As indicated earlier, this information is then used in the process of determining the proper match of (1) mission, (2) external factors, and (3) internal strengths and capabilities.

While somewhat oversimplified, table 1.1 does provide the basic building blocks for the development of decisions on priorities. Once all programs (existing and proposed) have been sorted as described above, there remains the issue of how to ensure that priority decisions are reflected in the budgetary process. It is very important to note, however, that a ranking of programs in terms of *developmental priorities* is *not* the same as a ranking of *resource allocation priorities* in any given year. For instance, frequently it is necessary for an institution to first provide increased support for continuing programs that have not been funded at an acceptable level of quality in the past, with the secondary priorities being to provide those resources needed to facilitate the attainment of national leadership in those programs that are already at or near that level of quality. The integration of decisions on priorities with decisions on resource allocations is perhaps the most important function of the leadership of an academic institution. Before this integration process is discussed further, it is important to review the nature of the budgeting process in higher education.

Budgeting

The essential purposes of budgeting in higher education are to translate plans into actions, to distribute resources, and to foster accountability. The traditional view of the budget as simply a statement regarding expenditure and revenue projections for a future period of time is really much too limited in terms of scope and function. In colleges and universities, the development, communication, and execution of the budget lie at the heart of the management process and affect, either directly or indirectly, most leadership and management decisions.

Some authors distinguish between the passive nature of a budget and the active process of budgeting. Herman Heiser (1959) defined a budget as an overall blueprint or a comprehensive plan of operations and actions, expressed in financial terms. He viewed budgeting, on the other hand, as the process of preparing a budget, a function that is used for coordination as well as control of an organization. From either point of view budgets are, in reality, a representation of expectations about the future, a portrayal of all the planning of the organization.

Most business organizations now have, and have had for a long period of time, well-developed, comprehensive budgets that encompass every phase of their plans and operations. The same statement, however, generally cannot be said of higher education.

Alfred D. Chandler has reported that the Du Pont Corporation was making advanced use of statistical and budgeting data well before 1918. At that time, one of the functions of that company's treasury department was to assist the functional departments and the company's executive committee to "allocate rationally funds and other resources by providing forecasts of probable conditions extending 12-months in advance . . . revised every 12 months" (1966, p. 81). Each specific request for capital appropriations at Du Pont had to include the particulars of the cost of, need for, and estimated rate of return, for any proposed project. The various budgets of the Du Pont Corporation were quantatively and logically related to form an integrated system.

This same era was really just the beginning of what Allen Schick (1966, p. 243) describes as the executive budget movement in governmental budgeting. Before that time, municipal budgets had concentrated on functional accounting designed to facilitate program decisions. The 1912 Taft Commission (U.S. President's Commission on Economy and Efficiency, 1912, p. 210), for example, strongly recommended that expenditures be classified in categories such as class of work, organizational unit, character of expense, and method of financing. However, the mood soon turned to using budgets to develop a system of expenditure control. In an age when personnel and purchasing controls were unreliable, the main consideration became how to prevent administrative improprieties. In 1917 the New York Bureau of Municipal Research (p. 10) recommended the total "defunctionalization" of budgets in order to give more priority to the object and control orientation. Once installed, object controls rapidly gained status as an indispensible deterrent to administrative misbehavior in the area of governmental finance. Although the planning and management functions of budgeting were not absent during this time period, they were clearly subordinate to the control function. During the period between about 1920 and 1935, most states adopted some type of budget innovation which is now generally considered to have been control oriented. Other state-level reforms during this period generally resulted in reinforcing a strong role for the governor in the development of the state's budget. The idea was that the state's chief executive was the only one who could be made responsible for leadership (Schick, 1966, p. 246). At the federal level, this movement took the form of the Budget and Accounting Act of 1921, which established the Bureau of the Budget. The executive budget movement led to such innovations as centralized purchasing, competitive bidding, civil service reform, uniform accounting procedures, and expenditure audits.

The second major era of reform in public administration budgeting has been described by Schick as a period of performance budgeting. From the mid-1930s until the late 1960s, the focus in governmental budgeting was on good management to achieve stated goals. This represented a shift from the use of the budget as an instrument of expenditure control, to its use as a means of promoting effective management of public activities. This period saw a greatly increased scope of governmental activity, with New Deal projects, World War II, and various postwar economic recovery programs. The emphasis during these times was thus placed on output, and the "management" of activities to best achieve the needed output. Many of the techniques used in the performance budgeting movement were derived from cost accounting and scientific management studies, including the use of detailed workload studies that were compiled rigorously by administrators to justify their requests for funds. On a higher level of sophistication, there were attempts to develop work and productivity standards. One widespread artifact of the performance budgeting era and the desire to relate output to resource input, is the concept of formula budgeting.

The third budgeting movement focused on planning. During the 1960s and 1970s, the planning orientation began to dominate public-administration budgeting. This increased emphasis on planning, accompanied by new economic theories and the widespread availability of computers, led to the development of Planning, Programming, and Budgeting Systems (PPBS) in public administration. Charles Hitch (1967), for instance, contends that the separation of the planning and budgeting functions was one of the major sources of difficulty in the Department of Defense and quickly led Robert McNamara to introduce PPBS into that agency of the federal government. Reports of success with PPBS in the Department of Defense later prompted President Lyndon Johnson to issue an executive order that directed all federal agencies to implement the PPBS approach to their budget planning. Additionally, changing the name of the federal government's Bureau of the Budget (BOB) to the Office of Management and Budget (OMB) in 1970 was in part based on a recognition of the potential planning and management role that a budgeting office should play in coordinating organizational units. The importance of decision-making techniques such as cost-benefit analysis, systems analysis, and operations research also increased considerably during this period.

Today, many of the aspects of these three governmental reform eras can be observed in the budgeting practices in postsecondary education: many institutions still employ the position and line-item controls of the executive-budget movement; formulas that resemble performance-budgeting work-load measurements remain common in many states; and variations of PPBS or zero-based budgeting are the accepted practice at many institutions (Caruthers and Orwig, 1979, p. 28).

Functions of Budgets

In its most important role, the budget is the formal mechanism through which plans become undertakings. Clearly, organizational plans of any type must first be translated into a formal budget request if they are later to become operational activities. Subsequently, the turning point for plans to become programs is the authorization of budgetary spending authority for the program's activities. Decisions to begin programs, to modify their scope, or discontinue them, are most directly declared through the budgetary process. This method of structuring the approved financial plans and policies of an institution so that they are carried out in an efficient and effective manner is the *management* function of a budget.

While budgets translate plans into actions they also provide messages that are effective communication devices throughout the organization. The efficiency of budgets as communication devices is dependent upon the extent to which they transmit the same meaning to different people. Some aspects of the budgetary system are highly efficient in this respect. For example, the quantitative information about specific material requirements found in purchasing budgets for capital construction projects transmits meaning in very exact terms. But the quantitative preciseness of budgets does not eliminate other kinds of distortion. Budget information is often subject to different interpretations and may convey a variety of meanings. For instance, the president of a university may view a reduction in a department's budget as an inducement to that department to increase productivity, perhaps by increased faculty workloads; the department head, however, may see it as an unjustified attempt to curtail the department's activities; junior faculty members, on the other hand, may feel that it threatens such dire consequences as unemployment!

Budgets also serve as an instrument for achieving internal and external accountability. Internally, budgets provide a mechanism for the control of operational activities. This control function is usually effected through accounting and reporting procedures that restrict the transfer of funds from one account to another, limit the number of positions available to a department, do not allow for the future expenditure of funds once departmental balances are depleted, and so on. Furthermore, the budget provides important documentation for reporting purposes and allows for the fulfillment of legal requirements often required by funding agencies. Externally, the budget also helps to communicate to constituencies the activities that will be supported by the allocation of funds and the expected results of those activities.

Some Issues in Budgeting for Higher Education

Considering the importance of budgeting to institutions of higher education, it should not be surprising that many points of contention surround the budgeting process. J. Kent Caruthers and Melvin Orwig (1979, p. 13) have organized the major issues of budgeting in postsecondary education into five categories: participation, centralization of authority, equity, information burdens, and cost, outcomes, and performance information. These will be briefly reviewed below.

There are many diverse groups that desire to participate in the budgeting process in higher education. Furthermore, the unique and often conflicting roles of the various members of these groups becomes a complicating factor in the decision-making process in colleges and universities. For example, faculty members on the one hand are managers of the institution; among other things, they initiate new areas of academic inquiry, direct research projects, teach courses, and advise students. On the other hand, however, discussions between faculty members and higher-level administrators often take on a labor-management relationship. Faculty members' claims to participation in the development of the budget are therefore made on the basis of two roles of equal importance (AAUP, 1976). In a similar fashion, students function in a multipurpose capacity: as consumers, as participants in campus governance organizations, and as products of the institution. The roles of legislators, state government department heads, alumni groups, and the general public are also complicated by multiple-role relationships with the institution. Balancing the diverse interests of these many participant groups in postsecondary education, and satisfying their claims for equal participation is a major challenge in the development of budgets (Caruthers and Orwig, 1979, p. 14).

The issue of centralization of authority through budgeting is closely tied to the issue of participation. For example, faculty members who feel that their department head did not consult them sufficiently in the preparation of the departmental budget are likely to think that the budgeting process was too centralized. A similar relationship exists between the department head and the dean, between the dean and the appropriate vice president of the institution, and so on up the line. Furthermore, the issue of centralization of budgetary responsibility does not stop within the institution. The Carnegie Foundation for the Advancement of Teaching has noted an "overall tendency towards centralization of authority over higher education—from the campus to the multi-campus system and from governing boards to state mechanisms." The Carnegie Commission went on to voice its regret for this trend because "it reduces the influence of students and faculty members and of campus administrators and of members of campus governing boards. . . . it also reduces their sense of responsibility" (1976, p.11).

Perhaps the most widespread concern about budgeting and the allocation of resources in higher education, is the question of equity. The concept of equity implies that similar resources will be provided for similar individuals, similar programs, and so on. Issues of equity range from the prevalent concerns of faculty members about salaries and programatic support, to questions about the costs of parking spaces. Other concepts of equity relate to having all programs evaluated by the same technique and maintaining consistent quality standards. The resolution of many equity issues has been difficult to achieve and thus has led to numerous grievances, court cases, and new public laws.

Some states and institutions have turned to the use of formula budgeting in order to overcome some of the concerns about equity, by relating the allocation of resources to "standard" measures of activities. The unique characteristics of individuals, programs, and institutions, however, has limited the usefulness of these types of formulas and has brought about criticism of their use from many of the participants in the budgeting process. A further discussion of economic comparisons, formula funding, and equity appears in Chapter 2 of this book.

One of the more recent issues relating to the development of budgets in higher education is the desire for standardized cost information. Pressure from the federal-government level for submitting standardized unit cost information about budgets for institutions of higher education was reflected in recommendations made in 1973 by the National Commission on the Financing of Post-Secondary Education. Since that time several states, as well as governing boards of higher education, have mandated that institutions develop both request budgets and report budgets by the use of standardized costing formats and categories.

In recent years, several efforts have been undertaken on a national basis to achieve better consistency in the information used in postsecondary education. For instance, the National Center for Higher Education Management Systems has developed information procedures which are now widely used by institutions and state agencies throughout the United States and Canada. Also, the National Center for Educational Statistics publishes several manuals to support the annual Higher Education General Information Survey. Because of these developmental efforts, it has been possible to improve somewhat the comparability of the budgeting information coming from colleges and universities. However, many authors and many faculty and administrators still feel quite strongly about the diversity of institutional needs and argue strongly against standardized costing systems.

As noted by Caruthers and Orwig (1979) in their outline of the issues relating to budgeting in higher education, the amount of information needed for budgeting is not the only concern. Questions are often raised about the nature of the information as well as the validity of measurements in general. The quantification of costs, outcomes, and performance information for higher education is a very difficult task. There are questions as to whether the outputs of higher education can or should be measured; and even if they can be, it is equally questionable whether it is economically feasible to do so on any long-term repetitive basis. In addition, the structure of higher education is complicated by the presence of numerous partial, complementary, and joint products. Educational systems are not organized in such a way that provides information particularly relevant to the development of production-function types of cost reporting procedures. In other words, many feel that education should not be viewed as a product but rather as a process (Thompson and Carter, 1973, p. 1). These issues will also be discussed in greater depth in Chapter 2 of this book. They are mentioned here because of their importance to the information burdens of the budgeting process.

Budgetary Time Cycles

Budgeting in higher education can generally be broken down in four time cycles: (1) fiscal year operations; (2) annual budgeting; (3) short-term academic staff planning; and (4) long-term staff planning. Each of these cycles requires different types of information and support.

Fiscal year operations. During the fiscal year, a department or school generally has some control over expenditures for many parts of its budget, including such things as filling vacancies caused by leaves or attrition, expenditures for supplies and materials, expenditures for equipment, and for travel. A department or school can also hope to influence spending for new programs by acquiring grants or contracts from external agencies, or by obtaining gifts. If however, problems develop with either the lack of income or increased expenses, a department or school will run a deficit that represents additional implicit funding from the institution. If the department or school should run a surplus, the surplus is generally used to meet other needs of the institution. Generally deficits or surpluses can be carried forward on a departmental level into a subsequent fiscal year, thus providing some management incentive for departments to balance their budgets.

To facilitate control to a balanced fiscal-year operation, schools and departments are generally provided with periodic reports. One of the most useful ones is a monthly income-expense report which lists and categorizes expenditures. Often, these reports project year-end balances or variances in advance, based on linear approximations.

Annual budgeting. The second major time cycle for budgeting is the annual fiscal-year budget. In the development of the annual budget, a school or department must decide, consistent with general guidelines, what it can and should do to influence items such as: enrollments and tuition income; grant, contract, and gift income; overhead recovery income; faculty and staff salary and benefit expenses; operating and travel expenses; and controllable overhead costs.

The annual budgeting process usually proceeds through several phases ranging from the presentation of an outline budget, to the formal approval of detailed departmental budgets. The outline budgets should be prepared early in the budgeting cycle by the budget office of the institution for presentation to the colleges and departments. These initial budgets are, in essence, an extension of the previous year's income-expense budget, with projections forward to include all known and probable changes for the coming year. These projections should reflect university trial guidelines for tax-based increases, tuition increases, gifts, salary increases, the effects of inflation, and new overhead rates. At the University of Pennsylvania these outline budgets are called "default" budgets in order to stress that the projections indicate what is likely to happen by default if the school does not take corrective action (Strauss, et al., 1979, p. 160).

Starting from the outline-budget projections, schools and departments then work closely with deans, the campus vice presidents, and the budget office to develop an acceptable, balanced budget plan for the coming year. Of course, care should be taken to assure that these annual budgets are compatible with previously approved, longer-term budget plans. In addition, considerable emphasis should be given during the discussion stages of budget development to determining the specific amount of tax-based allocation to be provided to a school or department for the coming year. Typically, however, there is only a small amount of flexibility in this area when dealing with the annual budgeting period.

Once a satisfactory agreement is reached regarding the annual budget, the outline budgets are formally approved and detailed budgets and payroll documents are prepared.

Biannual budget planning. The third major time cycle for financial decision making is biannual budget planning. This cycle is needed in order to be more effective in terms of academic staff planning, particularly at institutions where contracts require a full year's notification of intent not to reappoint faculty members. Biannual budget planning allows for a more appropriate emphasis on short-term (two to five years) academic staff planning.

Academic staff planning. The fourth major time cycle for financial decision making is the five-year academic staff and program plan. This planning concentrates on projecting the resources that will be available with some confidence to support long-term commitments. On the income side, five-year financial planning must include a review of such things as undergraduate tuition, graduate and professional tuition, state tax-base support, federal funds, gifts and nonfederal funds, yield from endowments, and sales and service income for *each* of the institution's programs. On the expense side, consideration must be given to the flow of faculty and staff, tenure guidelines, prudent staffing levels, and instructional workloads, again for *each* of the institution's programs. The five-year financial planning cycle must then allow for analyzing decisions on campus priorities and program offerings as part of the "matching" process described in figure 1.4.

It is imperative that colleges and universities develop longer-range projections for both the income and expense portions of all of their planning alternatives. Often institutions are not fully aware of the long-term costs of many of their major decisions. For example, an appointment to tenure is an obligation on the part of an institution to maintain a professor in his area of expertise for a period of perhaps thirty years or more. In constant dollars, that commitment is an obligation to expend on behalf of that professor an amount very close to one million dollars; when adjusted for inflation at the rate of only 8 percent per year, the sum is well over three million dollars!

Integration of Planning and Budgeting

To be effective, the planning and budgeting processes in higher education must be closely integrated. The typical academic planning process has been for institutions to (1) define their philosophy and mission, (2) establish goals in keeping with that mission, (3) devise programs to attain such goals, and (4) *then* attempt to marshal the human and financial resources necessary to maintain the institution and to achieve the goals established in the earlier parts of the planning process. All too often, however, the last phase of this process is the most difficult and leads to frustration and disappointment for all parties involved.

Unfortunately, the planning and budgeting processes in higher education inherently conflict. Planning is a very positive, developmental kind of process; budgeting, on the other hand, is usually a constraining influence. Because of these distinctively different characteristics, the two processes cannot be viewed as one undertaking. The relationships between budgeting and the functions of leadership planning and decision making in higher education are depicted in figure 1.5. As shown in this figure, the correct role for budgeting in the academic management process is to provide for the analysis and synthesis of financial information, within the leadership, planning, and decision-making processes. Budgeting is thus a part of the "matching" process outlined in figure 1.4.

The synthesis role of budgeting is an extremely important one but is often misunderstood. For example, a classic flaw in much of the planning that is done in higher education is to assume that conclusions come directly from the data that are being analyzed or reviewed. This is simply not true. Rather, the conclusions flow from the perceptions and values of the decision maker. This simple relationship is depicted in figure 1.6.

A more correct view of the analysis/synthesis process, and the way in which recommendations are made, has been explained by Henry Levin (see Frances, 1980, p. 12) and is depicted in figure 1.7. In most real-world situations, and particularly in institutions of higher education, conclusions that are reached and decisions which are made are based on the values and perceptions of the decision makers. Furthermore, the recommendations which come from these conclusions are built not only on values and perceptions, but are also derived from a set of ambitions.

The need for tying together the planning and budgeting processes in higher education has been emphasized by several major studies. One of these, reported by J. Victor Baldridge and Michael L. Tierney (1979), summarizes the impact of the Exxon Education Foundation's Resource Allocation Management Program (RAMP) on forty-nine institutions which had received grants under Exxon's program. The fundamental goal of the study was to determine

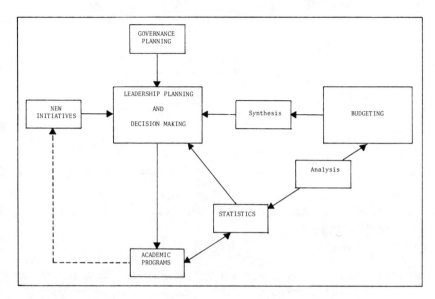

Figure 1.5
Relationship of Budgeting to the
Leadership, Planning, and Decision-Making Functions

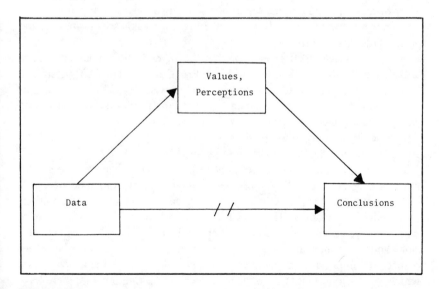

Figure 1.6
The Role of Values and Perceptions in the
Decision-Making Process

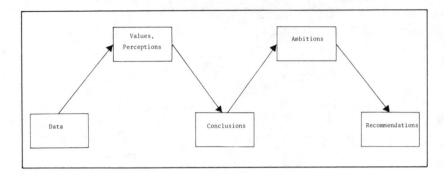

Figure 1.7
The Role of Values, Perceptions, and Ambitions in the
Decision-Making Process

whether improvements in management techniques have a measurable impact
on institutions of higher education. One of the major conclusions of this extensive research project was that planning and budgeting are more successful
when they are closely tied together. In the words of these authors, "Planning
becomes a farce when it is not clearly tied to budgets and money" (p. 164).
They further reported that the separation of the two functions of planning and
budgeting was unquestionably one of the biggest weaknesses in most of the
projects they studied (p. 11).

A separate research effort sponsored by the W. K. Kellogg Foundation, and
undertaken by the Academy for Educational Development (AED), studied
"change" management at sixty colleges and universities. The report on this
project concludes that management information is a primary concern in
change management. According to the project's director, John D. Millett,
"Too often the search on a college or university campus, as in society, is for a
simple solution rather than for an intelligent choice" (1977, p. 14).

If better information and more intelligent decisions are to become part of
the planning and budgeting processes in higher education, then decision-
makers must be able to structure their own values, perceptions, and ambitions
in a meaningful manner. They must also be able to see the impact of these
factors, as well as those of a host of other considerations, on their own conclusions and recommendations. While most management researchers have recognized the importance of being able to model these types of value trade-offs
which are so important to the academic decision-making process, there have
been very few attempts to actually demonstrate a methodology for their
examination. This book provides insights and directions to this dilemma

through the application of goal programming to the management of institutions of higher education.

References

American Association of University Professors. *AAUP Policy Documents and Reports*. Washington, D.C.: AAUP, 1977.

American Association of University Professors, Committee T on College and University Government. "The Role of the Faculty in Budgetary and Salary Matters." *AAUP Bulletin* 62 (December 1976): 379–81.

Baldridge, J. Victor, and Tierney, Michael L. *New Approaches to Management*. San Francisco: Jossey-Bass, 1979.

Carnegie Commission on Higher Education. *The More Effective Use of Resources*. New York: McGraw-Hill, 1972.

Carnegie Foundation for the Advancement of Teaching. *The States and Higher Education: A Proud Past and a Vital Future*. San Francisco, Jossey-Bass, 1976.

Caruthers, J. Kent, and Orwig, Melvin. *Budgeting in Higher Education*. Washington, D.C.: American Association for Higher Education, 1979.

Chandler, Alfred D., Jr. *Strategy and Structure*. Garden City, New York: Doubleday, 1966.

Cooke, Morris L. *Academic and Industrial Efficiency*. New York: Carnegie Foundation for the Advancement of Teaching, 1910.

Frances, Carol. *The Short-Run Economic Outlook for Higher Education*. Washington, D.C.: American Council on Education, 1980.

Franz, Lori Sharp. "Elicitation of Decision Maker Preference Structure for Multicriteria Optimization Through Interactive Goal Programming." Ph.D. dissertation, University of Nebraska–Lincoln, 1980.

Gray, Paul. *University Planning Models*. Los Angeles: University of Southern California Center for Futures Research, March 1975.

Heiser, Herman C. *Budgeting: Principles and Practices*. New York: Ronald Press, 1959.

Hitch, Charles J. *Decision-Making for Defense*. Berkeley: University of California Press, 1967.

Hopkins, David S. P., and Massey, William F. "Long Range Budget Planning in Private Colleges and Universities." In *Applying Analytical Methods to Planning and Management*, ed. David S. P. Hopkins and Roger G. Schroeder, pp. 43–66. San Francisco: Jossey-Bass, 1977.

"Interview with Shirley Hufstedler." *Educational Record* 61, no. 2 (Spring 1980): 6–9.

Mahew, Lewis B. *Surviving the Eighties*. San Francisco: Jossey-Bass, 1980.

Millett, John D. *Higher Education Planning*. Washington, D.C.: Academy for Educational Development, 1977.

Monical, David G., and Schoenecker, Craig V. "Marginal Funding: A Difference that Makes a Difference?" *Research in Higher Education* 12, no. 1 (1980): 67–82.

Mortimer, Kenneth P., and Tierney, Michael L. *The Three "R's" of the Eighties: Reduction, Reallocation, and Retrenchment*. Washington, D.C.: American Association for Higher Education, 1979.

National Center for Higher Education Management Systems. *An NCHEMS Progress Report*. Boulder, Colorado: National Center for Higher Education Management Systems, September 1978.

New York Bureau of Municipal Research. "Some Results and Limitations of Central Financial Control in New York City." *Municipal Research*, 1917.

Schick, Allen. "The Road to PPB: The Stages of Budget Reform." *Public Administration Review*, December 1966, pp. 243–58.

Shelby, Cecily Cannan. "Better Performance from Nonprofits." *Harvard Business Review*, September–October 1978, pp. 92–98.

Shirley, Robert C., and Volkwein, J. Frederick. "Establishing Academic Program Priorities." *Journal of Higher Education*, 49, no. 5 (1978): 472–88.

Strauss, Jon C.; Porter, Randall; and Zernsky, Robert. "Modeling and Planning at the University of Pennsylvania." In Wyatt, Joe B.; Emery, James C.; and Landis, Carolyn P., eds, *Financial Planning Models: Concepts and Case Studies in Colleges and Universities*. Princeton, N.J.: EDUCOM, 1979.

Thompson, Frederick G., and Carter, George C. "CUPID 2: Thoughts on the Notion of Production Functions in Higher Education." Los Angeles: Systems Research Inc., 1973.

U.S. President's Commission on Economy and Efficiency. *The Need for a National Budget*. Washington, D.C., 1912, pp. 210–13.

Chapter 2

Systems Analysis in Higher Education

Budgetary behavior and the decision-making processes in higher education today reflect the continuum of decision theories. At one end of the continuum, as shown in figure 2.1, are the rational comprehensive, or systems, theories that emphasize economic rationality in decision making. At the other end of the spectrum are the incremental theories that emphasize political criteria and group decision making and limit the scope of individual decisions (Kramer, 1979, p. 2).

The systems analysis, or systematic, approach to planning and budgeting in higher education is generally concerned with production-function type relationships. Technical efficiency denotes the degree to which an organization produces a set of outputs of specified quality and quantity using the least cost set of inputs. The primary objective is to systematically examine alternative courses of action in terms of utility and cost.

Technical approaches to budgeting attempt to (1) achieve better coordination between the planning and budgeting functions; (2) allow for the consideration of future consequences of budget decisions; (3) improve the understanding of how proposed expenditures influence other programs; and (4) make the budget an instrument for achieving increased efficiency. However, the specification of production functions in higher education has not turned out to be an easy task (Fox, et. al., 1972; Verry and Davies, 1976; and Psacharopoulos, 1973). As mentioned earlier, in Chapter 1, in assessing the productivity of higher education, the most obvious difficulty is measurement —determining the value of inputs and quantifying the value of outputs. In addition, the structure of higher education is complicated by the presence of numerous, partial, complimentary, and joint products. Most analysts recognize that the outputs of higher education are related to the inputs, but they are

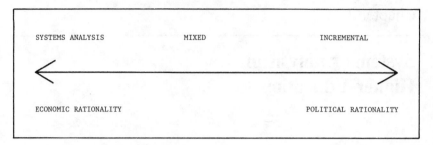

Figure 2.1
Decision-Theory Continuum

also a function of the educational process and a host of other factors, such as the environment in which higher education operates, the attributes and attitudes of students, and the staff and citizenry who participate. Recognition of these factors limits somewhat the usefulness of the systems-analysis approach to decision making in higher education.

At the other end of the decision-theory continuum are the incremental theories which recognize that any suggested course of action must be evaluated first by its effects on the political structure of the organization and its environment. These theories would hold that a course of action which corrects economic deficiencies but increases political difficulties should be rejected, while a decision which contributes to political improvement is desirable even if it is not entirely sound from an economic standpoint (Wildavsky, 1974, p. 191).

In part, the political-rationality criterion recognizes that many decisions do not "open up" for straightforward systematic or allocative analysis and, as a consequence, require a decision-making process that permits discussion and negotiation. Additionally, the need for politically rational decision making derives from the "political costs" which campus leaders may incur when one of their decisions antagonizes someone either within the organization, or externally. If such hostilities mount, they may result in a lack of credibility and a lack of leadership effectiveness.

Because of the importance of finding solutions that are both economically efficient and politically acceptable, administrative decisions in higher education today are rarely based solely on either economic or political rationality. Clearly, both politics and quantitative analysis have important contributions to make to the planning and budgeting processes. Political negotiation provides a mechanism through which social and human values can be reflected in budgetary decisions; quantitative analysis helps to refine options, and explore the consequences of alternatives. Therefore, most decisions made in government and higher education today are based on a "mixed" decision model.

This mixture of the multiple criteria brought out by the desire for political rationality on the one hand, and the need for economic rationality on the other hand, calls for the application of decision-making techniques that can help structure the trade-offs between these often conflicting values. The goal-programming methodology, described thoroughly in Chapter 3 of this book and then demonstrated through examples in Chapters 4 and 5, provides an ideal solution procedure for decision making in higher education. Before examining the goal programming technique, however, it is first important to review more thoroughly some of the existing models of educational planning.

Overview of Existing Models of Higher Education

The range of existing model forms for institutions of higher education is wide and varied. The distinction is usually made between nonquantitative models, mathematical models, and computer-simulation models.

Nonquantitative Modeling

There are many varieties of nonquantitative modeling forms, most relying on some technique of focusing the informed judgment of experts on the problems at issue. Three methods are often discussed: scenario writing, operational gaming, and the Delphi method, with Delphi being perhaps the most popular.

The Delphi Method. In the Delphi method, experts exchange information and opinion through a carefully designed series of questionnaires. It is an attempt to improve on the panel or committee approach by subjecting the views of individual experts to the criticism of fellow panel members without actual confrontation.

Olaf Helmer (1967, pp. 74–95) has suggested the use of the Delphi technique in educational planning. Helmer suggested, among other things, that a group of experts be used to arrive at a convergence of opinion as to the location of the "relevant section" of the cost-effectiveness curve for a particular educational program. For example, by looking at the curve in figure 2.2a, it can be seen that expenditures below g yield insignificant returns and expenditures above h are subject to rapidly diminishing returns. Through the Delphi method, the diagram could clearly be extended, as in figure 2.2b, to the determination of a set of cost-effectiveness curves for alternative programs I, II, and III.

Helmer described a number of Delphi pilot experiments carried out at the Educational Innovations Seminar at the Institute of Government and Public Affairs at the University of California in 1965, in which a hierarchial listing of

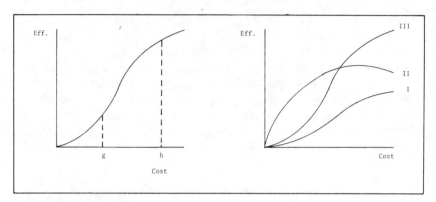

Figures 2.2a, 2.2b
Hypothetical Cost-Effectiveness Curves

educational innovations was arrived at by a first group of experts using Delphi questionnaires. The assignment of these proposals to one of four cost categories (essentially free, low cost, medium cost, and high cost) was consensually arrived at by a second group, and the hypothetical allocation of various fixed budgets to these proposals carried out by yet a third group. The proposal is reported to have provided considerable insight into the nature, the quality (as determined by professional judgments), the cost-effectiveness, and the weighting assigned to the various educational problems (Cutt, 1972, p. 125).

CUPID/Outcomes Budgeting. A method very similar to the Delphi technique was used in 1973 at the Fullerton campus of the California State University (CSUF) to study the impact of outcomes-oriented budgeting (Trask, 1973). In this experiment, the participants were divided into two groups, with each group including representatives from academic affairs, student services, and administration. The first group was asked to allocate a $20-million CSUF budget among the five program classifications of instruction, research, public service, academic support, and student services. The second group was asked to divide its $20 million into those particular amounts it thought warranted by each of six outcome categories including cognitive knowledge, noncognitive knowledge, personal growth, social growth, image development, and autotelic (institutional development) activity. Each group was asked to reach an internal consensus on its initial allocation "mix," and the members were asked to agree on a complete budget matrix. Those who had originally divided the budget by activity completed all individual cells, thereby indicating what particular outcomes they expected from activity performance. For exam-

Table 2.1

Allocation of a $20-Million CSUF Budget
by Indicated Outcomes Using Two Methodologies

Programs	(1) Allocation by Outcome Chancellor's Office Staff	(2) Allocation by Outcome CSUF Faculty and Staff	(3) Allocation by Activity Chancellor's Office Staff	(4) Allocation by Activity CSUF Faculty and Staff
Outcomes				
Internally Desirable				
Cognitive Knowledge	7.0	8.5	5.75	12.60
Non-cognitive Knowledge	7.0	4.0	6.75	3.85
Personal Growth	2.5	3.0	2.75	1.75
Social Growth	2.0	2.0	2.75	1.20
Externally Necessary				
Image Development	1.25	2.0	1.5	.6
Autotelic Activity	.25	.5	.5	0

SOURCE: Tallman Trask, *CUPID: An Exploratory Construct for Outcomes Budgeting*, Los Angeles: Systems Research Inc., 1973, p. 16.

ple, if a group indicated a $10-million expense for instruction, it was asked to divide the $10 million by anticipated value of the outcomes which result from instructional activities. The second group, having begun with an outcome distribution, completed its matrix to indicate which particular activities would need to be required (and their relative weights) in order to produce the desired mix of outcome benefits.

The experimental results presented some surprising patterns as shown in table 2.1. The important distinction was that the budgets for those groups which began with outcomes were amazingly similar (see tables 2.1 and 2.2), indicating that the groups had a consistent concept of what they wanted accomplished. But the outcome budgets derived from activity allocations showed no such similarities, suggesting that when the budget begins with activities, there is no clear agreement as to anticipated outcomes.

Operational gaming and Delphi-oriented modeling are finding increased use in educational planning. The merit of the Delphi method lies in the explicit focusing of expert opinion on problems. As such, these types of models may become invaluable in setting up the more explicit "quantitative" models.

Table 2.2
Allocation of a $20-Million CSUF Budget by Activities Using Two
Methodologies and as Compared with Actual Spending Patterns

Programs		Instruction	Research	Public Service	Academic Support	Student Services
Historical Pattern	(1)	$15.2	$0	$0	$2.3	$2.5
Allocation by Activity						
Chancellor's Office Staff	(2)	13.0	0	.25	3.75	3.0
Allocation by Activity						
CSUF Faculty and Staff	(3)	14.0	2.0	1.0	2.0	1.0
Allocation by Outcome						
Chancellor's Office Staff	(4)	10.85	1.225	1.65	2.375	3.9
Allocation by Outcome						
CSUF Faculty and Staff	(5)	7.1	3.85	2.25	3.95	2.85

SOURCE: Tallman Trask, *CUPID: An Exploratory Construct for Outcomes Budgeting*, Los Angeles: Systems Research Inc., 1973, p. 15.

The technique of Planning, Programming, and Budgeting System (PPBS) should also be mentioned in this section as a model currently being applied to the management of higher education. PPBS is most easily defined in terms of its name: planning refers to the setting of organizational objectives and goals; programming refers to the identification and evaluation of programs or alternatives which meet those objectives; and budgeting refers to obtaining and providing the resources to support the programs. PPBS, though, is really more than simply a method of planning and budgeting; it also includes an analysis function. The analysis part of PPBS is usually accomplished by the application of cost-utility analysis.

The fundamental characteristic of cost-utility analysis is the systematic examination and comparison of alternative courses of action that might be taken to achieve specified objectives for some future time period. Cost-utility analysis not only calls for the systematic examination of all relevant alternatives, but also for the design of additional ones if those examined are not found to be sufficient. This critical examination of alternatives typically involves numerous considerations, but the two main ones are the assessment of the economic resource costs, and the utility (in terms of benefits or gains) pertaining to each of the alternatives. The central idea behind PPBS, and cost-utility analysis for that matter, is that the techniques themselves, if thoroughly and imaginatively done, may result in a modification of the initially-specified objectives.

PPBS was used extensively in the late 1960s, with the impetus coming from federal and state governmental agencies. In 1973, however, Roger G. Schroeder reported that there was "no successful ongoing application of a comprehensive PPBS in higher education" (p. 896). A similar conclusion was also reached more recently by William Massy and David Hopkins (1979, p. 21). One very important effort along the lines of PPBS, though, is the Information Exchange Program (IEP) which has been established at the National Center for Higher Education in Management Systems (NCHEMS). This program is aimed at the development of standard program classification structures so that institutions can have comparable data on cost programs in order to facilitate state-wide, regional, and national planning. Furthermore, programs for comparing and collecting data across institutions are being carried out at the American Council on Education, and under the auspices of the Consortium on Financing Higher Education (COFHE).

Management information systems (MIS) have also been extremely helpful to planning in higher education. MIS refers to the collecting, storing, and retrieving of information for planning and control. Relevant information to be included in college and university management information systems includes financial and budgetary data (both historic and projected), faculty employment records, departmental course offerings, student enrollments, historical student demand statistics, anticipated future student demand, operating budget expenditures, cost trends, and so on. Perhaps the greatest difficulty in the development and implementation of a management information system relates to the design of the data base. One approach is to include a very large amount of data, based on the assumption that it is impossible to predict exactly what information management decisions will need in future years. The other approach concludes that decision-making should be analyzed and analytical models constructed, where possible, to determine what data to include in the data base (Schroeder, 1973, p. 896).

Management information systems, as such, are not models. However, many of the models discussed in this book, and particularly the goal programming methodology recommended in Chapters 4 and 5 of this book, have specific implications for the design of institutional data bases.

Mathematical models

A mathematical model is one in which the relationships between the variables and parameters can be presented by mathematical relationships. Mathematical models employ a range of techniques such as linear and dynamic programming, queueing theory, network theory, game theory (when conflict is involved), and various statistical analysis techniques, for their solution procedures.

Some common aspects characterize the mathematical optimization approaches to university planning. First, they usually assume linear relationships among all decision variables involved in administrative decision policies. Second, they usually hypothesize that input and output variables are measurable on a continuous scale. Third, they take the position that the decision maker seeks to achieve the allocation pattern for the available resources which will attain a maximum value of the desired objective. And finally, they are frequently concerned with the operations of a single department in a college and/or a whole college.

For example, Lawrence Southwick (1967 and 1979) constructed a linear-programming model which was designed to maximize the utility function of a university. He regarded the university as an entity whose function is the production and sale of services and products, and whose organizational structure is much the same as that of a profit-oriented corporation.

Southwick argued that the university as a continuing entity desires to produce current outputs but also to continue indefinitely to produce its own services. These "own services" are similar to the autotelic activities of the CSUF experiment described earlier in this chapter. Therefore, according to Southwick, the chief administrator's objective becomes the maximization of the utility function of the institutional outputs over continuous periods of time. Because outputs in future time periods are conditional on outputs in the current period, "profit" or "current fund surplus" is included in the administrator's utility function as a proxy for the future.

Ismail Turksen and A. G. Holzman (1970) developed two sets of mathematical models for allocating resources available to an academic department for its activities of teaching, research, and other services. Among the available faculty resources they used were faculty time and space.

Some of the best-known applications of management science to higher education planning have come from the Department of Economics at Iowa State University. In 1967, Karl Fox, et al. published their final report on *Formulation of Management Science for Selected Problems of College Administration*, and Francis McCamley (1967) completed a paper on *Activity Analysis Models of Educational Institutions* (Ph.D. dissertation, Iowa State University). In 1968, Fox and J. K. Sengupta published "The Specification of Econometric Models for Planning Educational Systems: An Appraisal of Alternative Approaches." And in 1969, Yakir Plessner, et al. constructed a model "On the Allocation of Resources in a University Department."

Probably the best known of these Iowa State models are the three developed by Fox, et al. Their first was a departmental staff-allocation model constructed as a transportation-type problem, including such variables as amount of teaching and research inputs available from each staff member, the demand on staff services, and departmental objectives as determined subjectively by departmental heads. The second Fox et al. model was constructed for examining the effect of the current period's resource allocation policies on the alternatives of the succeeding periods. The idea was that decisions made about the admission of new students this year may affect the number that can be admitted in subsequent years, and so on. Recursive programming techniques were used in this model. The third model was a two-level decision-making procedure for allocating college resources and used the Danzig-Wolfe decomposition technique.

One type of quantitative planning model that has been explored rather extensively is the faculty-flow model. Several sophisticated flow models exist that provide potential means for predicting the efforts of various policy changes on the future size and composition of a university faculty. Such models have particular utility in situations where stabilized or declining enrollments have raised the issues of tenure quotas and/or retrenchment.

Typically, a faculty-flow model is based on assumptions regarding retention and attrition rates as affected by natural factors and policy decisions in the areas of retirement and promotion. Stephen Hoenack and William Weiler (1977) have postulated a faculty-flow model that also considers and predicts the effects of policy decisions in the areas of tuition rates and student recruitment, especially in nontraditional instruction.

The potential utility of a faculty-flow model has been illustrated by Stefan Bloomfield (1977) in his assessment of a comprehensive faculty-flow model developed at Oregon State University. In his estimation, the most significant benefits derived from implementation of the model were the insights it provided into the problem of an assumed "bulge" in the tenured population that would result from the hiring that took place to accommodate the rapid growth of the mid-sixties. Results from the model seemed to indicate that the tenured/nontenured ratio was much more stable than anticipated, and only "drastic" changes in hiring and promotion policies would affect its future stability (Bloomfield, 1977, p. 15).

More recently, William A. Simpson has used EDUCOM's Financial Planning Model (EFPM) to develop a nonstochastic faculty-flow model at Michigan State University. The model was developed essentially to address two issues: the proportion of tenured faculty, and distribution of faculty by age. A diagram of the final model is shown in figure 2.3 and shows why this is considered a "flow" model. In the situation depicted, Simpson has chosen to model a zero-growth policy so that faculty coming into the institution equals faculty leaving. Simpson has further reported that, by setting constraints on the tenure ratios, the flow of new faculty into the institution, and on the number of older faculty, he was able to find feasible solutions that involved the major policy variables such as the reappointment rate for nontenured faculty (the flow into NT#2), the rate of reappointment to tenure (the flow into T1, T2, and T3), the rate at which temporary faculty enter the tenure system, and the number of faculty allowed to remain on Michigan State's staff after age 65 (*EFPM Newsletter*, March 1980, p. 1).

The models developed by Sang M. Lee (1972) should also be included under the rubric of mathematical models. Lee has constructed two planning models for academic institutions. Both models utilize goal programming and were designed to be used by academic department heads and college deans for the purpose of determining the size, type, rank, and salaries of the academic staff required for the operations of an academic institution.

Computer-Simulation Models

The distinction between the use of a computer in a mathematical model and computer-simulation models is sometimes blurred. Resource allocation optimization models generally go beyond the simulation approach and actually attempt to specify an optimal or best feasible resource allocation pattern. Practical limitations with respect to the specification of objective functions, data collection, and solution algorithms for models of realistic size currently keep such models in the realm of the conceptual rather than the operationally useful (Lawrence and Service, 1977, p. 59).

Simulations can be viewed as the "playing through" of a model of reality in order to investigate the consequences or outputs of particular variables and parameters developed in a specific case-by-case approach. Factors that are irreducible to quantitative terms or logical statements play an important part in many system simulations. Only if qualitative factors are deliberately included in such models is the completeness of the simulation assured (Van Court, 1967, p. 366). An algorithmic simulation may fail because of the exclusion of highly variable human factors, or other political or social factors; thus the use of computer simulation is usually called for where the relevant factors in the real system are too numerous, too qualitative, or their relationships too complex to be easily comprehended by individuals or described in a set of mathematical equations.

Campus. The pioneering work in simulation modeling for higher education was accomplished in Toronto, Canada, by R. W. Judy and J. B. Levine in 1965. Their effort, initially funded by a Ford Foundation grant, resulted in the development of CAMPUS (Comprehensive Analytical Methods for Planning in University/College Systems), a relatively large-scale modeling system. Their model was later extended to the versions labeled CAMPUS V, VI, and

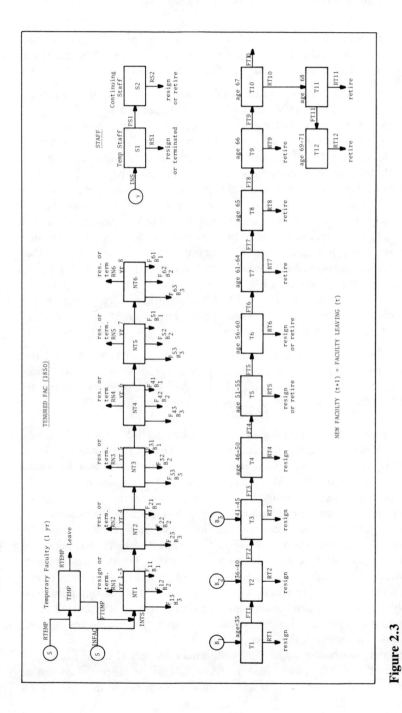

Figure 2.3

Faculty Flow Model for Michigan State University

SOURCE: William Simpson, *EFPM Newsletter* 2, no. 2 (March 1980): 2.

VII (Judy, et al., 1970). The CAMPUS system included a planning and budgeting procedure and standardized data collection definitions. The model was designed to answer questions such as those listed below:

1. Assuming that forecasts existed for the coming decade, what resource inputs in facilities would be required to meet the demand?
2. Assuming that forecasts for manpower needs for a decade were available in terms of various educational programs, what staff and facilities would be needed to meet the manpower requirements? How sensitive would the input requirements be to changes in factors beyond the control of educational decision makers? For specific type of graduates, what would be the incremental costs of producing additional graduates or changing curriculum? As an example, if the medical student graduates were to be produced at a rate of two hundred fifty per year, instead of one hundred fifty at present, what resource implications would it have for the university and also on the various departments offering courses for medical students?
3. Assuming a multicampus university with decentralized campuses, what would be the resource implications of providing facilities for graduate instruction at the decentralized campus?

The CAMPUS model answered these types of questions using simulation techniques. The output from the model provides reports on personnel, space allocation, student loads, and costs. In the reports, the operator may call for historical data, presentations of current data, or projections.

California Cost-Simulation Model. The first well-developed simulation model for higher education was that provided by George B. Weathersby (1967) which became the basis for the University of California Cost Simulation Model (CSM). The California CSM was an analytical model designed to help university decision makers determine intermediate and long-term resource requirements and, through a price vector, the budgetary costs of instructional programs. It calculated resource requirements in five major areas of university activity (instruction, instruction support, organized research and organized activities, campus-wide administration, and physical facilities), distinguishing twelve major subject fields, seven levels of students, seven ranks of faculty, three levels of instruction, and two categories of supporting personnel. Analytical flexibility and the simulation of alternatives were facilitated by incorporating all functional relationships in a computer program and all numerical values in a separate data deck.

The most interesting stage of the California CSM model was the first stage in which the induced course load matrix (ICLM) is established. This pivotal transformation, which is expressed in student credit hours, indicates how a student of each level in each major field distributes his or her course load in all fields of study and over the three levels of instruction, i.e., the formal course load induced by students both within their major field and in all other major fields. Calibration and verification of the California CSM structure were done by comparing the forecasted university budgets with actual budgets for the period 1960 to 1967; accuracy was obtained within a range of 1 percent to 5 percent (Cutt, 1972, p. 36).

Michigan State Model. In 1968, Koenig, Keeney, and Zemach presented the results of a major research and development effort carried out under a National Science Foundation Grant (C-518) in a document titled *A Systems Model for Management, Planning, and Resource Allocation in Institutions of Higher Education.* The model has since become known as the Michigan State Systems Model.

The stated purpose of the Michigan State Systems Model was to provide a rational basis for evaluating alternative resource allocation policies within the university on the assumption of varied and perhaps conflicting goals. The model was broken into two levels of analysis and consisted of sets of equations which described the relationships of resources to production. Based on these relationships, the model calculated unit costs of production for university products—defined as developed manpower, research, and public or technical services. The resources of the university are described broadly as personnel, space and equipment.

Using a systems approach, the Michigan State Model defined five sectors: personnel, physical facilities, academic production, nonacademic production, and students as shown in figure 2.4. At the first level of analysis, equations were developed for each sector to describe the relationship between the identified input, and output prices and flows. In the case of the student sector, the model was developed largely from historical records and represented primarily a behavioral pattern. By contrast, the models of the production sectors recorded the allocation policies implicit in such things as teaching assignments, the research commitment, and classroom and laboratory use.

At the second level of analysis, the models characterizing the input-output relationships of the functional sectors were coupled together by the requirement that the outputs from one sector are used as resources by other sectors and by the requirement that the imputed price of the resources available to any given sector depends upon the production costs associated with the sector from which its resources are derived.

In its final form, the model was an intensely structured, explicit mathematical construct of the entire educational institution viewed as an input-output process with the outputs of the institution being developed manpower, research, and public or technical services. No attempt was made to specifically

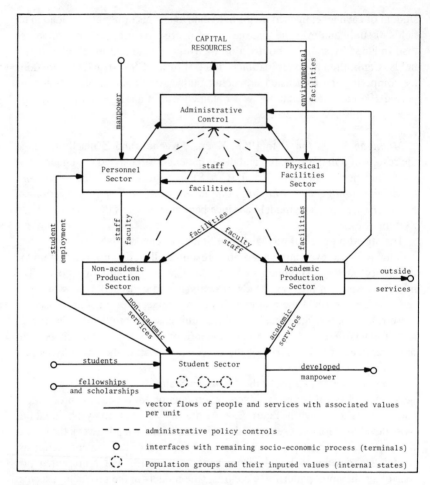

Figure 2.4
Basic Structure of a Typical Institution of Education
as a Socioeconomic Process
SOURCE: Herman E. Koenig, "A Systems Model for Management, Planning, and Resource
Allocation in Institutions of Higher Education," NSF Contract C518 Abstract, p. 34.

define the academic goals of higher education or to establish operational
measures of quality or performance. The objective was to provide a description of the mechanism by which resources are transformed into the resulting
products; in effect, the model was a mathematical description of the way in
which the university utilizes its resources in production. In particular, certain
variables were identified as controlled input variables which could be manipu-

lated by decision makers in order to study the effect on the future state of the university system.

The approach used in the Michigan State Model is interesting in its view of university operations as a set of interrelated subsystems. However, its production-function type formulation and the accompanying detailed information and costing requirements severely limited its usefulness. Professor Koenig himself has commented that "A *de novo* implementation of the total system model as a computer simulation, with all the attendant problems of data acquisitions and processes and computer input-output format, is likely to be both very costly and disappointing in the actual capability it provides" (NSF Contract C-518 Abstract, p. 35).

RRPM 1.6. The Resource Requirements Prediction Model 1.6 (RRPM) was developed by the National Center for Higher Education Management Systems (NCHEMS) at the Western Interstate Commission for Higher Education (WICHE) in 1973. RRPM 1.6 is an evolutionary model which grew out of institutional experiences with other NCHEMS products, specifically RRPM 1.3 and the NCHEMS Cost Estimations Model. In essence, the original conceptualization for all of the RRPM models was provided by Weathersby's earlier works (1967).

The RRPM 1.6 is a widely known, instructional cost-simulation model for postsecondary institutions. The primary purpose of RRPM 1.6 is to generate information necessary for the preparation of instructional program budgets. Institutional data, either historical or projected, is put into the model; then RRPM 1.6 calculates the program-cost information and the resource requirements necessary to undertake a given series of programs.

The key elements in the RRPM 1.6 model are the Induced Course Load Matrix (ICLM) and the Instructional Work Load Matrix (IWLM). Both constructs are quite similar to the ICLM used in the California Cost-Simulation Model. In the NCHEMS nomenclature, the ICLM is a table defining the relationships between the instructional programs and the teaching disciplines or departments that provide instructional services for those programs. The ICLM displays the *average* number of credit hours taken at various course levels in each instructional discipline by a typical student in each program. The IWLM is a matrix indicating the total number of credit hours demanded by *all* students in each program at each student level from each of the instructional disciplines or departments at each course level.

The RRPM 1.6 software program then allows the user to use either a short method or a long method to calculate program-level and per-student costs under varying assumptions about faculty workloads, class meeting time to faculty contact hour ratios, and so forth. The model generates four different types of reports, including: (1) organizational unit reports providing line-item budgets for various organizational units within the institutions, (2) program budget reports indicating the discipline or department contributions to various instructional programs, (3) institutional summary reports, and (4) formatted display reports that show all parameter data for the institution.

The WICHE project has been specifically concerned with the development and implementation of data storage, management, and retrieval systems that will allow interinstitutional comparisons and promote efficient reporting to state and federal agencies. Although the RRPM approach permits fine-grained estimations of resources used in instruction, it does not treat the problems of joint processes and joint products, and, thus research universities can make use of it in only a very limited way (Balderston, 1974, p. 243).

THE TRADES MODEL TRADES is an interactive financial-planning model developed by Stanford University in 1977 in order to help university administrators forecast income and expenses. The goal of the TRADES model is to display the financial impact of trade-offs (hence its name, TRADES) between as many as two hundred working variables. The model is described in detail in the March 1978 issue of *Business Officer.*

In the TRADES model, the most used of the working variables are put forth as a subset called Primary Planning Variables (PPVs). These are the variables considered of high importance to the decision maker and are generally of three types: (1) base values, such as the number of students, the number of faculty members, and so forth, (2) growth rates, such as the rate of tuition price increases, the rate of salary increases for faculty and staff, and (3) coefficients, such as the percentage of faculty who are tenured, the percentage of budget dedicated to new, incremental programs, and so forth. These PPVs are then used to drive submodels. The submodels, in turn, provide forecasts of income, expense, and asset items which the trades model allows to be displayed in as many as fifty categories for up to twenty-five years.

While some of the submodels are fairly simple and apply linear growth rates to project the cost of a particular line item (such as equipment), other submodels are quite complex and actually derive their growth rates from other items, such as endowment income flows, which must be computed from other portions of separate submodels. The sophistication of the TRADES model comes in the aggregation of these variables into an overall forecast. The model allows for both fixed and variable constraints over policies governing planning variables. For instance, it is possible to acquire a balanced budget, where expenses equal revenues; alternatively, it is possible to specify that future students should not have a greater burden for financing the university than present students, necessitating a type of stationary equilibrium so far as a certain planning variable (i.e., tuition rate) is concerned.

In looking at financial trade-offs, the model allows for the graphical presentation of interacting or constraining values. For instance, in the above example relating to the desire to restrict the relative level of financing provided by tuition income to its current level, the model might show a graph of the real growth rate of tuition, displayed against a variable called "budget enrichment" (the fraction of the previous year's budget used to fund incremental programs and improvements). This graph would then allow the decision maker to evaluate the possibilities of using one variable to improve the "standing" of a higher priority variable. As an example, the decision maker might note that a 1 percent increase in tuition income would allow a .5 percent increase in "budget enrichment." This information facilitates decision making by allowing for both a graphical and a quantitative analysis of trade-offs (Dickmeyer, et. al., 1979, p. 69).

A further option of the TRADES model allows for the listing of variables by their "distances" from the feasible boundary. In other words, the decision maker can begin to see how much of a change could be made in a nonconstraining variable before it would begin to impact the policy decision currently being reviewed.

The main thrust of the TRADES model is clearly toward strengthening the understanding of primary planning variables and the difficulties which decision makers have in being directed toward "optimal" feasible university financial configurations. When viewed in this light, the real significance of the model is that it takes care of the tedious financial calculations, thus freeing the decision maker to focus on his preferences for alternative financial policies (Dickmeyer, et al., 1979, p. 76).

EDUCOM Financial Planning Model. Under a grant provided by the Lilly Endowment, EDUCOM has developed a generalized version of the Stanford TRADES model, called the EDUCOM Financial Planning Model (EFPM). The original study of the feasibility of generalizing the Stanford model was done by Joe B. Wayatt, and William F. Massey. The model has further been extended and documented by Daniel A. Updegrove (1979).

EFPM users start with a blank matrix of five hundred sixty rows and ten time periods, each usually set at one year. The contents of the matrix are determined by user-defined variables whose relationships are contained in a set of six on-line data files labeled as follows: (1) data descriptions, (2) budget function, (3) growth functions, (4) report formats, (5) discontinuance, or step functions, and (6) feasibility constraints.

As explained by Updegrove (p. 200), these files contain specifications for the calculations to be used throughout the model. These fundamental relationships between variables must be provided on a case-by-case (institution-by-institution) application. Once the variables and relationships are defined, EFPM can be used to forecast from one time period to the next by first calculating new values for exogenous variables (using growth functions) and then calculating new values for endogenous variables (using budget functions). Discontinuous or step increments for growth or budget functions may be inserted by the user at specified future dates. Using all of these specifications, EFPM can then fill the entire matrix for the five hundred sixty variables for ten years. Once the matrix of variables is complete, selected rows and columns can be printed on a computer terminal, under the control of the user. Other files specify the subsets of variables to be included together with report members and titles. Up to thirty reports can be specified, each using up to forty-five variables. EFPM also has a constraint option which allows for the "flagging" of individual forecasts and the performance of feasibility "matches" in an attempt to find boundaries between feasible and infeasible policies. Once these constraining variables are found by the model, trade-offs can be examined and graphed in a manner similar to that described for the TRADES model.

EFPM is operational on an IBM 370/168 computer at Cornell University in Ithaca, New York. The system operates under VM-CMS which allows multiterminal access to one program while providing secure data storage for each user. By this method, the model is easily available to users in cities throughout the United States and Canada.

EFPM is an extremely flexible, simple, conversational, and relevant system. However, the model itself is really a file management and forecasting system which allows for the analysis of policies, policy variables, and constraints, but does so only for relationships that are developed and specified by individual users.

The Role of Data and Management Information Systems

Over the past decade, there has been a phenomenal growth in the number of institutions that use some type of computer-based information system to support various administrative functions. Some of these systems require extreme sophistication in their data bases, as well as complex data-analysis methods, while others are quite simple. Some systems incorporate many different types of data into one system, while others have each area in a different system; still others simply do not have much data. Some systems use the data primarily for current reports, with little impact on decision making, while other systems are highly integrated into the decision process, with advanced capacity to predict the future impact of current decisions.

As Baldridge and Tierney (1979, p. 26) have stated, "It would clear the air of much nonsense if everyone understood that the overwhelming majority of the so-called 'management information systems' currently in use in higher education are really nothing more than simple data banks." Colleges have always gathered a large amount of information about students, faculty, alumni, finances, and many, many other items. In earlier years, these records were simply kept by a member of the clerical staff. More recently, many institutions formally established offices of institutional research. These offices were established to consolidate the statistics gathered from the various sectors of college campuses. The office usually serves as a focal point for information which is funneled, synthesized, and translated into reports.

It is important to note that, for the vast majority of colleges and universities, a discussion of a "management information system" would almost exclusively mean a discussion of the simple data banks compiled by the institutional research office. Using computers to compile these statistics has given them increased credibility, at least in some arenas.

What are Data?

Before progressing further, it is important to consider a more formal definition of data and systems. Data are usually defined as facts or concepts which are known or assumed and which are usually expressed in numerical form. As we know, nearly all organizations maintain voluminous quantities of data. While some of the data are dictated by the government, or other regulating organizations, the preponderance of data are collected and kept because they are deemed important by the organization. Data usually reflect what has happened in the past, in the form of historical trends, but frequently they are used to describe current situations. Perhaps of most importance, data may also be useful in helping make decisions about the future.

It is frequently assumed that the data needed for the development of a model will be easily available. Unfortunately, as real-world analysts know, this is not always the case. Data collection is frequently the most expensive and time-consuming step in the application of advanced quantitative methods. As will be shown later in this book, however, one of the main advantages of the goal programming model is the relatively small amount of data needed in order to analyze important relationships.

Types of Data

Gallagher and Watson (1980, p. 29) discuss the types of data as: transactional, internal, and external, or environmental. The most common type of data maintained by organizations are the transactional data. This is information or statistics which accrue as a result of the everyday business transactions of an organization. For colleges and universities, transactional data include student and course registrations, fees income, salaries paid, and so forth. Most of the data which an organization maintains can also be classified as internal data. These are data which are associated with the internal workings of the organization. Transaction data are also internal data, but there are internal data which are not transactional. For example, estimates of future enrollment patterns in college courses would be internal, but not transactional, data.

Most organizations also maintain a considerable amount of external, or environmental data. This is information about the environment in which the organization operates. For colleges and universities, examples might include the estimates of future high school graduates, by state or region, estimates of changes in the tax base supporting the institution, estimates of gross national product, and so forth.

Another way that data can be categorized is by whether they are objective or subjective. Objective data reflect facts or concepts which require no subjectivity in their interpretation. For example, if university records indicate that twenty thousand students were enrolled during first semester of the current academic year, this would be an example of objective data. On the other hand, if the estimate for next year's enrollment is twenty-two thousand students, this is an example of subjective data, since it reflects subjective beliefs. Organizations generally store much more objective data than subjective data.

Data Requirements at Different Organizational Levels

The type of data required to carry out decision-making responsibilities varies within an organization according to the managerial level. As described in table 2.3, lower management is generally concerned with assuring that specific tasks are carried out effectively and efficiently and thus rely primarily on internal and objective data. For instance, generally a department head, while developing his department's teaching assignments and class schedule for the coming semester, would rely primarily on specific information regarding resources which would be available during the coming fiscal period, as well as fairly well-known information about the levels of demand for the courses to be taught. By its very nature, activity at this level focuses mostly upon what is going on within the organization. Consequently the data needed to support this decision making tends to be internal. As chairpersons and directors of departments involve themselves with the longer-range planning for the institution, they move up more to the middle-management level and thus require more external and subjective data. Generally speaking, deans or heads of

Table 2.3
Managerial Levels, Decision-Making Responsibilities,
and Data Requirements in Higher Education

Managerial Level	Important Decision-making Responsibilities	Data Requirements
Top administrators (President, Vice Presidents, Chancellors)	Strategic planning	Considerable external and subjective data
Middle management (Deans and Directors)	Management control and planning	Some external and subjective data
Lower management (Departmental Chairmen)	Operational control	Primarily internal and objective data (for short-term decisions); External data (for longer planning horizons)

schools would typically occupy middle-management positions and thus need the type of data illustrated on table 2.3.

Middle management, as also indicated in the table, must assume more responsibility for assuring that resources are obtained and used effectively and efficiently in the accomplishment of the organization's objectives. While internal, objective data is still needed by middle managers in colleges and universities, the responsibility for obtaining resources from the external environment creates a demand for external and subjective data.

Top college administrators, such as campus chancellors or system presidents, must assume most of the responsibility for strategic planning. Robert N. Anthony (1965, p. 18) has defined strategic planning as the process of deciding on the objectives of the organization, on changes in these objectives, on the resources used to obtain these objectives, and on the policies that are to govern the acquisition, uses, and disposition of these resources. Because of the rapidly changing environment in which colleges and universities are functioning today, it is essential for their strategic planning purposes that they obtain a considerable amount of external and subjective data.

Whereas nearly all of lower management's and much of middle management's needs call for internal and objective data, top management, whether in colleges and universities or other organizations, must rely on an increasing amount of external and subjective data. This latter requirement is the most difficult for organizations, but is also the most important in terms of the long run viability of the organizations.

Data Base

As used in higher education, a data base refers simply to a machine-readable file of information. For example, a student data base could include the social security number, name, address, list of courses taken, and grades of each student. The principle difference between a machine-readable data base and a file is the resulting ease with which the information can be manipulated. For example, consider a report requiring the number of students from each postal zip code area. While this could be done manually, the amount of clerical effort for a large institution would clearly be exorbitant; such summary reports are relatively trivial when machine-readable data bases are used.

Experience has shown that there must be consistent and high standards for the editing and auditing of machine-readable data bases. A data base is considered "clean" only when there have been sufficient checks to insure that the data are internally valid and reasonably error free.

Data Elements and Data-Element Dictionaries

A data element is a single item of data. Typical data elements include the student identification number, student name, course number, grade, and so forth. In order to permit an exchange of data between institutions, or the use of computer programs developed at one institution by another, a series of documents called the Data-Element Dictionaries have been developed. These dictionaries provide the definition, format, codes, and classifications of specific data. For example, the format of a student's name could be twenty-four characters—last name, followed by first name or initials. For the computer programmer, the format is twenty-four characters; the embedded comma distinguishes the last name from the first name and initials. Perhaps the most important purpose of a data-element dictionary, however, is concerned with definition and classification. For example, a full-time equivalent (FTE) student, in many state recording systems, is defined as fifteen credit hours of instruction taken while a lower-division student. Potentially, a full-time equivalent student could be five part-time students taking three hours each, a full-time student taking fifteen hours, or .83 of a student taking eighteen hours. FTE is only a construct used in the representation of instructional work-loads, and is a *derived* data element, defined in a data-element dictionary. Similarly, levels of students are also specified. For example, lower division can be defined as a student who has completed less than sixty credit hours, while an upper-division student is one who has completed sixty or more semester hours but has not yet received his undergraduate degree. Definitions such as these become extremely important when comparing one institution to another, since the validity of comparisons is often determined by consistency in the measurements used.

To facilitate the exchange of data, codes may be chosen to represent various levels. For example, in the NCHEMS cost estimation model, "LD" is used to represent lower division and "UD" is used to represent the upper division. As indicated by James Farmer and Tallman Trask (1973, p. 10), data-element dictionaries are used (1) to provide definitions of the representation of data in terms of codes and formats which are useful to programmers, and (2) to permit institutions to make better comparisons, assuming the other requirements for data exchange are met. Several institutions or systems have used data element dictionaries, and those of the National Center for Higher Education Management Systems are quite well known.

Operating Data Systems

Most of the transactional data developed by colleges and universities are the result of the operations of their operating data systems. These elementary systems are sometimes called operating data systems since they directly support the day-to-day operations of the institution through the automation of clerical tasks. In many management-information systems, operating data systems perform a central role, providing the machine-readable data bases which are, in turn, used by the management system itself. Because operating data systems which produce transactional data are so closely related to the daily operation of the institution, they tend to require modification as the underlying processes change. For example, when the tax laws are changed, the payroll system has to reflect the new tax rates. Similarly, as academic policies change, the student record system has to be modified to accommodate new regulations. These types of systems are generally fairly complex, and usually expensive to develop and maintain.

Management-Information Systems

There are considerable differences of opinion as to what constitutes a management-information system. At one extreme is the view that it is a further integration of the processing of transactional data and the preparation of an expanded set of scheduled reports. At the other extreme is the belief that an MIS should provide all organizational elements with the information needed to manage effectively. Somewhere in between is what most people mean by an MIS, i.e., a system featuring structured reporting, an integrated data base, and a decision-support orientation.

There are two characteristic differences between management-information systems and operating-data systems. First, management-information systems, when appropriately designed, are primarily used for planning and control. Thus, they produce information used for management decisions as contrasted to operating-data systems, in which the immediate result, such as student grade reports and employee paychecks, are administrative documents themselves. Second, management-information systems should involve manipulation of the data in the sense that they produce summaries, calculate statistical measures, and use mathematical models of the underlying processes. For example, a management-information system could yield the cost of a student as $1,700 per year; this may represent the computation of the cost per each credit hour of instruction by discipline and level and the number of credit hours by discipline and level taken by an average student, with a specified faculty rank distribution, by area of subject expertise, and so forth. The resulting value— $1,700—has meaning only within the context of management decisions.

Because the term *management-information systems* frequently includes all of the data processing systems necessary to maintain data bases and support administrative applications, the term *planning and management systems* has come to refer to those specific analytic tools which can be used for planning in institutions of higher education. Since these tools also can be used to describe current operations, they may also be used by management for control purposes. At the present time, however, most of these planning tools emphasize the allocation and use of resources and are frequently implemented as *cost* models. Management information systems in higher education should include methods of evaluation and comparison and should help in understanding the relationships between the use of resources and their benefits. As will be shown later in this book, the goal-programming model is ideally suited to the development of these types of evaluations.

The problem of lack of integration among models, data bases, and decision makers is being reduced or eliminated somewhat by the development of decision-support systems. Such systems treat models, data bases, and decision makers as subsystems in an overall system designed to supply information to support decision-making responsibilities. An illustration of the components of a decision support system is shown in figure 2.5. Chapter 7 of this book describes a specific application of a decision-support system to an institution of higher education.

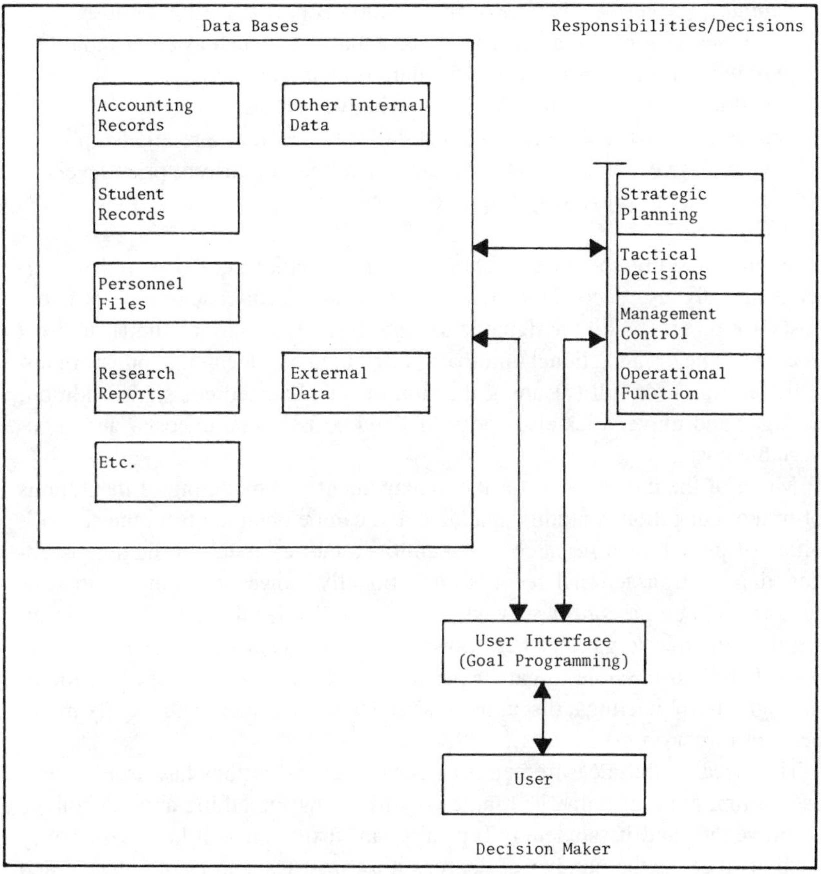

Figure 2.5
Components of a Decision-Support System for Higher Education

Data Collection and Use

Against this discussion of the role of data and data bases in the modeling and management of higher education, it is important to examine how relevant data is usually gathered and used.

At the institutional level, there are many ways and places in which data can be obtained. When viewed in this manner, the normal categories are:

Historical data—the information is derived directly from past records
Projected—these types of data are not based on historical records, but
rather on a judgment regarding future expectations

Standard (target)—this type of information is normative in that it expresses a judgment as to what a particular item (such as cost) should be
Imputed—a relationship where the data is estimated under some objective and based on the assumption of alternative actions.
Replacement—usually refers to cost data and provides a relationship where the estimate is based on the assumption of current price levels attributed to previously acquired assets.

When speaking specifically about cost information, colleges and universities usually use secondary characteristics and further determine whether costs are direct (readily assignable to a specific organizational unit), indirect (a cost of one organizational unit that is attributed or allocated to other organizational units), or full (meaning the sum of the allocated costs). In addition, colleges and universities also speak of fixed costs, variable costs, and semivariable costs.

Much of the data needed for the management and modeling of institutions of higher education is readily available and can be obtained from the school's office of institutional research. As mentioned earlier, much of the data is obtained from transactional records. Additionally, however, many institutions require the completion of surveys and reports by faculty, staff, and administrators in order to gain further information about the institution and its activities. It is also possible to gather pertinent information about specific topics through group meetings, discussions with deans, chairmen, and faculty members, or direct observation.

Historically, the measurement of educational institutions has been viewed as a compilation of numerical indicators to tell us something about a college or university and its students. Typically, an institution will be measured by such artifacts as the number of degrees it awards, test scores of entering and completing students, the percentage of students who continue on to graduate school, the number of graduate fellowship winners, student-faculty ratios, and the like. In and of themselves, these data are descriptive, not normative; they simply explain the characteristics of the institution. It is only when the data from one institution are compared to those from another institution that indications of quality result. Even then these indications, by their very nature, are quite relative.

Intrainstitutional comparisons are also quite important. When undertaking this type of comparison, it is imperative to begin by compiling an appropriate reference group for the institution being judged. In this manner, cost data and outcome measures, once collected, can be profitably compared. Unfortunately, it is often difficult to determine an appropriate reference group of peer-group institutions. Among other things, peer groups are often defined for use in examining a certain set of relationships; when another set of decisions must be made, it may be necessary to develop a completely different group of comparison institutions. Once an appropriate reference group has been agreed upon, it is then important to make certain that all data collected have been defined in the same manner by the respective institutions.

State-wide and regional information may also be helpful, depending upon the type of problems being examined by a particular college or university. Frequently, colleges and universities will turn to other state agencies to obtain the type of information needed (e.g., demographic trends, high school enrollment, economic indicators, income figures, and so forth).

Today, most institutions of higher education also have numerous sources of information available to them regarding national and international concerns. Furthermore, these data sources, which may be public or private, usually cover a very broad range of issues and frequently do so with a very high level of sophistication. Examples of the types of information that are available range from "futures" scenarios (such as those published by the Center for Futures Research at the University of Southern California) to the publication of National Manpower Planning Needs Statistics by federal government agencies.

When collecting and using data from various sources, it is essential to make certain that:

1. Data definitions are standardized. The constant plague of information systems is the lack of standardized terms. Unfortunately, different agencies often use different definitions, and thus the resulting figures may not be comparable. This problem exists in many operational areas. The standardizing of definitions is often a very difficult task, but it is a first step which must be taken before data systems can be used.
2. The data must be clearly trackable. In other words, the source of the data must always be well documented.
3. The information must be condensed. In the early stages of building a data bank, the emphasis is almost always on collecting information. Later, however, it becomes apparent that much of the information must undergo a process of condensation. Frequently, concerns about how to condense, synthesize, and organize the information becomes a highly debated issue. A move to condense data early on in the process can help overcome some of these difficulties.
4. The assumptions behind the data must be clearly stated. When gathering data and preparing reports, many questions inevitably appear: Do part-time faculty count in the total number of faculty? Do they count on some fractional basis? Are laboratories counted the same as lecture halls? In

many cases, assumptions and decision points are lost in the recording of the data; later, a decision maker may need to know the change of assumptions that led to the numbers in the final report.

Summary

It is important to stress that data collection is a *continuing* process. Even with well-defined data definitions and with clear goals and objectives, an institutional researcher may end up with incomplete data. When this occurs, it is frequently necessary to modify the model, to change data definitions, or to find an alternative method of measuring or identifying the particular concept being examined. As stressed in previous chapters, the appropriate approach to management of colleges and universities entails the systematic development of institutional goals and objectives. This process involves the proper "matching" of (1) mission, (2) external factors, (3) internal strengths and capabilities. As the administration-by-objectives (ABO) process proceeds, the issues or relationships to be modeled are then elucidated, and the data collection process is undertaken. This does not mean, however, that the data-collection process is the last step in the management chain. In order to make certain that the data and the models are compatible, the information needs and data requirements should be an integral part of development of the goals and objectives.

One of the strengths of the goal-programming models recommended in this book lies in the fact that they do not require the use of extensive information structures or data banks. More specifically, the sources of data for the models demonstrated in Chapter 6 included only the following: the registrar's reports of enrollment, credit hours, and degrees conferred; budget and financial reports routinely provided by the campus budget and accounting offices; instructional staff and AAUP salary summaries; and instructional load and other activity data (obtained from departmental records). These data were collected from the institutional sources and put together by clerical and work-study help under the supervision of the authors. Most of the compilation work involved the transfer of data elements from standard reports (some computerized) and other documents, to the formats needed by the goal-programming algorithm. After the data were collected, some modifications were made in the specification of the constraint equations in order to more clearly represent the issues at hand or to better accommodate the intended users of the model.

It is important to understand that good information becomes the basis for good decisions. The role of management science models, such as goal programming, is the structured analysis of information, within the context of specific relationships and well defined goals and objectives of the institution. The next chapter will more specifically expand on these ideas and concepts.

State of the Art

To date, modern management techniques and modeling in higher education have not been readily accepted by academic administrators. To a large extent, this failure can be attributed to the types of assumptions made in most of the currently available models. The following is an overview of some of these limiting characteristics:

1. The student credit hour, a unidimensional measure, is often assumed to be a proxy for the multiple outcomes of higher education.
2. Differences in quality or skill imparted over time are not reflected in any measurable units.
3. Decision makers are not allowed to systematically structure their preferences, and thus learn of the trade-offs inherent in the policies they are examining.
4. Many of the measures currently used are not capable of reflecting "jointness"—joint inputs, joint activities, joint products, joint beneficiaries.
5. The use of these types of measures takes no account of fixed-versus-variable inputs, or constraints of a technical policy or environmental nature (such as tenure, scale economics, and market factors).
6. For most models, the use of historical data (or average data) often builds in the assumption of linearity and thus implies perfect substitutability of resources over time. Since cost is frequently the only resource measure involved, there is no possibility (without further analysis) of addressing the trade-off possibilities among the resources that underlie the costs.
7. Readily available models do not allow for a full examination of multiple objectives; in the cases where multiple objectives can be analyzed, the reviews cannot be done simultaneously.

Perhaps the biggest challenge to the analytical approaches to management of higher education comes from the very heart of these approaches, namely, quantification. Proponents of quantitative approaches must repeatedly ask themselves: Can these limitations be overcome? Are they inherent in the methodology? How can we advance the art of quantification and still maintain a focus on the centrality of human values in education?

A further challenge is the need to focus more on the end results or the "effectiveness" of higher education, as opposed to efficiency methodologies or means used to reach those ends. Efficiency must continue to be taken into consideration, but not at the expense of overall effectiveness.

Because of the above factors, it is clear that the debate surrounding the political versus the technical dimensions of budgeting is not likely to diminish. Increasing demands for social accountability and the prospect of constantly changing missions and roles will continue to lead to a vigorous political review of all academic institutions. Similarly, the need to be able to examine more explicitly the impact of such items as limited resources, continuing inflation, the financial costs of serving new markets, and the cost of labor proposals will clearly demand the application of more sophisticated technical analysis. Needed is a model which can allow for the "mixing" of this type of combined political and economic rationality. The following chapters will demonstrate that the goal-programming technique is capable of meeting these needs.

References

Anthony, Robert N. *Planning and Control Systems: A Framework for Analysis*. Boston: Division of Research, Graduate School of Business Administration, Harvard University, 1965.

Balderston, Frederick E. *The University of California: A Program Budget FY 1970–71: FY 1973–74*. Berkeley: University of California, April 1969.

————. "Thinking about the Outputs of Higher Education." In *Outputs of Higher Education: Their Identification, Measurement, and Evaluation*, ed. Ben Lawrence, G. Weathersby, and V. W. Patterson. Boulder, Colorado: WICHE, 1970.

————. *Managing Today's University*. San Francisco: Jossey-Bass, 1974.

Baldridge, J. Victor, and Tierney, Michael L. *New Approaches to Management*. San Francisco: Jossey-Bass, 1979.

Bloomfield, Stefan. "Comprehensive Faculty Flow Analysis." In *New Directions for Institutional Research*, ed. David S. P. Hopkins and Roger G. Schroeder, no. 13 (Spring 1977).

Clark, David G.; Huff, Robert A.; Haight, Michael J.; and Collard, William J. *Introduction to the Resource Requirements Prediction Model 1.6*. Technical Report No. 34A. Boulder: NCHEMS-WICHE, 1973.

Cutt, James. "Program Budgeting and Higher Education." Canberra, Australia: Department of Accounting and Public Finance, Public Finance Monograph No. 1, Australian National University, 1972.

Dickmeyer, Nathan; Hopkins, David S. P.; and Massey, William F. "TRADES: A Model for Interactive Financial Planning." In *Financial Planning Models: Concepts and Case Studies in Colleges and Universities*, ed. Joe B. Wyatt, James C. Emery, and Carolyn P. Landis. Princeton: EDUCOM, 1979.

Educational Testing Service. *Increasing Productivity in Higher Education*. Princeton, New Jersey: 1974.

EFPM Newsletter 2, no. 2 (March 1980).

Farmer, James, and Trask, Tallman. "Management Information Systems for Nebraska Higher Education: A Report to the Legislative Interim Study Committee on Higher Education." Guthrie, Oklahoma: Systems Research, Inc., 1973.

Fox, Karl A., ed. *Economic Analysis for Educational Planning*. Baltimore: Johns Hopkins University Press, 1972.

Fox, Karl A.; McCamley, Francis P.; and Plessner, Yakir. *Formulation of Management Models for Selected Problems of College Administration*. Ames: Iowa State University, 1967.

Fox, Karl A., and Sanyol, B. C. *On the Optimality of Resource Allocation in Educational Systems*. Ames: Iowa State University, 1967.

Fox, Karl A., and Sengupta, J. K. "The Specification of Economic Models for Planning Educational Systems: An Appraisal of Alternative Approaches." *Kyklos* 21, no. 4 (1968): 665–94.

Gallagher, Charles H., and Watson, Hugh J. *Quantitative Methods for Business Decisions*. New York: McGraw-Hill, 1980.

Grinold, Richard C.; Hopkins, David S. P.; and Massey, William F. "A Model for Long-Range University Budget Planning Under Uncertainty." Stanford: Stanford University, 1977.

Gross, Edward, and Grambsch, P. V. *University Goals and Academic Power*. Washington, D.C.: American Council on Education, 1969.

Gross, Francis M. "Comparative Analysis of the Existing Budget Formulas Used for Justifying Budget Requests or Allocating Funds for the Operating Expenses of State-Supported Colleges and Universities." Knoxville: Office of Institutional Research, University of Tennessee, 1973.

Haight, Mike, and Martin, Ron. "An Introduction to the NCHEMS Costing and Data Management System." Boulder: NCHEMS-WICHE, 1975.

Haight, Mike, and Romney, Leonard C. "NCHEMS Overview—A Training Document." Boulder: NCHEMS-WICHE, 1975.

Harwood, Gordon B., and Lawless, Robert W. "Optimizing Organizational Goals in Assigning Faculty Teaching Schedules." *Decision Sciences* 6, no. 3 (July 1975): 513–23.

Heesterman, A. R. G. *Allocation Models and Their Use in Economic Planning*. Dordrecht, Holland: Dreidel Publishing Co., 1971.

Helmer, Olaf. "The Delphi Technique and Educational Innovation." In *Inventing Education for the Future*, ed. W. Z. Hirsch. San Francisco: Chandler Publishing Co., 1967.

———. *Social Technology*. New York: Basic Books, 1966.

Hoenack, Stephen A., and Norman, Alfred L. "Incentives and Resource Allocation in Universities." *Journal of Higher Education* 45 (January 1974): 21–37.

Hoenack, Stephen A., and Weiler, William C. "A Comparison of Effects of Personnel and Enrollment Policies on the Size and Composition of a University's Faculty." *Journal of Higher Education* XLVIII, no. 4 (July/August 1977): 432–52.

Huckfeldt, Vaughn. "An Introduction to the State Postsecondary Education Planning Model." Boulder: NCHEMS-WICHE, 1976.

Huff, Robert A., and Young, Michael E. "Profiles of Management Information Uses." Boulder: NCHEMS-WICHE, 1974.

Johnston, William, ed. *Proceedings of the 1976 National Assembly.* National Center for Higher Education Management Systems. Boulder: NCHEMS-WICHE, 1976.

Judy, Richard W. "A Research Progress Report on Systems Analysis for Efficient Resource Allocation in Higher Education." Report for the University of Toronto, January 1970.

———. "Simulation and Rational Resource Allocation in Universities." In *Technical Reports on Efficiency in Resource Utilization in Education.* Paris, France: Organization for Economic Cooperation and Development, 1969.

Judy, Richard W., and Levine, J. B. *A New Tool for Educational Administrators.* Toronto, Canada: University of Toronto Press, 1965.

Koenig, H. E.; Keeney, M. G.; and Zemach, R. *A Systems Model for Management Planning and Resource Allocation in Institutions of Higher Education.* East Lansing: Michigan State University, 1968.

Kramer, Fred A. *Contemporary Approaches to Public Budgeting.* Cambridge, Massachusetts: Winthrop Publishers, Inc., 1979.

Lassiter, Roy L., Jr. "Instructional Productivity and the Utilization of Faculty Resources in the State University System of Florida." Gainesville, Florida: Institute of Higher Education, 1976.

Lawrence, G. Ben. *Goal Programming for Decision Analysis.* Philadelphia: Auerbach Publishers, 1972.

Lawrence, G. Ben, and Clayton, E. R. "A Goal Programming Model for Academic Resource Allocation." *Management Science* 18, no. 8 (April 1972): 395–408.

Lawrence, G. Ben, and Service, Allan L. "Quantitative Approaches to Higher Education Management." Washington, D.C.: American Association for Higher Education, 1977.

Lawrence, G. Ben; Weathersby, G.; and Patterson, V. W., eds. *Outputs of Higher Education: Their Identification, Measurement, and Evaluation.* Boulder: WICHE, 1970.

Lawrence, G. "The Implementation of Campus Simulation Models for University Planning." In *Management Information Systems: Their Development and Use in the Administration of Higher Education,* ed. J. Minter and B. Lawrence. Boulder: WICHE, 1969.

McCamley, Francis P. "Activity Analysis Models of Educational Institutions." Ph.D. dissertation, Iowa State University, 1967.

Massey, William F., and Hopkins, David S. P., "The Case for Planning Models." In *Financial Planning Models: Concepts and Case Studies in Colleges and Universities*, ed. Joe B. Wyatt, James C. Emery, and Carolyn P. Landis. Princeton: EDUCOM, 1979.

Micek, Sidney S., and Arney, William Ray. "Outcome-Oriented Planning in Higher Education: An Approach or an Impossibility?" Boulder: NCHEMS-WICHE, June 1973.

Micek, Sidney S.; Service, Allan.; and Lee, Yong S. "Outcome Measures and Procedures Manuel Field Review Edition." Boulder: NCHEMS-WICHE, 1975.

Plessner, Yakir; Fox, Karl A; and Sanyal, B. C. "On the Allocation of Resources in a University Department." *Metroeconomica* 20, no. 3 (1969): 256–571.

Psacharopoulos, George. *Returns to Education*. San Francisco: Jossey-Bass, 1975.

Said, Kamal el-Dien. *A Budgeting Model for an Institution of Higher Education*. Austin: University of Texas, 1974.

Schroeder, Roger G. "A Survey of Management Science in University Operations." *Management Science* 19, no. 8 (April 1973): 895–906.

Schroeder, Roger G., and Adams, Carl R. "The Effective Use of Management Science in University Administration." *Review of Educational Research* 46, no. 1 (Winter 1976): 117–31.

Southwick, Lawrence, Jr. "The Economics of Higher Education: The University as a Firm." Ph.D. dissertation, Carnegie-Mellon Institute, 1967.

———. "The Role of Profits in the University." WP Series No. 57. Buffalo: State University of New York at Buffalo, School of Management, 1969.

Thompson, Frederick G., and Carter, George C. "CUPID 2: Thoughts on the Notion of Production Functions in Higher Education." Los Angeles: Systems Research Inc., 1973.

Trask, Tallman. *Cupid: An Exploratory Construct for Outcomes Budgeting*. Los Angeles: Systems Research Inc., 1973.

Turksen, Ismail B., and Holzman, A. G. "Micro Level Resource Allocation Models for Universities." Washington, D.C.: Paper presented at the 37th National Meeting of the ORSA, April 1970.

Updegrove, Daniel A. "EFPM: Generalizing the Stanford TRADES Model." In *Financial Planning Models: Concepts and Case Studies in Colleges and Universities*, ed. Joe B. Wyatt, James C. Emery, and Carolyn P. Landis. Princeton: EDUCOM, 1979.

Van Court, Hare, Jr. *Systems Analysis: A Diagnostic Approach*. New York: Harcourt, Brace and World, 1967.

Verry, Donald, and Davies, Bleddyn. *University Costs and Outputs*. New York: Elsevier Scientific Publishing, 1976.

Weathersby, George B. *The Development and Application of a University Cost Simulation Model*. Berkeley: University of California, 1967.

————. "The Potentials of Analytical Approaches to Educational Planning and Decision Making." In *Proceedings of the 1976 National Assembly*, ed. William Johnson. Boulder: NCHEMS-WICHE, 1976.

Wildavsky, Aaron. *The Politics of the Budgetary Process*. 2d ed. Boston: Little Brown, 1974.

Part Two

Academic Administration by Multiple Objectives

This part of the book is devoted to the discussion of academic administration by multiple objectives. It presents the general background about the nature and needs of multiple conflicting objectives in the academic setting and how multiple goals should be analyzed in a systematic fashion.

Chapter 3 is an introduction to administration by objectives (ABO) as a basic approach to academic administration. Chapter 4 presents the concept and modeling aspects of goal programming as a systematic approach to implementing ABO in institutions of higher education.

Chapter 3

Administration by Objectives (ABO)

Chapter 1 of this book outlined the many aspects of planning and budgeting in higher education and emphasized the importance of integrating those functions into the decision-making processes at all levels of administration. Chapter 2 discussed the major modeling efforts which have been undertaken to assist academic administrators in carrying out their managerial responsibilities.

A critical implication of the foregoing reviews is that educational decision making must be viewed as a continuing process in which past choices constrain, but do not determine, current decisions, and decisions can, within limits, be modified in response to changing external (often environmental) conditions. More fundamentally, in this view it is impossible to divorce the process of educational decision making from the evolving processes of planning and budgeting.

It is clear that improvement of the administrative process in higher education can best be accomplished by the application of a systematic approach which can help clarify, tie together, and then strengthen the values and relationships on which the processes themselves are built. This chapter describes such an approach, called administration by objectives (ABO), and then introduces goal programming as a modeling technique that can truly help academic administrators structure the value tradeoffs which are such an important part of the choices they must make.

Administration by objectives (ABO) is simply a variation of management by objectives (MBO). While MBO has been popular in business firms, ABO is concerned more with public and nonprofit organizations. ABO, whether utilized simply as a concept or as a formalized system, has been accepted by scholars, practicing administrators, and consultants as a pragmatic management approach for public organizations. Many governmental agencies, nonprofit organizations, and educational institutions have applied or integrated some features of ABO into their administrative functions with varying degrees of success. We have seen some flowery praise as well as harsh criticism of the approach in the past; however, administration by objectives is now generally accepted as a sound normative approach to public administration.

The basic idea of ABO is that the best way to manage an organization is to involve people in setting objectives and then direct needed resources toward these objectives in a systematic manner (Lee, 1981). The basic problem with ABO is not in its concept but rather in its weakness as a functional system. Because of this weakness, ABO has thus far been more of a philosophy than a self-contained operational system.

A key problem with the ABO process remains in the methodological area—pulling all the relevant parts together in a systematic way to achieve the basic goal(s) of ABO. Thus, quite frequently the ABO implementation process becomes an exercise in wishful thinking, generation of self-justifying or self-protective paperwork, and the creation of unmanageable mish-mash. It is, of course, true that the ABO implementation process provides an opportunity for administrators to gain broader insights about the functions and interrelations among various departments and personnel. Such a secondary benefit, however, without the achievement of the basic purpose may not warrant the efforts, resources, and organizational turmoil that are usually required of an ABO implementation process.

There is no singularly correct way to develop and implement ABO, just as there is no one best way to manage all organizations. The appropriate ABO approach to a university or college depends upon the particular circumstances and conditions under which the institution functions. The objective of this chapter is to provide the basic approach and understanding that are required to implement the features of ABO in any educational institution.

Administration by Multiple Objectives

The specific origin of the concept of ABO, or MBO for that matter, is not known, just as the beginning of management is not known. Although some academicians suggest that the concept of ABO can be traced to the days of the Old Testament, Koran, and ancient Greek or Oriental philosophers, there is no value in establishing such a genealogy. It should suffice to state that the idea of defining objectives and implementing organized resource allocation schemes for specific results can be readily found in the management styles of many early military leaders and entrepreneurs as well as in some early management texts.

The basic theoretical foundation of ABO, if such a thing ever exists, can perhaps be found in management science. Management science is a popular substitute for operations research, which originated in the United Kingdom during the early part of World War II. In order to develop the most effective military strategies and operations, there was an urgent need for scientific approaches which could be used to analyze logistics problems. The British and later the American military authorities formed groups of scientists to do research on military operations. Their studies were instrumental in the achievement of victories in the air battle of Britain, the island campaign in the Pacific, the battle of the North Atlantic, and other phases of the war.

After the war, there was a natural progression of operations research from military operations to nonmilitary organizations. Thus, the name *management science* became a substitute for operations research, as the concept and areas of application were broadened to general management-decision problems.

Management science is concerned with the application of scientific tools, models, and computer-based analysis to provide concrete information relevant to managerial problems. The management science approach emphasizes the following aspects of the decision situation:

1. Analysis of the nature of the management problem or an opportunity.
2. Analysis of the decision environment and its interaction with the organization.
3. Definition of organizational objectives.
4. Definition of system constraints and priorities of the decision maker.
5. Determination of available resources.
6. Analysis of technological activities of the system.
7. Determination of decision and activity levels to achieve objectives.

Traditional management theorists have concentrated only on the human side of enterprise, seeking improved management effectiveness through objective-oriented performance appraisals, incentive systems, training and development programs, participative management processes, and the like (McGregor, 1969). They often neglected the interrelationships among system components, environmental factors, system constraints, priorities of the decision maker, and so forth. Thus, many behaviorally oriented ABO or MBO processes have resulted in less-than-anticipated results. In order to develop an operational ABO program, one must consider both the systematic as well as the human aspects of management.

Management science permits a more scientific approach to administration by objectives. Management science and systematic approaches to decision making have perhaps contributed more for the acceptance of ABO than is usually appreciated by administrators or scholars. This is especially true when the organization involves complex technologies, conflicting interests, increasingly scarce resources, and rapidly changing environmental conditions. Although management science has contributed a great deal in systematizing and operationalizing the ABO process, it has often neglected the human aspect of organizations. Management systems, regardless of how well conceived, modeled, analyzed, and solved, cannot exist in a vacuum. The system functions and disfunctions because of people. The human side of management—motivation, leadership, psychological needs, and so forth—must be the core of any successful ABO system.

In today's complex organizational environment, administrators attempt to achieve a set of objectives to the fullest possible extent in an environment of conflicting interests, incomplete information, and limited resources. The effectiveness of the administrative process is measured by the degree to which organizational objectives are achieved. Therefore, the recognition and definition of organizational objectives provides the foundation for administration (Lee, 1972, p. 7).

Administrative functions are also constrained by environmental factors such as governmental regulations, economic and political developments, as well as other sociological concerns. In order to determine the best course of action, therefore, a comprehensive analysis of multiple and often conflicting organizational objectives and environmental factors must be undertaken.

Regardless of the type of administrative problem at hand, it is indeed very difficult to answer questions such as what should be done now, what can be deferred, what alternatives are to be explored, and what should be the priority structure for the objectives. Recent developments in the field of management indicated that "administration by multiple objectives" is perhaps the most difficult but also the most important topic in the field (Lee, 1979). Martin K. Starr, editor of *Management Science* and a past president of The Institute of Management Science (TIMS), states that, in his opinion, the most important research topic in the area of management and administration today is the area of multiple-objective decision making. Warren Bennis, eminent scholar in the field of organizational development, states that organizations, as well as society in general, have become so fragmented into various interest and value groups that there is no longer one predominent objective for any organization. Consequently, one of the most important and difficult decision problems is to achieve an equilibrium among the multiple and conflicting interests and objectives of the various components of the organization (Lee, 1981, p. 9).

Several recent studies concerning the future of the industrialized society have echoed this same theme: when a society is incurring enormous technological development and rapid change, the stability of the system must be assured by achieving a delicate balance among such multiple objectives as food production, industrial output, pollution control, population growth, use of natural resources, international cooperation for economic stability, and civil rights and equal opportunity provisions (Lee, 1979). Administration by multiple objectives is clearly a very important element of public administration today, and it will certainly be the central issue in the 1980s.

The multiplicity of organizational objectives is even more apparent in the academic setting. For example, as we mentioned in Chapter 1, the present situation in many universities is one of compromise and tense coexistence among all parties involved—taxpayers, the state legislature, the university administration, faculty and staff, students, and the general public. Any effective administrative decision must, therefore, be capable of reflecting the various concerns, aspirations, and priorities of the many interest groups seeking satisfaction. The academic administrator must be able to demonstrate to the various forces demanding justification for his or her actions, the basis for the decision process. This requires the development of a methodology which includes explicit consideration of the multiple and often conflicting objectives of the various interest groups. ABO based on a modern management science methodology is proposed here as such a decision system.

ABO as a System

The application of the ABO concept in organizational planning has gone through three distinct stages: (1) performance appraisal, (2) management planning, and (3) an integrated administrative process. In the early state of ABO's development, its concept was adopted as a better way to appraise an administrator's performance. The scope of this application was generally limited to the first-line supervisors and their subordinates. As Douglas McGregor (1969) pointed out, the administrator was put in a very uneasy position in evaluating individual subordinates' personal worth to the organization.

In the second stage of ABO development in the 1960s, its concept was used for organizational planning. No doubt the influence of the Planning Programming and Budgeting System (PPBS), widely touted during the early 1960s in the federal government, was a strong impetus for the ABO application. ABO thus evolved as a scheme to tie planning, budgets, and programs to objectives. In the 1970s, ABO reached the third stage and has now become an integrated administrative process that includes the formulation of organizational objectives, long-range strategic plans, operational objectives, action plans, and feedback and control.

ABO should not be merely a style, philosophy, or procedure. It is an integrated management system—a way to pull administrative functions together in a systematic and logical manner in order to formulate and achieve a set of

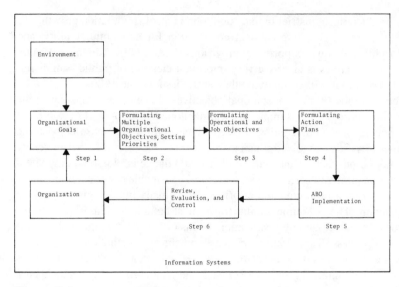

Figure 3.1
Major Elements and Steps of ABO

objectives. The major elements of the system and key steps of ABO are presented in figure 3.1. The key steps of the system can be identified as follows (Lee, 1981):

ABO Steps

1. Set Organizational Goals: Evaluate environmental conditions and the organization's unique factors, and then formulate broad, long-range organizational goals.

2. Formulate Multiple Objectives: Formulate explicit organizational objectives and analyze them in terms of their priorities for the organization.

3. Formulate Operational Objectives: Formulate specific, detailed, short-term work objectives at the divisional, departmental, or individual administrator's level.

4. Formulate Action Plans: Develop a set of action plans to achieve operational work objectives. Action plans should include manpower needs, training and manpower

	planning, performance-appraisal plans, and employee-motivation plans. Also, it is essential to establish plans to secure, control, and systematically allocate resources to implement the action plans.
5. Implement the System:	Determine the system-implementation strategies in terms of personnel, resource requirements, planning, and expected problems and strategies to resolve them.
6. Review, Evaluation, and Control:	Evaluate the results of the action plans and make necessary modifications based on periodic reviews for the entire system.

As a working system, the ABO process is composed of certain elements and their relationships to achieve a set of objectives. To make the system function effectively, important and timely information must be retrieved, processed, stored, and utilized. Since ABO is also a human process, it requires a good communication system that can serve as the catalyst in pulling all the human efforts together.

The primary functions of management information systems for ABO involve the following:

To identify and obtain information, both from external and internal sources, that would be required in setting long-range organizational goals.

To analyze relationships among organizational objectives, priorities of objectives, and alternative courses of action, and work activities. Process this information for use in various elements of the ABO system.

To identify data-input requirements, data-collection methods, and information-flow patterns for systematic analysis and decision making.

To design a system of information and communication flows for feedback control and updating of the ABO support elements.

The major elements of the ABO system will now be discussed in greater detail:

1. Setting Organizational Goals

This step involves the following basic questions: What is the basic purpose or mission of the organization in the society? Why and how does the organization exist? What type of organization does it want to become? Any human organization must serve a purpose and satisfy certain needs in the society. It exists in a given environment with its unique set of factors. Also, it has certain organizational characteristics, such as the size, location, management philosophy, stage of its growth, physical and human capabilities, and the like. Based on all such information, management must formulate broad, long-range organizational goals.

2. Formulating Multiple Objectives

Broad organizational goals present the general direction in which the organization should move. However, such a direction alone cannot provide explicit targets toward which the organization should direct its resources. Formulating organizational objectives in explicit and measurable criteria is the most important element of the ABO process. Once organizational objectives are formulated, they can be further refined and broken down into departmental objectives and personal work objectives. In this way, work activities will be coordinated toward achieving the overall organizational objectives.

3. Setting Priorities

It is human nature to desire more than one can possibly achieve. Organizational objectives are no exception to this rule. Since multiple objectives are competing for organizational resources, there is a need to set priorities so that important organizational objectives are achieved *before* less important objectives are considered. This is one aspect of the ABO process which has been generally neglected by administrators. A *sound priority structure is as essential as formulating realistic objectives.*

4. Analyzing Alternative Courses of Action

It has been said that any decision problem which does not have alternatives will result in a poor decision. Once multiple objectives are formulated and their priorities determined, strategies or possible ways to achieve these objectives should be explored. The set of available alternatives may not be exhaustive. It is sometimes necessary to develop new alternatives through systems analysis. However, it is extremely difficult to determine how exhaustive the alternative search should be, because the process may cost a great deal of money, time, and effort. Once all feasible alternatives have been determined, they should be carefully analyzed in terms of their cost-effectiveness in achieving organizational objectives. This process is further complicated when we introduce the time dimension—short-term vs. long-term—to the effectiveness. This is where management-science models are most useful—in determining the relative merits of available alternatives.

5. Decision Making

When all relevant information is obtained about feasible courses of action, decisions have to be made regarding the choice of specific courses of action. The decision-making process should be as rational and systematic as possible. However, quantitative data or model results do not automatically become decisions. We must recognize the fact that the decision-making process is based on the personal style and perceptions of the administrator. The administrator may use his or her intuition and judgment about many other factors that are not quantitative and could not be examined explicitly—i.e., organizational politics, personal insights about future outcomes, environmental factors, and so forth. The administrator uses all available data and information to enrich and sharpen his judgment so that the final decision will be at least "intentionally rational" in the environment of uncertainties and intangibles, as well as incomplete information.

6. Developing Action Plans

When a set of alternatives is selected through the decision-making process, action plans must be developed. This step essentially involves scheduling activities, resource allocations, manpower needs, and the proper control of event sequences. A host of network and planning models can be applied so that the objectives will be achieved effectively.

7. Human Resources Management

The ABO is a human process. Without effective human resources management, an effective ABO system cannot be expected. Thus, it is essential to develop a well-planned and coordinated human-resources-management process encompassing: performance appraisal; behavior reinforcement; employee motivation with appropriate compensation plans, training and development, and career paths; and long-range organizational manpower planning.

8. Feedback Control System

In the ABO processs organizational goals, plans, and objectives are to be achieved by a set of action plans. However, it would be indeed rare if action plans resulted in the exactly expected attainment of objectives. Thus, there is a need to evaluate the results of the action plans and personnel performance and then to make necessary modifications so that the desired results are obtained. Also, since the environment changes, it is quite possible that previously established goals, plans, objectives, criteria for cost-effectiveness, and so forth are no longer appropriate. Thus systematic feedback evaluation and control of the ABO process are essential to the maintenance of a current and effective system.

Administrative Approaches with the ABO System

As a result of the ABO system and the acceptance of some of its important features by organizations, several changes are likely to occur in administrative approaches.

1. Purpose-Oriented Administration

The ABO system requires an organization to be purpose oriented, from the work of the top administrator to that of the employee in the lowest echelon. The work activities will be planned and carried out according to organizational objectives rather than just "by the book" of organizational procedures. The question "What does this activity contribute toward important organizational objectives?" will continually be asked before resources are committed. There will be more emphasis on such things as zero-base budgets, cost-effectiveness, and priorities for objectives.

2. Information and Analysis-Based Administration

An effective ABO system also requires an efficient management information system (MIS) and systematic decision making. With the ever-increasing complexity of the environment and its vital impact on the organization's survival, information management becomes extremely important. Accurate and timely information must be processed in order to predict the future state of affairs with an acceptable degree of accuracy.

There will be more widespread application of management-science models to generate additional information. The use of computers for everyday administration will be more prevalent. With the availability of inexpensive but powerful micro- and minicomputers, even small organizations can be more systematic in handling materials, inventory control, research, payroll, scheduling, and resource allocation. Decentralization of decision making will be more common in large organizations with economical installations of departmental computing facilities. Administrators, especially at the lower and middle levels, will be required to be more knowledgeable about computers and management science.

3. Management of Multiple Objectives

Organizations will be vitally concerned with the analysis of multiple objectives, not only with their formulation, but with priorities and trade-offs. There exists an ever-increasing pressure for the simultaneous satisfaction of government regulations, economic optimization, and other organizational goals. Materials shortage (e.g., energy) and their increasing costs are forcing administrators to be more concerned with the economic optimization (minimizing operational costs). Yet, government regulations to cope with the same basic problems have forced organizations to be further removed from the economic optimization. Undoubtedly, there will be more direct conflict between an organization's economic survival and other objectives that are related to the social responsibilities of the organization.

Administrators will be held increasingly accountable for the legitimacy of their objectives, priorities, and the resolution of conflict among their objectives. Thus, we will see greater application of systematic approaches in dealing with multiple goals and their trade-offs. Computer-based interactive approaches will be more widely used in objective formulation and priority setting.

4. Increased Concern for Productivity

The essence of ABO is to increase the efficiency of the organization. Productivity of human, physical, and financial resources will continue to be the central concern of administration. In order to improve the cost-effectiveness of the administrative process, three important areas should be evaluated: (1) productivity of personnel; (2) more effective management of resources; and (3) more efficient administrative process. In order to implement an effective ABO system, administration must commit itself to the training, development, self-improvement, and motivation of human resources. The human resource and its effective utilization will continue to hold the key to the survival and prosperity of the organization under the ABO system.

5. Increased Attention to Group Behavior

As we focus our attention on the human resource, group behavior will become increasingly more important than the individual's behavior. It has been pointed out by many scholars that one of the important reasons for the poor showing of Americans' productivity is the failure to recognize the importance of people's group behavior. Harvard sociologist Ezra F. Vogel (1979) contends that perhaps the most important reason for the phenomenal productivity increase of the Japanese human resource is their group-conscious behavior patterns. It is terribly important for Japanese to belong to groups. Group loyalty and confidence in group values are driving forces for Japanese workers. The study of group behavior, especially the importance of the sense of shared purpose to motivation and productivity, will receive greater attention from administrators under the ABO system.

6. Management of Capital, Energy, and Materials

With the increasing scarcity and cost of acquiring capital, energy, and materials, an effective management of these resources will become almost as important as the management of human resources. As many economists point out, the American economy suffers from a lack of capital formation due to low savings. They single out inflation and government taxes that penalize savings as the main causes of declining savings. The efficient management of capital, energy, and materials will further require systematic approaches based on computer-based information systems and management-science techniques.

7. More Systematic Contingency Management

Future changes in the environment will clearly be more drastic than those of the past. Shortages of energy, materials, water, clean air, and many other resources can be no doubt expected. Also, some important technological breakthroughs—cheaper and more powerful microcomputers, new inventions concerning energy, new transportation methods, as well as new leisure approaches to work and productivity, and so on, will be forthcoming. Moreover, most experts expect the future to hold many political and economic crises on the international scene. These changes will have varying impacts on organizations.

An organization cannot be totally *reactive* to new developments, functioning without plans. Nor could it be totally *proactive* with every possible contingency planned for changing situations. Under the ABO system, however, the basic targets are clearly defined, and thus people can use imagination to get to them. With the availability of improved information systems, management-science models, and computational facilities, contingency management will be more systematic and orderly.

8. Closer Interaction with External Factors

The ABO system is an open system. It breathes in external factors in the form of environmental constraints, needs, and information. The feedback-control system monitors such information so that the entire ABO system remains current and effective. Thus, the organization can be expected to have closer interaction with external forces: government agencies; international situations; socio-economic factors of the environment; concerns of taxpayers; and changing markets.

Key Terms of ABO

At this point it is appropriate to define a number of terms which are widely used in ABO. For example, the reader needs to understand the terms *mission*, *goals*, *objectives*, and *targets*.

Mission: This is a very broad and general statement about the basic purpose of the organization.

Goals: This is a more precise statement of a purpose than is the mission, but may not be a quantifiable description of a hoped-for accomplishment. It tends to be relatively long-range in its time frame—five years or longer.

Objective: An objective is an explicit, clear, and specific statement about a desired accomplishment, in quantifiable terms. Objectives are based on goals and they are to lead toward accomplishing goals. Objectives can be long term (up to five years). Usually, however, they are short term, ranging from six months to three years. It is necessary to define objectives in quantitative criteria with specific time constraints.

Target: A target is a finer breakdown of an objective. It is a very specific desired state that contributes toward achieving an objective. Targets are expressed in a very short-term time frame (e.g., to introduce a new curriculum for the college by November 15 for review by the academic committee).

Priority Structure for Objectives: This represents an ordering of objectives in terms of their importance to the organization. Priorities may be either numerical or hierarchical weights. The numerical weights in terms of utilities or coefficients of regret are also called cardinal weights. The hierarchical weights are ordinal, preemptive, or lexicographic priority weights. Thus, the most important objective should be pursued until it is attained or until the point is reached beyond which no further improvement is possible, before the second most important objective is considered.

Rationality in Decision Making

According to conventional dogma, human decision-making behavior in organizations has been analyzed in two broad theoretical foundations—normative (prescriptive) and descriptive (behavioral). The normative theories are concerned with how rational decisions *ought to* be made, whereas the descriptive theories are concerned with how decisions are *actually made* in reality (Simon, 1955; "On How To Decide" 1978; "Rationality" 1978; 1979). The distinction between the two theories of decision-making behavior has been clearly established. However, in reality they are closely related, particularly to the extent that each has been greatly modified by new development in the other (Becker, 1962).

The normative theories emphasize substantive rationality (*what* decisions are to be made) while generally neglecting procedural rationality (*how* decisions are actually made) (March, 1978). As the environment becomes increasingly complex, decision making becomes increasingly more concerned with how the decision maker utilizes limited human cognitive powers in coping with the complexity involved in the decision problem. Thus, the descriptive theories are primarily concerned with procedural rationality.

The classical theory of rational decision making is theoretically neat. It assumes the decision maker is an "economic man" who has an omniscient rationality. In other words, the decision maker as an economic optimizer is assumed to have complete information about all relevant aspects of the decision environment, possesses a stable system of preferences, and also has the ability to analyze the alternative courses of action. However, developments in the organizational behavior field during the past two decades have cast considerable doubt about whether the classical theory of rationality can be applied to decision makers in today's complex organizations (Cyert, March, 1963; March and Simon, 1958).

According to broad empirical investigations, there is no evidence that an individual decision maker is capable of performing a completely rational analysis for complex decision problems. Also there is considerable doubt that the individual value (preference) system is exactly identical to that of the organization in determining what is best for the organization. Furthermore, the decision maker in reality is often quite incapable of identifying the optimum choice because of a lack of analytical ability, incomplete information, or the complexity of the decision environment (Simon, 1955).

The emphasis of substantive rationality coupled with the concept of "economic man" naturally leads the classical theory toward the achievement of global optimization as its objective. Thus, the global optimization process is concerned with the achievement of a single overall organizational effectiveness measure such as finding the least cost, maximum profit, or maximum utility. The criterion of global optimization (regardless of exactly what kind of measure is used) is extremely difficult to define. Even if it can be defined, there exists considerable doubt about whether such a global goal of an organization that cannot be readily connected operationally with administrative actions can be used as the objective criterion.

The descriptive theories, based on an abundance of empirical data, proposed the now celebrated "bounded rationality." H. A. Simon (1979) explains in his Nobel Prize lecture as follows:

> What then is the present status of the classical theory of the firm? There can no longer be any doubt that the micro assumptions of the theory—the assumptions of perfect rationality—are contrary to fact. It is not a question of approximation; they do not even remotely describe the process that human beings use for making decisions in complex situations.
>
> Moreover, there is an alternative. If anything, there is an embarrassing richness of alternatives. Today, we have a large mass of descriptive data, from both laboratory and field, that show how human problem solving and decision making actually take place in a wide variety of situations.

. . . In one way or another, they incorporate the notions of bounded rationality: the need to search for decision alternatives, the replacement of optimization by targets and satisficing goals, and mechanisms of learning and adaptation. If our interest lies in descriptive decision theory (or even normative decision theory), it is now entirely clear that the classical and neoclassical theories have been replaced by a superior alternative that provides us with a much closer approximation to what is actually going on.

Bounded rationality does not mean irrationality on the part of decision makers (March, 1978). Rather, it does mean that individual decision makers strive to be as effective as possible in achieving organizational goals, given their information-processing capabilities. In other words, the decision maker employs an "approximate" rationality in the process of attempting to do the best to achieve organizational goals within the given set of constraints. This idea of "intentionally" rational decision behavior is the foundation of bounded rationality. The same basic theses, although not in the same vein of terminology, have been presented by scholars of management concerning functions of practicing managers (Mintzberg, 1973; Sayles, 1979).

Decision models developed under the stringent and unrealistic conditions of complete rationality have very limited real-world implications. In order to implement decision models, then, one must either sufficiently simplify the model so that the optimum solution can be easily derived, or design a realistic model and seek satisfactory solutions. The first is the so-called "quick and dirty" approach, while the second approach attempts to retain a richer set of properties of the real decision environment by giving up optimization. Although the two approaches are quite different, they are both "satisficing" approaches based on the concept of bounded rationality and have been widely applied by management scientists. In the satisficing approach, one attempts to attain satisfactory levels of goals rather than optimizing each of the goals.

Perhaps the most realistic procedure for developing a decision model would be to replace abstract and global organization goals with tangible and measurable subgoals. The subgoals may be formulated on the basis of certain aspiration levels that are related to the organizational goals. Once a decision alternative satisfies a set of aspirations (or at least important ones), the search activity could be terminated. This is also a satisficing approach. Undoubtedly, aspiration levels are dynamic, always changing in accordance with changing environmental conditions. Nevertheless, the important thing is that the use of aspiration levels instead of global optimization goals through the search-and-satisficing approach would allow for a bounded rational decision with reasonable amounts of computational efforts and incomplete information about the decision environment.

The global optimization model has a single criterion objective function (e.g., cost minimization, profit maximization, or utility maximization). On the other hand, the satisficing model based on aspiration levels typically has a multiple criterion objective function. Since some aspirations may be competitive or in conflict, and thus all aspirations may not be achieved within the given system constraints, there is a need to attach some form of preferences (either weighted or prioritized) to the aspirations. The multicriteria-satisficing approach to decision making is a practical way to search for "good" decisions with limited information, resources, and computational skills.

In his Nobel Prize lecture, Simon (1979) continues:

> It would take a much more extensive review than is provided here to establish the point conclusively, but I believe it is the case that specific phenomena requiring a theory of utility or profit maximization for their explanation rather than a theory of bounded rationality simply have not been observed in aggregate data. In fact, as my last two examples (first-degree homogeneity of production functions and executive salaries) indicate, it is the classical rather than the behavioral form of the theory that faces real difficulties in handling some of the empirical observations.

The classical optimization model generally attempts to find the optimum solution through economic models or certain operations research techniques (especially linear programming). On the other hand, the satisficing model attempts to find a satisfactory solution through computer-based search routines, heuristics, artificial intelligence, cognitive simulation, and some operations research techniques with varying degree of success.

Goal Programming for ABO

Goal programming is an extension of a classical optimization technique (i.e., linear programming). Yet, its ability to incorporate the decision maker's multicriterion aspiration levels, the relaxation of system constraints, and the decision maker's preference system for multiple conflicting goals transforms it into a satisficing model. Although goal programming can be used strictly as an optimization model, its real purpose and value are in the domain of the satisficing decision-behavior of bounded rationality.

In addition to the satisficing behavior, the decision maker in reality is extremely conscious of the implications of the decision, and its solution, on the surroundings in terms of the decision maker's own welfare. We are only beginning to recognize the importance of the decision maker's personal goals and perceptions about the organizational environment (politics) in the decision-making process. Goal programming is capable of reflecting such personal judgmental factors in the environment of bounded rationality.

From the days of early scholars of management theories, such as Henri Fáyol, Mary Parker Follet, Frederick W. Taylor, Elton Mayo, and others, to modern-day scholars, such as Peter Drucker, Henry Mintzberg, Leonard Sayles, and many others, it has been firmly established, through normative as well as descriptive theories of managerial functions, that management is a function of achieving a set of organizational objectives in the most efficient way. In order to coordinate human efforts, management must identify organizational objectives and their priorities *before* organizing and controlling. Some of the well-established motivational theories, especially the social exchange theory of G. C. Homans (1961), the inducement-contributions theory of Chester Barnard (1938), the cognitive dissonance theory of L. Festinger (1957), the equity theory (Adams, 1963), and the like, have clearly demonstrated that expected work performance toward explicitly stated organizational objectives is an essential requirement for employee motivation. Thus, the development of organizational objectives, policies, and work procedures is important for allowing organizational members to experience a sense of challenge and accomplishment while fulfilling organizational as well as personal goals. The basic ABO process also recognizes that the vertical and horizontal work coordination in an organization must be achieved through communicated objectives (organizational aspirations), their priorities, and the reward-punishment system connected with them.

Modern motivation theories recognize that one of the most important motivators of organizational members is the determination of appropriate aspiration levels for individual work efforts. These aspiration levels must be challenging, attainable with good efforts, and related to the achievement of an individual's personal goals. Furthermore, the aspiration levels should be operational and tangible, to the extent that human efforts and other organizational resources can be directed toward the achievement of such aspirations (Lee, 1981).

A decision-making approach that can improve the actual management decision-making practices will have the greatest impact. The thesis of this book is that goal programming accommodates most of the above-described aspects of reality better than other approaches suggested for multicriterion decision making. Thus, in this book goal programming is presented as the means to implement the basic concepts of ABO to academic administration.

Summary

This chapter has presented the basic concepts and elements of ABO. ABO should not be regarded simply as an administrative style for public organizations but as a self-contained, *operational* system that gets things done in a *systematic* way. In utilizing ABO, either in its entirety or through some of its important features, we must recognize many relevant factors that influence the organization, such as the changing concept of rationality, importance of establishing operational objectives, the multiplicity and conflicting nature of objectives, and the need for systematic approaches for decision making. Goal programming is proposed in this book as a systematic approach to implement ABO for public organizations, especially academic institutions.

References

Adams, J. S. "Toward an Understanding of Inequity." *Journal of Abnormal and Social Psychology* 67 (1963): 422–36.

Barnard, Chester I. *The Functions of the Executive.* Cambridge, Massachusetts, 1938.

Becker, G. S., "Irrational Behavior and Economic Theory." *Journal of Political Economy* 70 (1962): 1–13.

Cyert, R. M., and March, J. G. *A Behavioral Theory of the Firm.* Englewood Cliffs, New Jersey: Prentice-Hall, 1963.

Festinger, L. *Theory of Cognitive Dissonance.* Stanford, California: University Press, 1957.

Homans, G. C. *Social Behavior: Its Elementary Form.* Lexington, Massachusetts: Brade & World, 1961.

Lee, Sang M. *Goal Programming for Decision Analysis.* Philadelphia: Auerbach Publishers, 1972.

———. *Goal Programming for Multiple Objective Integer Programs.* Monograph 2. American Institute of Industrial Engineers, Atlanta, 1979.

———. *Management by Multiple Objectives.* Princeton: Petrocelli Books, 1981.

McGregor, Douglas. *The Human Side of Enterprise.* New York: McGraw-Hill, 1969.

March, J. G. "Bounded Rationality, Ambiguity, and the Engineering of Choice." *Bell Journal of Economics* 9, no. 2 (1978): 587–608.

March, J. G., and Simon, H. A. *Organizations.* New York: Wiley, 1958.

Mintzberg, Henry. *The Nature of Managerial Work.* New York: Harper, 1973.

Sayles, L. *Leadership.* New York: McGraw-Hill, 1979.

Selznik, P. *Leadership in Administration.* Evanston, Illinois: Row, Peterson, 1957.

Simon, H. A. "A Behavioral Model of Rational Choice." *Quarterly Journal of Economics* 69 (1955): 99–118.

———. "On How to Decide What to Do." *Bell Journal of Economics* 9, no. 2 (1978): 494–507.

————. "Rational Decision Making in Business Organizations." *American Economic Review* 69, 4 (1979): 493–513.

————. "Rationality as Process and as Product of Thought." *American Economic Review* 68, 2 (1978): 1–16.

Vogel, E. F. *Japan as Number One: Lessons for America.* Cambridge: Harvard University Press, 1979.

Chapter 4

Goal Programming for
Administration by Objectives

The Concept of Goal Programming

For over thirty years, the student of management science has been taught that in order to develop a decision model one must follow the set of steps listed below:

1. Define the decision variables for the problem.
2. Develop an objective criterion which should be maximized or minimized depending upon the nature of the problem.
3. Formulate constraints that describe either environmental restrictions imposed upon the activities of the system, or resource limitations.
4. Then, seek a solution to the model which optimizes the single objective function while all the constraints are absolutely satisfied.

The methodological approach described above has been so deeply ingrained that people tend to develop decision models by following the procedure without ever pausing to consider the limitations of the approach. However, as we discussed in Chapter 3, the classical optimization approach for a single objective criterion is incapable of handling real-world decision problems in any meaningful way.

In order to be practical, a modeling approach should be able to perform the following important functions:

1. It should be capable of obtaining a satisficing solution for a set of multiple, conflicting objectives.
2. It should distinguish the truly binding system constraints, those representing environmental and fact-of-life type restrictions, and goal constraints, those reflecting organizational objectives expressed in terms of aspiration levels.

3. It should reflect the decision maker's judgments concerning the unique aspects of the decision environment and the priorities of organizational objectives.

Numerous approaches have been developed in the field of management science during the past fifteen years concerning multiple-objective decision making. Among them are the indifference-curve analysis, the multiattribute utility analysis, search routines, heuristics, multiobjective linear programming, goal programming, and many others. Several promising techniques and their applications to real-world decision problems are providing new dimensions for ABO as an operational system. Perhaps the most pragmatic technique for multiple-objective decision making is goal programming. Goal programming is not only a powerful tool which draws upon the highly developed and tested technique of linear programming, but it also closely resembles the primary features of ABO in dealing with multiple-objective administrative problems.

The most important characteristic of goal programming is its realistic and practical approach to decision making. It has the following special features:

1. An explicit consideration of the existing decision environment— constraints for the environmental factors, organizational climate, and management philosophy, as well as the judgment of the decision maker.
2. A flexible approach to formulating tangible and realistic objectives as aspiration levels.
3. Incorporation of the decision maker's priorities for the objectives as an integral part of the model analysis.
4. Capability to perform an interactive analysis for feedback and control of the system (trade-offs among objectives; effects of changing technological coefficients, levels of objectives, and priorities; addition or deletion of objectives or variables).
5. Capability to perform computer-based solution and model simulations with various combinations of inputs.
6. Recognition of the human side of administration in the ABO process.

In order to operationalize the ABO process for academic administration, we propose goal programming as the basic methodological tool. Goal programming can handle decision problems having a single goal with multiple subgoals, as well as cases having multiple goals and subgoals. It should be noted here that in goal programming the term *goal* is used interchangeably with the terms *objective* and *aspiration level*.

Often goals set by an organization compete for scarce resources. Furthermore, these goals may be incommensurable. Thus there is a need to establish a hierarchy of importance among these conflicting goals so that higher-order goals are satisfied or have reached the point beyond which no further improvements are desirable before lower-priority goals are considered. If the decision maker can provide an ordinal ranking of goals in terms of their contributions or importance to the organization, and if all relationships of the model are linear, the problem can be solved by goal programming.

In goal programming, instead of attempting to maximize or minimize the objective criterion directly, as is the case in linear programming, the deviations between goals and what can be achieved within the given set of constraints are minimized (Charnes and Cooper, 1961; Charnes, Cooper, and Ferguson, 1955). In the simplex algorithm of linear programming, such deviations are called slack variables. These variables take on a new significance in goal programming. The deviational variable is represented in two dimensions: both positive and negative deviations from each subgoal or goal. Then the objective function becomes the minimization of these deviations based on the relative importance or priority assigned to them (Ijiri, 1956; Lee, *Goal Programming for Decision Analysis*, 1972; Lee, *Goal Programming Methods*, 1979).

The solution of any linear programming problem is based on a numerical (cardinal) value such as profit or cost. The distinguishing characteristic of goal programming is that it allows for an ordinal solution. The decision maker may be unable to obtain information about the value or cost of a goal or a subgoal, but often can determine its upper or lower limits. Usually, the decision maker can determine the priority of the desired attainment of each goal or subgoal and can rank the priorities in an ordinal sequence. Obviously, it is not possible to achieve every goal to the extent desired. Thus, with or without goal programming, the decision maker attaches a certain priority to the achievement of a particular goal. The true value of goal programming, therefore, is its contribution to the solution of decision problems involving multiple and conflicting goals according to the decision maker's priority structure (Ijiri, 1965; Lee, 1971; Lee, 1972; Lee, 1973).

Goal programming has been applied to a wide range of planning, resource allocation, policy analysis, and functional problems. The first application was made by A. Charnes et al ("Note on the Application," 1968) for advertising-media planning. However, the first real-world application was in the area of manpower planning, again by Charnes, and W. W. Cooper and R. J. Neihaus (August 1968). Subsequently, goal programming has been applied to aggregate production planning (Jaaskelainen, 1969; Lee, Moore, "A Practical Approach," 1974), transportation logistics (Lee, Moore, 1973), academic resource planning (Lee, Clayton, 1972), hospital administration (Lee, 1972, pp. 320–50), marketing planning (Lee, Nicely, 1974), financial planning (Lee, 1972, pp. 208–16), portfolio selection (Lee, Lerro, 1974), municipal economic planning (Lee, 1972, pp. 299–318), resource allocation for environmental protection (Charnes, et al, 1975), and many other real-world problems.

The Goal Programming Model

Goal programming is a linear mathematical model in which the optimum attainment of multiple goals is sought within the given decision environment. The decision environment determines the basic components of the model, namely, the decision variables, the constraints, and the objective function.

In the goal programming model there are two types of constraints: system constraints and goal constraints (Lee, 1979). The system constraints represent the absolute restrictions imposed by the decision environment on the model. For example, there are only seven days in a week (time constraint), the physical capacity in a short run is limited to certain available facilities (space constraints), and the production of goods and services should be limited to demand and storage capacity (physical constraint). The system constraints must be satisfied before any of the goal constraints are considered.

The goal constraints represent those functions that present desired aspiration levels of certain measures. The desired level for a budget, faculty-student ratios, faculty-staff ratios, undergraduate-graduate program relationships, and the like are several illustrations of goal constraints. Through the use of goal constraints, a goal programming model can perform three types of analysis: (1) determining the input (resource) requirements to achieve a set of goals; (2) determining the degree of attainment of defined goals with given resources; and (3) providing the optimum solution under the varying combinations of inputs and priority structures of goals.

Let us now consider the goal programming model through a simple illustration. First, goal programming involving a single goal with multiple subgoals will be discussed, followed by an analysis of multiple goals.

A. Single Goal with Multiple Subgoals

Example 4.1. An organization produces two products: A and B. The unit profit of A is $80 and of B is $40. The goal of the manager is to earn a total profit of exactly $640 in the next week.

The profit goal can be interpreted in terms of subgoals, which are sales volumes of A and B. Then a goal programming model can be formulated as follows:

Minimize $Z = d_1^- + d_1^+$

subject to $\$80X_1 + \$40X_2 + d_1^- - d_1^+ = \$640$

$X_1, X_2, d_1^-, d_1^+ \geqslant 0$

where

X_1 = number of units of A sold

X_2 = number of units of B sold

d_i^- = underachievement of the profit goal of \$640

d_i^+ = overachievement of the profit goal of \$640

If the profit goal is not completely achieved, then obviously the slack in the profit goal will be expressed by d_i^-, which represents the underachievement of the goal (or negative deviation from the goal). On the other hand, if the solution shows a profit in excess of \$640, the d_i^+ will show some value. If the profit goal of \$640 is exactly achieved, both d_i^- and d_i^+ will be zero. It should be noted that d_i^- and d_i^+ are complementary. If d_i^- takes a nonzero value, d_i^+ will be zero, and vice versa. Since at least one of the deviational variables will always be zero, $d_i^- \times d_i^+ = 0$. In the above example, there are an infinite number of combinations of X_1 and X_2 that will achieve the goal. The solution will be any linear combination of X_1 and X_2 between the two points ($X_1 = 8$, $X_2 = 0$) and ($X_1 = 0$, $X_2 = 16$). This straight line is exactly the isoprofit function when total profit is \$640.

The objective function can be expressed solely in terms of deviational variables based on the desire of the decision maker. For example, if a goal constraint is expressed by a function $\Sigma\, a_{ij}\, X_j = b_i$, then the three primary goal constraint types can be formulated as follows:

Goal Type	Goal Constraint	Deviational Variable in the Objective Function
$\Sigma a_{ij} X_j \leq b_i$	$\Sigma a_{ij} X_j + d_i^- - d_i^+ = b_i$	d_i^+
$\Sigma a_{ij} X_j \geq b_i$	$\Sigma a_{ij} X_j + d_i^- - d_i^+ = b_i$	d_i^-
$\Sigma a_{ij} X_j = b_i$	$\Sigma a_{ij} X_j + d_i^- - d_i^+ = b_i$	$d_i^- + d_i^+$

The above example did not have any model constraints. Now suppose that in addition to the profit goal constraint considered in example 4.1, the following two constraints are imposed. The marketing department reports that the *maximum* number of units of A that can be sold in a week is six. The *maximum* number of units of B that can be sold is eight.

Now the new goal programming model can be presented in the following way:

Minimize $Z = d_i^- + d_i^+$

subject to $\$80X_1 + \$40X_2 + d_1^- - d_1^+ = \$640$

$$X_1 \leq 6$$

$$X_2 \leq 8$$

$$X_1, X_2, d_1^-, d_1^+ \geq 0$$

The solution to the above problem can be easily calculated on the back of an envelope. The solution is $X_1 = 6$ and $X_2 = 4$. With this solution the deviational variables d_1^- and d_1^+ will both be zero. The manager's profit goal can be achieved under the new constraints imposed on the subgoals.

B. Analysis of Multiple Goals

The model illustrated above can be extended to handle cases of multiple goals. Let us assume that these goals are conflicting and incommensurable.

Example 4.2. Let us consider the case illustrated in example 4.1. Now the manager desires to achieve a weekly profit as close to $640 as possible. He also desires to achieve sales volumes for A and B as possible to six and to four, respectively. The manager's decision problem can be formulated as a goal programming model as follows:

Minimize $Z = d_1^- + d_2^- + d_3^- + d_1^+$

subject to $\$80X_1 + \$40X_2 + d_1^- - d_1^+ = 640$

$$X_1 + d_2^- = 6$$
$$X_2 + d_3^- = 4$$

where d_2^- and d_3^- represent underachievements of sales volume for A and B, respectively. It should be noted that d_2^+ and d_3^+ are not included in the second and third constraints, since the sales goals are given as the *maximum* possible sales volume. The solution to this problem can be found by a simple examination of the problem: If $X_1 = 6$, and $X_2 = 4$, all goals will be completely attained. Therefore,

$$d_1^- = d_2^- = d_3^- = d_1^+ = 0$$

C. Ranking and Weighting of Multiple Goals

In example 4.2 we had a case in which all goals are achieved simultaneously within the given constraints. However, in a real decision environment this is rarely the case. Quite often, most goals are competitive in terms of need for scarce resources. In the presence of incompatible multiple goals the manager needs to exercise his judgment about the importance of the individual goals. In other words, the most important goal must be achieved to the extent desired before the next goal is considered.

Goals of the decision maker may simply be meeting a certain set of constraints. For example, the manager may set a goal concerning a stable employment level in the plant, which is simply a part of the production constraint. Or the goal may be an entirely separate function from the constraints of the system. If the latter is the case, the goal constraint must be generated in the model. The decision maker must analyze the system and investigate whether all of his goals are expressed in the goal-programming model. When all constraints and goals are completely identified in the model, the decision maker must analyze each goal in terms of whether over- or underachievement of the goal is satisfactory or not. Based on this analysis the manager can assign deviational variables to the system and/or goal constraints. If overachievement is acceptable, positive deviation from the goal can be eliminated from the objective function. On the other hand, if underachievement of a certain goal is acceptable, negative deviation should not be included in the objective function. If the exact achievement of the goal is desired, both negative and positive deviations must be represented in the objective function.

In order to achieve the ordinal solution—that is, to achieve the goals according to their importance—negative and/or positive deviations about the goal must be ranked according to the "preemptive" priority factors. In this way the low-order goals are considered only after high-order goals are achieved as desired. If there are goals in several ranks of importance, the preemptive priority factor p_k ($k = 1, 2, \ldots, k$) should be assigned to the negative and/or positive deviational variables. The preemptive priority factors have the relationship of $p_1 >>> p_2 >>> p_3 \ldots p_k >>> p_{k+1}$, where $>>>$ means "very much greater than." The priority relationship implies that multiplication by n, however large it may be, cannot make the lower-level goal as important as the higher goal. It is, of course, possible to refine goals even further by means of decomposing (subdividing) the deviational variables. To do this, additional constraints and additional priority factors may be required.

One more step to be considered in the goal-programming model formulation is the weighting of deviational variables at the same priority level. For example, if the sales goal involves two different products, there will be two deviational variables with the same priority factor. The criterion to be used in determining the differential weights of deviational variables is the minimization of the opportunity cost or regret. This implies that the coefficient of regret, which is always positive, should be assigned to the individual deviational variable with the identical p_k factor. The coefficient of regret simply represents the relative amount of unsatisfactory deviation from the goal. Therefore, deviational variables on the same priority level must be commensurable, although deviations that are on different priority levels need not be commensurable.

Example 4.3. Consider the following modified case of the illustration given in the previous examples. Production of either a unit of A or B requires 1 hour of production capacity in the plant. The plant has a normal production capacity of 10 hours per week. Because of the limited sales capacity, the *maximum* number of units of A and B that can be sold are six and eight per week, respectively. The unit profit for A is $80 and for B $40.

The manager has set the following goals, arranged in order of importance.

1. Avoid any underutilization of production capacity (providing job security to the plant employees).
2. Sell as many units of A and B as possible. Since the unit profit of A is twice the amount of profit of B, the manager has twice as much desire to achieve the sales goal for A as for B.
3. Minimize overtime operation of the plant as much as possible.

In the above example, the manager is to make a decision that will achieve the goals as closely as possible with the minimum sacrifice. Since overtime operation is allowed in this example, production of A and B may take more than the normal production capacity of 10 hours. Therefore, the operational capacity can be expressed as

$$X_1 + X_2 + d_1^- - d_1^+ = 10$$

where X_1 = number of units of A to be produced

X_2 = number of units of B to be produced

d_1^- = idle (underutilization of) production capacity

d_1^+ = overtime operation

Accordingly, the sales capacity constraints can be written as

$$X_1 + d_2^- = 6$$

$$X_2 + d_3^- = 8$$

where d_2^- = underachievement of sales goal for A

d_3^- = underachievement of sales goal for B

It should be noted that d_2^+ and d_3^+ are not in the equation, since the sales goals given are the *maximum* possible sales volume.

In addition to the variables and constraints stated above, the following preemptive priority factors are to be defined:

P_1: The highest priority, assigned by the manager to the underutilization of production capacity (i.e., d_1^-).

P_2: The second priority factor, assigned to the underutilization of sales capacity (i.e., d_2^- and d_3^-). However, management puts twice the importance on d_2^- as that on d_3^- in accordance with respective profit figures for A and B.

P_3: The lowest priority factor, assigned to overtime in the production capacity (i.e., d_1^+).

Now the complete model can be formulated. The objective is the minimization of deviations from the goals. The deviant variable associated with the highest preemptive priority must be minimized to the fullest possible extent. When no further improvement is desirable or possible in the highest goal, then the deviations associated with the next highest priority factor will be minimized. The model can be expressed as:

$$\text{Minimize } Z = P_1 d_1^- + 2P_2 d_2^- + P_2 d_3^- + P_3 d_1^+$$

$$\text{subject to } X_1 + X_2 + d_1^- - d_1^+ = 10$$

$$X_1 + d_2^- = 6$$

$$X_2 + d_3^- = 8$$

$$X_1, X_2, d_1^-, d_2^-, d_3^-, d_1^+ \geq 0$$

From the simple investigation of the model we can derive the following optimal solution:

$$X_1 = 6, X_2 = 8, d_1^- = d_2^- = d_3^- = 0, d_1^+ = 4.$$

The first two goals are completely attained, but the third goal is only partially achieved, since the overtime operation could not be minimized to zero. This result is due to the direct conflict between the second (sales) goal and the third (minimization of overtime) goal. This kind of result reflects the everyday problem experienced in organizations when there are several conflicting goals.

Now, the general goal programming model can be presented as below:

$$\text{Minimize } Z = \sum_{k=1}^{K} \sum_{i=1}^{m} P_k(w_i^- d_i^- + w_i d_i^+)$$

$$\text{subject to } \sum_{j=1}^{n} a_{ij} X_j + d_i^- - d_i^+ = b_i \ (i = 1, \ldots m)$$

$$X_j, d_i^-, d_i^+ \geq 0$$

In this model, P_k is the preemptive priority factor assigned to goal k; w_i^- and w_i^+ are numerical weights assigned to the deviations of goal i at a given priority level; d_i^- and d_i^+ are the negative and positive deviations, respectively; a_{ij}

is the technological coefficient of X_j in goal i; and b_i is the right-hand-side value of goal i.

Goal Programming Model Formulation

It is important to consider formulation of the model before we discuss the solution methods and other topics of goal programming. The most difficult aspect of the application of goal programming is, in fact, the formulation of the model for a real-world situation. Model formulation is the process of transforming a decision problem into a management-science model. With the great advances in solution algorithms and computer software, the solution is not generally as difficult a problem as the model formulation.

In order to provide some experience and insight into formulating and analyzing the goal-programming model, several examples will be presented in this section. One key to successful application of goal programming is a person's ability to recognize when a problem can be analyzed by goal programming, and then to formulate the corresponding model.

Example 4.4 The registrar at a state university has a decision problem that involves multiple goals. The registrar's office currently employs 5 full-time clerical and 4 part-time student workers. The normal working hours per month for the clerical staff are 160, and 80 hours per month for student workers. According to past performance records of the workers, the average number of cases (either mail or window requests) handled has been 5 per hour for full-time clerical staff and 2 per hour for part-time student workers. The average wage rates are $6 for full-time staff and $3 for student workers.

In view of the increasing enrollment at the university, the registrar feels that the total number of cases or requests to be processed should be at least 5,500 per month. Since the office is open only for five days a week, overtime is often required of the workers (not necessarily overtime but extra hours for the student workers).

The registrar has set the following goals in terms of their priorities:

1. The first goal is to handle at least 5,500 cases for the next month.
2. The second goal is to limit the overtime work of clerical staff to a total of 100 hours for the month.
3. The third goal is to provide job security for all employees. The registrar feels that the full utilization of full-time clerical staff is twice as important as the full utilization of student workers.
4. The last goal is to minimize the overtime for full-time and student workers.

Based on the problem described above, the following goal constraints can be formulated:

1. Case Clearance Goal
    Achievement of the case clearance goal, which is set at 5,500, is a function of total working hours of the full-time clerical staff and part-time student workers and their productivity (cases handled per hour) rates.

$$5X_1 + 2X_2 + d_1^- - d_1^+ = 5,500$$

where X_1 = total full-time clerical staff hours/month

X_2 = total part-time student worker hours/month

d_1^- = underachievement of the case clearance goal

d_1^+ = overachievement of the case clearance goal

5 = case clearance rate/hour for full-time staff

2 = case clearance rate/hour for part-time student workers

5,500 = case clearance goal for the month

2. Regular Working Hours
    Office employees' working hours are determined by the regular monthly working hours for each type of employee and the number of full-time staff and part-time student workers. Since we denoted X_1 as the total full-time staff hours per month, with 5 full-time employees the total regular working hours per month will be $5 \times 160 = 800$. For the part-time student workers, the total working hours/month will be $4 \times 80 = 320$. Thus we have:

$$X_1 + d_2^- - d_2^+ = 800$$

$$X_2 + d_3^- - d_3^+ = 320$$

where d_2^- = underutilization of regular working hours of full-time staff

d_2^+ = overtime hours given to full-time staff

d_3^- = underutilization of regular working hours of student workers

d_3^+ = extra working hours given to student workers

3. Overtime
    In the goal-programming approach, to achieve a certain goal we must have a deviational variable to minimize. If there is no deviational variable to minimize to achieve a certain goal, one must be created by introducing a new goal constraint. In this problem, the second goal is to limit the

overtime of full-time staff to 100 hours. We do not have a deviational variable to minimize in order to achieve this goal in the above-formulated goal constraints. Therefore, we must introduce a new constraint as follows:

$$d_2^+ + d_4^- - d_4^+ = 100$$

where d_2^+ = actual overtime of full-time staff

d_4^- = difference between the actual overtime and the allowed overtime of 100 hours

d_4^+ = overtime in excess of 100 hours

We introduced both the negative and positive deviations from the allowed 100 hours of overtime because the actual overtime can be less than, equal to, or even greater than 100 hours. Now we have a deviational variable to minimize to achieve the second goal, i.e., d_4^+. It should be noted that the above constraint can also be expressed in a different way by adding 100 to the right hand side value of the regular working hour constraint for full-time staff as below:

$$x_1 + d_4^- - d_4^+ = 900$$

In this problem either of the above two constraints can be used to formulate the model.

The goal-programming model for the above problem is thus formulated as below:

Minimize $Z = P_1 d_1^- + P_2 d_4^+ + 2P_3 d_2^- + P_3 d_3^- + P_4 d_2^+ + P_4 d_3^+$

subject to $5X_1 + 2X_2 + d_1^- - d_1^+ = 5{,}500$

$$X_1 \qquad + d_2^- - d_2^+ = \quad 800$$

$$X_2 + d_3^- - d_3^+ = \quad 320$$

$$X_1 \qquad + d_4^- - d_4^+ = \quad 900$$

Example 4.5 The Management Training and Development Institute is again planning the annual "Summer Management Skills Workshop Series" during the summer months. All management workshops will be conducted at the continuing education center. The Institute is currently planning the following programs:

Program 1: First-Line Supervisor Management Skills Workshop
Program 2: Middle Management MBO Workshop
Program 3: Executive Management Seminar

Program 1 is a one-day workshop, whereas Program 2 is for three days, and Program 3 lasts for a whole week (five days). The workshop series is usually planned for a duration of eight weeks. Because of limited accommodations, dining, and conference room facilities at the continuing education center, only one workshop can be provided at a given time. Each type of workshop can be repeated as long as there are enough applicants. The desired class sizes for the workshops are as follows:

Program 1—30 participants
Program 2—25 participants
Program 3—15 participants

The Institute workshop coordinators report that, because of the reputation of the Institute's programs and nationally known lecturers participating in the programs, all regularly planned programs are expected to "make." As a matter of fact, the following applications have already been received:

Program 1—462
Program 2—206
Program 3—42

The director of the Institute has the following goals as listed by their priorities:

1. The Workshop Series should be run at least the planned forty program days (eight weeks).
2. Satisfy the following special requests of the Great Plains Chamber of Commerce:
   Program 1: 3 workshops
   Program 2: 2 workshops
   Program 3: 1 workshop
3. Limit the duration of Summer Management Skills Workshop Series to no longer than forty-five program days (nine weeks).
4. Meet the demand for the workshop series as closely as possible.

The constraints can thus be formulated as follows:

1. Planned Workshop Duration
   The normal planned workshop duration is for a period of forty program days or eight weeks.

   $$X_1 + 3X_2 + 5X_3 + d_1^- - d_1^+ = 40$$

   where X_1 = number of supervisory workshops

   X_2 = number of middle management workshops

X_3 = number of executive seminars

2. Program Demands
First, the Institute has outstanding requests from the Great Plains Chamber of Commerce as follows:

$X_1 + d_2^- - d_2^+ = 3$

$X_2 + d_3^- - d_3^+ = 2$

$X_3 + d_4^- - d_4^+ = 1$

The Institute has the following total number of applications:

$X_1 + d_5^- - d_5^+ = 15$

$X_2 + d_6^- - d_6^+ = 8$

$X_3 + d_7^- - d_7^+ = 3$

In the above goal constraints, it should be noted that the number of each program sessions was determined by dividing the applications by the desired class size and rounding off the product as shown below:

Program 1: 462/30 = 15.4 or 15
Program 2: 206/25 = 8.24 or 8
Program 3: 42/15 = 2.8 or 3

3. Limiting the Extension of the Planned Program Duration
We have already mentioned that frequently we have to introduce new constraints in order to define deviational variables that must be minimized to achieve certain goals. The director of the Institute desires to limit the extension of the planned program duration to five program days or one week so that the entire program duration would be no longer than forty-five program days, or nine weeks. As we do not have a deviational variable to minimize in order to achieve this goal, we introduce the following goal constraint:

$d_1^+ + d_8^- - d_8^+ = 5$ or

$X_1 + 3X_2 + 5X_3 + d_8^- - d_8^+ = 45$

Now, the problem can be formulated as a goal programming model.

Minimize $Z = P_1 d_1^- + P_2 (d_2^- + d_3^- + d_4^-) + P_3 d_8^+ + P_4 (d_5^- + d_6^- + d_7^-)$

subject to $\quad X_1 + 3X_2 + 5X_3 + d_1^- - d_1^+ = 40$

$\qquad\qquad X_1 \qquad\qquad\quad + d_2^- - d_2^+ = 3$

$$X_2 \qquad + d_3^- - d_3^+ = 2$$

$$X_3 + d_4^- - d_4^+ = 1$$

$$X_1 \qquad\qquad + d_5^- - d_5^+ = 15$$

$$X_2 \qquad + d_6^- - d_6^+ = 8$$

$$X_3 + d_7^- - d_7^+ = 3$$

$$X_1 + 3X_2 + 5X_3 + d_8^- - d_8^+ = 45$$

Example 4.6 The local college foundation has just completed a two-year fund raising campaign. The foundation has $2 million in hand and is planning to invest the money in four alternative plans: local banks stocks, municipal bonds, four-year certificates of deposit (CDs) at a local savings and loan, and real estate properties. Investments in stocks, bonds, and CDs are available at the beginning of each of the next six years. The investment analyst has filed the following detailed report.

Each dollar invested in stocks at the beginning of each year is expected to return an average of $1.30 (a return of $.30) two years later, in time for immediate reinvestment. Each dollar invested in bonds at the beginning of one year returns $1.50 three years later for possible reinvestment. Each dollar invested in a four-year CD returns $1.80 four years later. The investment opportunities in real estate (shopping centers and apartment complexes) are available only at the beginning of the fifth and sixth years. It is expected to return $1.25 (a return of $.25) one year later. Any money not in use is deposited in the passbook savings account at an annual interest rate of 6 percent.

The foundation board has established the following goals, in order of their importance.

1. Minimize the risk by diversifying the investment. No more than 30 percent of the total investment should be put into any one investment plan.
2. Since real estate is such a stable and attractive plan, try to invest at least $500,000 in this plan.
3. Make sure that at least $50,000 is available for emergency use in the passbook savings at all times.
4. Maximize the total cash value by the end of the sixth year.

This problem is unique in the sense that it involves time dimensions and compounding interests or returns. The cash flows involved in the problem can be depicted schematically as shown in figure 4.1. We can define decision variables as follows:

S_i = amount of money invested in the bank stocks at the beginning of the ith year

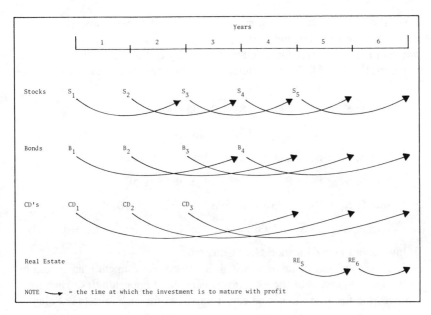

Figure 4.1
The College Foundation Investment Cash Flows

B_i = amount of money invested in the municipal bonds at the beginning of the ith year

CD_i = amount of money invested in the 4-year CDs at the beginning of the ith year

RE_i = amount of money invested in real estate at the beginning of the ith year

PS_i = amount of money not invested but put into the passbook savings account at the beginning of the ith year

1. System Constraints

In this problem, we have a set of system constraints that must be satisfied before any of the goal constraints are considered. The system constraints involved here are those that represent the cash outflow-inflow relationships. In other words, the amount of money the foundation can invest is restricted to the amount of funds available for investment.

At the beginning of the year, the foundation can invest only in stocks, bonds, and CDs. The amount of money available for investment for these plans at year one is $2 million. However, since the minimum length of maturity time (for the stocks) is two years, if the foundation invests the total amount of $2 million in S_1, B_1 and CD_1, there will be no funds available for investment at the beginning of the second year. Since one of the goals of this problem is to maximize the amount of funds by end of the sixth year, investments in S_i, B_i, and CD_i are limited to the first few years, as shown in figure 4.1.

Year 1: $S_1 + B_1 + CD_1 + PS_1 = 2,000,000$

Year 2: $S_2 + B_2 + CD_2 + PS_2 = 1.06 PS_1$

Year 3: $S_3 + B_3 + CD_3 + PS_3 = 1.06PS_2 + 1.3S_1$

Year 4: $S_4 + B_4 + PS_4 = 1.06PS_3 + 1.3S_2 + 1.5B_1$

Year 5: $S_5 + RE_5 + PS_5 = 1.06PS_4 + 1.3S_3 + 1.5B_2 + 1.8CD_1$

Year 6: $RE_6 + PS_6 = 1.06PS_5 + 1.3S_4 + 1.5B_3 + 1.8CD_2 + 1.25RE_5$

2. Investment Diversification Goal Constraint

The total amount of funds invested in any one investment plan should be limited to 30 percent of the total investment in all opportunities. Therefore, we need the following four goal constraints, one for each investment plan.

$$\sum_{i=1}^{5} S_i - .30 \left(\sum_{i=1}^{5} S_i + \sum_{i=1}^{4} B_i + \sum_{i=1}^{3} CD_i + \sum_{i=5}^{6} RE_i \right) + d_1^- - d_1^+ = 0$$

$$\sum_{i=1}^{4} B_i - .30 \left(\sum_{i=1}^{5} S_i + \sum_{i=1}^{4} B_i + \sum_{i=1}^{3} CD_i + \sum_{i=5}^{6} RE_i \right) + d_2^- - d_2^+ = 0$$

$$\sum_{i=1}^{3} CD_1 - .30 \left(\sum_{i=1}^{5} S_i + \sum_{i=1}^{4} B_i + \sum_{i=1}^{3} CD_i + \sum_{i=5}^{6} RE_i \right) + d_3^- - d_3^+ = 0$$

$$\sum_{i=1}^{6} RE_1 - .30 \left(\sum_{i=1}^{5} S_i + \sum_{i=1}^{4} B_i + \sum_{i=1}^{3} CD_i + \sum_{i=5}^{6} RE_i \right) + d_4^- - d_4^+ = 0$$

3. Investment in Real Estate Goal

The foundation desires to invest at least $500,000 because it represents such a stable and attractive opportunity.

$$\sum_{i=5}^{6} RE_1 + d_5^- - d_5^+ = 500,000$$

4. Minimum Balance in the Passbook Savings Goal

The foundation would like to maintain a minimum balance of $50,000 in the passbook savings at all times for emergencies.

$$PS_1 + d^-_{i+5} - d^+_{1+5} = 50,0000 \ (i = 1, 2, \ldots, 6)$$

Note that the above constraint has to be developed for each of the six years in the planning horizon.

5. Maximization of Cash Value Goal

The foundation attempts to maximize the cash value of investments by the end of the sixth year. From figure 4.1 it is clear that the amount of money at the end of the sixth year will be based on the returns of S_5, B_4, CD_3, RE_6, and PS_6.

$$1.3S_5 + 1.5B_4 + 1.8CD_3 + 1.25RE_6 + 1.06PS_6 + d^-_{12} - d^+_{12} = B$$

In the above constraint, the right-hand side value B is a very large number, let's say a billion dollars. If we minimize the negative deviation, d^-_{12}, we will actually be maximizing the cash inflows.

6. The Objective Function

Now the above objective function can be formulated as follows:

$$\text{Minimize } Z = P_1 \sum_{i=5}^{4} d^+_i + P_2 d^-_5 + P_2 d^-_5 + P_3 \sum_{i=6}^{n} d_i + P_4 d^-_{12}$$

Example 4.7 A state university system is considering ten capital improvement projects. The problem is a case of capital budgeting under a capital rationing situation where there are multiple conflicting objectives. Capital improvement projects require a special evaluation process because of the following considerations: (1) the state legislature takes a dim view of major new construction or capital improvement projects; (2) many existing physical facilities are old and energy inefficient; and (3) the maintenance costs of the existing facilities tend to be exorbitant.

The university system is considering the following ten projects:

1. Construction of a new agricultural experimentation facility—Main Campus.
2. Construction of a new wing and an additional floor for the College of Business Administration—Main Campus.
3. Renovating and refurbishing the Theater and Recital Hall—Main Campus.
4. Installation of a new boiler system—Main Campus.
5. Purchase of a new computer system and related equipment—Central Administration.
6. Construction of a married student housing apartment building—Main Campus.
7. Construction of a student activities center—Branch Campus A.

Table 4.1

Summary of Projects and Estimated Consequences

Project			NCF$_j$			CS$_j$			AMP
i	ICO	NPV	j = 1	j = 2	j = 3	j = 1	j = 2	j = 3	(FTE)
1	$3.75	$2.15	$0.70	$1.34	$1.75	$0.56	$1.15	$1.49	31
2	3.50	1.50	0.60	0.95	1.32	0.46	0.75	1.12	28
3	1.25	0.75	0.25	0.41	0.58	0.08	0.21	0.38	20
4	2.10	0.95	0.27	0.42	0.55	0.10	0.25	0.40	32
5	4.40	3.15	0.06	0.10	0.25	0	0	0.10	36
6	3.30	1.15	0.28	0.35	0.52	0.05	0.12	0.22	27
7	1.70	0.80	0.34	0.42	0.50	0.07	0.20	0.30	21
8	1.40	0.50	0.30	0.42	0.51	0.12	0.25	0.32	25
9	1.10	0.45	0.32	0.45	0.58	0.08	0.25	0.40	22
10	2.75	1.20	0.28	0.51	0.81	0.10	0.28	0.50	31

$ = millions of dollars.
ICO = Initial cash outflow of each project.
NPV = Net present value of cost savings of each project.
NCF$_j$ = Net cash flow requirement to maintain the project in year j.
CS$_j$ = Cost savings of each project in year j.
AMP = Administrative manpower requirement in terms of full-time equivalent (FTE).

  8. Renovating and refurbishing the Natural Sciences Building—Branch Campus B.
  9 Installation of a pollution control system at the coal-fired power generating plant—Main Campus.
10. Construction of a pollution-free new power generating plant—Main Campus.

The above listed projects are indivisible. In other words, if a project is accepted, it must be funded fully to complete the project. Thus, a partial funding of the projects is not feasible. Because of this special requirement, the problem needs a zero-one goal-programming approach.

Table 4.1 presents the pertinent information concerning the university system's capital budgeting problem in terms of the estimated consequences of the projects under consideration. The Board of Regents of the university system established the following set of goals, priorities, and constraints.

1. System Constraints

The zero-one requirement for the projects is automatically taken care of by the enumeration procedure of the zero-one goal programming approach. The mutually exclusive pollution-control projects (x_9 and x_{10}), one of which must be accepted to meet government guidelines, can also be easily handled by the zero-one goal programming algorithm as a goal constraint. Thus, the basic system constraints would be:

$$x_i = 0 \text{ or } 1 \ (i = 1, \ldots, 10)$$

2. Goal Constraints and Priorities

The Board of Regents has provided the following goals in the order of their importance:

P_1: The most important goal of the university system is to accept one of the two mutually exclusive antipollution projects. Thus, the goal constraint would be

$$x_9 + x_{10} + d_1^- - d_1^+ = 1$$

where d_1^- is to be minimized.

P_2: The second goal is to limit the total expenditure to the desired budget of $12 million.

$$\sum_{i=1}^{10} ICO_i\, x_i + d_2^- - d_2^+ = 12$$

where d_2^+ is to be minimized.

P_3: The third goal is to limit the total administrative manpower needs of the new projects to 100 FTEs.

$$\sum_{i=1}^{10} AMP_i\, x_i + d_3^- - d_3^+ = 100$$

where d_3^+ is to be minimized.

P_4: The fourth goal of the Board of Regents is to limit the net cash flow maintenance costs to certain desired levels during each of the next three years. The desired ceiling of the maintenance costs during the next three years are: year 1 = $1.5 million; year 2 = $2.3 million; and year 3 = $3.5 million. The goal constraints are

$$\sum_{i=1}^{10} NCF_1\, x_i + d_4^- - d_4^+ = 1.5$$

$$\sum_{i=1}^{10} NCF_2 \, x_i + d_5^- - d_5^+ = 2.3$$

$$\sum_{i=1}^{10} NCF_3 \, x_i + d_6^- - d_6^+ = 3.5$$

where d_4^+, d_5^+, and d_6^+ are minimized.

P_5: The fifth goal is to achieve satisfactory levels of cost savings from the projects. The desired levels of cost savings during the next three years are: year 1 = \$0.6; year 2 = \$1.2; and year 3 = \$1.6. The correspondence goal constraints are:

$$\sum_{i=1}^{10} CS_1 \, x_i + d_7^- - d_7^+ = 0.6$$

$$\sum_{i=1}^{10} CS_2 \, x_i + d_8^- - d_8^+ = 1.2$$

$$\sum_{i=1}^{10} CS_3 \, x_i + d_9^- - d_9^+ = 1.6$$

where d_7^-, d_8^-, and d_9^- are to be minimized.

P_6: The last goal of the Board of Regents is to maximize the net present value of cost savings from the selected projects. This goal constraint can be expressed by

$$\sum_{i=1}^{10} NPV_i \, x_i + d_{10}^- - d_{10}^+ = M$$

where M is a large arbitrary number and d_{10}^- is to be minimized.

This model contains a total of ten goal constraints, ten system constraints (which will be automatically taken care of by the zero-one goal programming algorithm), and the objective function. This problem can be easily solved by zero-one goal programming, which will be discussed briefly in a later section of this chapter.

The Modified Simplex Method of Goal Programming

In this section, the modified simplex method will be introduced as a solution method for the goal-programming mode. Although there have been several other techniques introduced, such as the generalized inverse technique (Ijiri, 1956), goal partitioning method (Arthur and Ravindran, 1978), and a revised simplex-based method, the modified simplex method provides for the most fundamental understanding of the goal programming solution procedure (Lee, 1972).

Before we discuss the modified simplex method, we should consider several unique aspects of the goal-programming model. First, in goal programming the purpose of the objective function is to minimize the total unattained portions of goals. This is achieved by minimizing the deviational variables through the use of certain preemptive priority factors and differential weights. There is no profit maximization or cost minimization *per se* in the objective function. Therefore, the preemptive factors and differential weights take the place of the C_j used in linear programming.

Second, the objective function is expressed by assigning priority factors to certain variables. These preemptive priority factors are multidimensional, since they are ordinal rather than cardinal values. In other words, priority factors at different levels are not commensurable. This implies that the simplex criterion (Z_j or $Z_j - C_j$) cannot be expressed by a single row as is done in the case of linear programming. Rather, the simplex criterion becomes a matrix of $k \times n$ size, where k represents the number of preemptive priority levels and n is the number of variables, including both decision and deviational variables.

Third, since the simplex criterion is expressed as a matrix rather than a row, we must design a new procedure for identifying the pivot column. The relationship between the preemptive priority factors is $P_k >>> P_{k+1}$, which means that P_k always takes priority over P_{k+1}. It is therefore clear that the selection procedure of the key column must be initiated from P_1 and move gradually to the lower priority levels.

In order to discuss the modified simplex method, let us consider the model formulated in example 4.4. The model is:

$$\text{Minimize } Z = P_1 d_1^- + P_2 d_4^+ + 2P_4 d_2^- + P_3 d_3^- + P_4 d_2^+ + P_4 d_3^+$$

$$\text{subject to} \quad 5X_1 + 2X_2 + d_1^- - d_1^+ = 5{,}500$$

$$X_1 + \quad\quad + d_2^- - d_2^+ = 800$$

$$X_2 + d_3^- - d_3^+ = 320$$

$$X_1 \quad\quad + d_4^- - d_4^+ = 900$$

$$X_j, d_i^-, d_i^+ \geq 0$$

Table 4.2 presents the initial tableau of the goal programming problem. The basic assumption in formulating the initial tableau of goal programming is

Table 4.2

The Initial Solution

C_j					P_1	$2P_3$	P_3			P_4	P_4	P_2
	v	rhs	X_1	X_2	d_1^-	d_2^-	d_3^-	d_4^-	d_1^+	d_2^+	d_3^+	d_4^+
P_1	d_1^-	5,500	5	2	1				−1			
$2P_3$	d_2^-	800	1			1				−1		
P_3	d_3^-	320		1			1				−1	
	d_4^-	100						1	1			−1
	P_4	0							−1	−1		
Z_j-C_j	P_3	1,920	2	1						−2	−1	
	P_2	0										−1
	P_1	5,500	5	2					−1			

identical to that of linear programming. It is assumed that the initial solution is at the origin, where values of all decision variables are zero. In the first constraint, therefore, the total number of cases handled by the registrar's office is, of course, zero, since, $X_1 = X_2 = 0$. Naturally, there cannot be any overachievement of the case clearance goal ($d_1^+ = 0$). Therefore, underachievement of the case clearance goal (d_1^-) will be 5,500 cases. Hence, the variable d_1^- is entered in the solution base and the right-hand side value (rhs) becomes 80. By the same token, d_2^-, d_3^-, and d_4^- are also in the solution base.

Now, let us examine C_j. In goal programming, C_j is represented by the priority factors and the differential weights as shown in the objective function. Most goal programming problems involve a large number of variables. For that reason, in order to make the tableau easier to read, empty spaces are left in the tableau where zero should appear.

The simplex criterion ($Z_j - C_j$) is a 4x10 matrix because we have four priority levels and ten variables (2 decision and 8 deviational) in the model. The goal-programming approach first achieves the most important goal to the fullest possible extent, then considers the second most important goal, and so on. It should be readily apparent that the selection of the pivot column should be based on the per-unit contribution rate of each variable in achieving the most important goal. When the first goal is completely attained, then the pivot-column selection criterion will be based on the achievement rate for the second goal, and so on. That is why we list the priority factors from the lowest to the highest so that the pivot column can be easily identified at the bottom of the tableau. To make the simplex tableau relatively simple, we have omitted the matrix of Z_j altogether. It requires a little more calculation this way, but the simplified tableau is well worth that inconvenience.

The goal programming model is a minimization model. In the minimization problem of linear programming, the Z_j values in the rhs column of the simplex criterion represent the total cost of the solution. By utilizing the same calculation procedure used in linear programming $[Z_j \text{ (rhs)} = \Sigma \, C_j \times \text{rhs}]$, we can obtain the Z_j value as $Z_j \text{ (rhs)} = (P_1 \times 5{,}500) + (2P_3 \times 800) + (P_3 \times 320) + (0 \times 100) = 5{,}500 \, P_1 + 1{,}920 \, P_3$. Now we can list these values at appropriate priority levels in table 4.2.

In goal programming, the Z_j values ($P_4 = 0$, $P_3 = 1{,}920$, $P_2 = 0$, $P_1 = 5{,}500$) in the rhs column represent the unattained portion of each goal. For example, in the initial tableau where the registrar's office is not providing any working hours to full-time or part-time workers, the second and the fourth goals are already attained. How could this be possible? Examining the objective function, we can find that the second goal is to limit the overtime work of full-time clerical staff to a total of 100 hours for the month, and the fourth goal is to minimize the overtime for full-time and student workers. It should be evident by now to the reader that since we are not providing any working hours to the employees at this point (we are at the origin), naturally there would be no overtime given to the employees. Consequently, we have already attained the second and fourth goals.

The underachievement of the first goal is 5,500 cases because none of the 5,500 cases to be cleared during the month has been taken care of as yet. For the third goal, the underachievement of the goal is 1,920. We remember that the differential weights of 2 and 1 are assigned to the full utilization goals for the full-time and part-time employees' regular working hours. Since these two goals are commensurable (in terms of working hours) and are at the same priority level, this procedure is absolutely appropriate. However, it is not so easy to interpret the underachievement of 1,920 for the third goal as other goals where no differential weights are assigned.

Now let us examine the calculation of $Z_j - C_j$ in table 4.2. We have already said that the C_j values represent the priority factors assigned to deviational variables and that Z_j values are products of the sum of C_j times rhs values or coefficients. Thus, Z_j values in the X_1 column will be $(P_1 \times 5 + 2P_3 \times 1)$, or $5P_1 + 2P_3$. The C_j value in the X_1 column is zero, as shown by the blank in the C_j row. Therefore, $Z_j - C_j$ for the X_1 column is $5P_1 + 2P_3$. Since P_1 and P_3 are not commensurable, we must list them separately in the P_1 and P_3 rows in the simplex criterion ($Z_j - C_j$). Consequently, the $Z_j - C_j$ value will be 5 at the P_1 row and 2 at the P_3 row in the X_1 column. By employing the same procedure, $Z_j - C_j$ of the X_2 column can be derived. It will be $(P_1 \times 2 + P_3 \times 1)$ $- 0$, or $2P_1 + P_3$. For the following three basic variable columns (those variables that are in the solution base, i.e., d_1^-, d_2^-, d_3^-, and d_4^-, $Z_j - C_j$ will be zero, since Z_j values are identical to the respective C_j values.

For the d_1^+ column, we can easily calculate the Z_j value of $-P_1$ from the tableau. Since the C_j value of the column is 0, $Z_j - C_j$ will be $-P_1$. Thus, -1 is listed at the P_1 row. In the d_2^+ column, $Z_j - C_j$ can be readily derived as $-2P_3 - P_4$. For the d_3^+ column, Z_i is $-P_3$ and C_j is P_4. Thus, we find $Z_j - C_j$ as $-P_3 - P_4$. In the last variable column, d_4^+, $Z_j - C_j$ is relatively easy to calculate. Z_j is zero and C_j is P_2. Thus, $C_j - Z_j$ is $-P_2$.

Now let us move on to find a new solution by taking the following steps of the modified simplex method of goal programming.

1. Determine the entering variable. This step is identical to the identification of the pivot column. First we find the highest priority level that has not been completely attained by examining the Z_j value in the rhs column. When the priority level is determined, we proceed to identify the variable column that has the largest positive $Z_j - C_j$ value. The variable in that column will enter the solution base in the next iteration. If there is a tie between the largest positive value in $Z_j - C_j$ at the highest priority level, check the next lower priority levels and select the column that has a greater value at the lower priority level. If the tie cannot be broken, choose one on an arbitrary basis. The other column will be chosen in subsequent iterations.

   In table 4.2., the highest priority goal not yet completely attained is P_1, as we can see the Z_j value of 5,500. In order to find the pivot column, we look for the largest positive $Z_j - C_j$ at the P_1 level. We identify 5 in the X_1 column. Thus, X_1 is the pivot column.

2. Determine the exiting variable from the solution base. This process is identical to finding the pivot row. Calculate the value of the rhs divided by the positive coefficients in the pivot column. Select the row which has the minimum nonnegative value. The variable in that row will be replaced by the variable in the pivot column in the next iteration. If there exists a tie when rhs values are divided by coefficients, find the row which has the variable with the higher priority factor assigned to it. If the tie cannot be broken, choose one on an arbitrary basis.

   In table 4.2, d_2^- is the pivot row since it has the smallest nonnegative value (800) when rhs values are divided by positive coefficients in the X_1 column. Therefore, in the second solution d_2^- will be replaced by X_1 in the solution base.

3. Determine the new solution. First we must find the new rhs and coefficients of the pivot row by dividing old values (values in the previous tableau) by the pivot element (the element at the intersection of the pivot column and

pivot row). Then find the new values for all other rows by following the calculational procedure presented below.

Pivot Row: New value = Old value/pivot row

Other Rows: New value = [old value—(intersectional element × new value in pivot row)].

The intersectional element for a given row is represented by the element which is at the intersection of the pivot column and a given row under consideration. The new value in the pivot row represents the new value we derived for the pivot row in the same column.

In our example, we can derive new values as below:

Pivot row

rhs:	$800/1 = 800$
X_1:	$1/1 = 1$
X_2:	$0/1 = 0$
d_1^-:	$0/1 = 0$
d_2^-:	$1/1 = 1$
d_3^-:	$0/1 = 1$
d_4^-:	$0/1 = 0$
d_1^+:	$0/1 = 0$
d_2^+:	$-1/1 = -1$
d_3^+:	$0/1 = 0$
d_4^+:	$0/1 = 0$

Other row: d_1^-

rhs:	$5{,}500 - (5 \times 800) = 1{,}500$
X_1:	$5 - (5 \times 1) = 0$
X_2:	$2 - (5 \times 0) = 2$
d_1^-:	$1 - (5 \times 0) = 1$
d_2^-:	$0 - (5 \times 1) = -5$
d_3^-:	$0 - (5 \times 0) = 0$
d_4^-:	$0 - (5 \times 0) = 0$
d_1^+:	$-1 - (5 \times 0) = -1$
d_2^+:	$0 - (5 \times -1) = -1$
d_3^+:	$0 - (5 \times 0) = 0$
d_4^+:	$0 - (5 \times 0) = 0$

New values in the remaining rows can be obtained by following the same procedure as applied to the d_1^- row.

Now we can complete the tableau by finding Z_j and $Z_j - C_j$ values for the priority rows. Table 4.3 represents the second solution.

4. Determine whether the solution is optimal. First analyze the goal attainment level of each goal by checking the Z_j value for each priority row. If the Z_j values are all zero, this is the optimal solution as all the goals are com-

Table 4.3
The Second Solution

C_j					P_1	$2P_3$	P_3		P_4	P_4	P_2	
	v	rhs	X_1	X_2	d_1^-	d_2^-	d_3^-	d_4^-	d_1^+	d_2^+	d_3^+	d_4^+
P_1	d_1^-	1,500	2	1	-5			-1	5			
	X_1	800	1			1			-1			
P_3	d_3^-	320		1			1			-1		
	d_4^-	100						1	1		-1	
	P_4	0						-1	-1			
$Z_j - C_j$	P_3	320	1		-2				-1			
	P_2	0								-1		
	P_1	1,500	2		-5			-1	5			

pletely attained. Such a situation can occur only when there exists no conflict among the goals.

If there exists a positive value of Z_j, examine the $Z_j - C_j$ coefficients for that row. If there are positive $Z_j - C_j$ values in the row, determine whether there are negative $Z_j - C_j$ values at a higher priority level in the same column. If there are negative $Z_j - C_j$ values at a higher priority level, this column cannot be selected as a pivot column. Such a case occurs when there exists a conflict between the goal under consideration and a higher priority goal. Since we are not willing to achieve a goal at the expense of a higher level goal, the column cannot be selected as a pivot column. Finally, if there exists a positive $Z_j - C_j$ value at a certain priority level and there is no negative $Z_j - C_j$ value at a higher priority level in the same column, the current solution is not optimal. Therefore, return to step 1 and continue the solution procedure.

In our example, the second solution shown in table 4.3 is not an optimal solution because we have the Z_j value of 1,500 at the P_1 level. Thus, we go back to step 1. The pivot column is d_2^+ and the pivot row d_4^-.

Table 4.4 presents the third solution and the subsequent iterations are also presented in tables 4.5, 4.6, and 4.7. Now let us evaluate the final solution presented in table 4.7. A quick glance of Z_j values in the rhs column indicates that the first three goals are completely attained but the fourth goal could not be attained completely as desired. The unattained portion of the fourth goal is

Table 4.4

The Third Solution

C_j			P_1	$2P_3$	P_3		P_4	P_4	P_2			
	v	rhs	X_1	X_2	d_1^-	d_2^-	d_3^-	d_4^-	d_1^+	d_2^+	d_3^+	d_4^+
P_1	d_1^-	1,000	2	1		−5		−5	−1			5
	X_1	900	1			1		1				−1
P_3	d_3^-	320		1			1				−1	
P_4	d_2^+	100							1	1		−1
	P_4	100							1		−1	−1
Z_j-C_j	P_3	320	1			−2					−1	
	P_2	0										−1
	P_1	1,000	2			−5		−5	−1			5

280. This amount represents the overtime hours given to the full-time and part-time workers that could not be minimized.

There are two positive Z_j-C_j values in the P_4 row. The largest positive Z_j-C_j of 3/2 is in the d_4^+ column. However, there is a −1 value at the P_2 level. Thus, d_4^+ cannot be selected as the pivot column. The other positive Z_j-C_j is in the d_1^- column. Again, there exists a Z_j-C_j value of −1 at the P_1 level. Therefore, d_1^- cannot be selected as the pivot column either. Consequently, this solution represents the optimal solution. Figure 4.2 presents a flowchart of the modified simplex procedure of goal programming.

The optimal solution can be summarized as follows:

A. *Basic Variables*
  X_1 = 900 (total working hours given to full-time workers)
  X_2 = 500 (total working hours given to part-time workers)
  d_2^+ = 100 (overtime hours given to full-time workers)
  d_3^+ = 180 (extra working hours given to part-time workers)
B. *Goal Attainment*
  P_1 = completely achieved
  P_2 = completely achieved
  P_3 = completely achieved
  P_4 = not completely achieved (d_2^+ = 100, d_3^+ = 180).
C. *Sensitivity Analysis*
  One more analysis that can be performed from the final simplex tab-

Table 4.5
The Fourth Solution

C_j					P_1	$2P_3$	P_3		P_4	P_4		P_2
	v	rhs	X_1	X_2	d_1^-	d_2^-	d_3^-	d_4^-	d_1^+	d_2^+	d_3^+	d_4^+
P_2	d_4^+	200		2/5	1/5	-1		-1	-1/5			1
	X_1	1,100	1	2/5	1/5				-1/5			
P_3	d_3^-	320		1			1				-1	
P_4	d_2^+	300		2/5	1/5	-1			-1/5	1		
	P_4	300		2/5	1/5	-1			-1/5		-1	
Z_j-C_j	P_3	320		1		-2					-1	
	P_2	200		2/5	1/5	-1		-1	-1/5			
	P_1	0			-1							

Table 4.6
The Fifth Solution

C_j					P_1	$2P_3$	P_3		P_4	P_4		P_2
	v	rhs	X_1	X_2	d_1^-	d_2^-	d_3^-	d_4^-	d_1^+	d_2^+	d_3^+	d_4^+
P_2	d_4^+	72			1/5	-1	-2/5	-1	-1/5		2/5	1
	X_1	972	1		1/5		-2/5		-1/5		2/5	
	X_2	320		1			1				-1	
P_4	d_2^+	172			1/5	-1	-2/5		-1/5	1	2/5	
	P_4	172			1/5	-1	-2/5		-1/5		-3/5	
Z_j-C_j	P_3	0				-2	-1					
	P_2	72			1/5	-1	-2/5	-1	-1/5		2/5	
	P_1	0			-1							

Table 4.7
The Final Solution

C_j					P_1	$2P_3$	P_3		P_4	P_4	P_2
	v	rhs	X_1	X_2	d_1^-	d_2^-	d_3^-	d_4^-	d_1^+	d_2^+	d_3^+	d_4^+
P_4	d_3^+	180			1/2	-5/2	-1	-5/2	-1/2		1	5/2
	X_1	900	1		1		1					-1
	X_2	500		1	1/2	-5/2		-5/2	-1/2			-5/2
P_4	d_2^+	100							1	1		-1
	P_4	280			1/2	-5/2	-1	-3/2	-1/2			3/2
	P_3	0				-2	-1					
$Z_j - C_j$	P_2	0										-1
	P_1	0			-1							

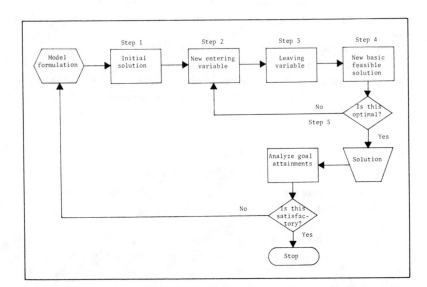

Figure 4.2
Flowchart of the Simplex Procedure of Goal Programming

leau is sensitivity analysis. Sensitivity analysis is concerned with analyzing the sensitivity of the optimal solution to (1) changes in the priority factors; (2) changes in the right-hand side values; (3) changes in the technological coefficients; (4) addition of a new constraint; and (5) addition of a new variable. Those who are interested in this topic of goal programming should consult Lee (1972; 1973; 1979).

Computer-Based Solution of Goal Programming

For any management science technique to be a truly valuable tool for administrative decision making, it must accommodate itself to a computer-based solution. The complexity of real-world problems usually compels the use of computers. Most simple hypothetical problems discussed really exist only in textbooks. This by no means suggests that simple examples are of no value. Actually, they provide the foundation for understanding complex concepts of various management science techniques. Nevertheless, in order to apply a technique to practical problems, computer-based analysis is usually required. Many powerful and mathematically sophisticated techniques have been developed—nonlinear programming, dynamic programming, game theory, etc.—that have found a disappointingly limited scope for practical applications to real-world problems. Modeling with such techniques is extremely hard for complex problems, and consequently a computer analysis is of little value.

In order for goal programming to be a useful tool for academic administration, a computer-based solution is an essential requirement. The modified simplex-method program is presented in Lee (1972; 1979). Although this program is not as efficient computationally as the revised simplex method of goal programming, it is quite simple to use.

Advanced Topics of Goal Programming

Thus far we have discussed the basic concept, model formulation examples, and the modified simplex method of goal programming. Here we shall briefly discuss several advanced topics of goal programming.

1. Integer Goal Programming Methods

In many practical decision problems with multiple conflicting objectives, the decision variables make sense only if they assume discrete values. The decision variables in this situation might be people, crews composed of various personnel and equipment, assembly lines, indivisible investment alternatives, construction projects, or large and expensive pieces of equipment. A simple rounding of values of the decision variables in the optimum solution obtained by the regular goal programming algorithm to the nearest integers can be easily accomplished. However, the rounding procedure frequently yields either an infeasible or a nonoptimal solution, and if the variable values are small numbers, such as those in $0 - 1$ programs, it can produce gross errors. Thus, there is a need to develop integer goal programming techniques (Lee, Morris, 1979).

2. Interactive Goal Programming

The ordinal solution approach based on the preemptive priorities makes goal programming a powerful decision aid. Yet, this very feature also makes it difficult to analyze the trade-offs among the goals. An equally important analysis that is useful for managerial decisions is the effects of changes in goal levels (b_i) and technological coefficients (a_{ij}), the addition or deletion of constraints, and addition or deletion of decision variables.

Perhaps the best way to analyze simultaneous changes in the model parameters would be an interactive mode where the decision maker and the goal programming model interact via a computer terminal. The interactive approach can be performed through an on-line analysis of the effect of changes in model parameters, as well as a complete sensitivity analysis of the optimal solution. The interactive goal programming approach provides a systematic process in which the decision maker seeks the most satisfactory solution. The process allows the decision maker to reformulate the model and systematically compare the solutions in terms of their achievement of multiple objectives.

3. Decomposition Goal Programming

Decomposition analysis was originally discussed as a computational device for solving large-scale linear programs. Recently, however, it has received increasing attention because of two important characteristics: (1) the decomposition technique can be utilized for resource allocation in the decentralized organization; and (2) it provides management in decentralized organizations with insights for developing organizational structure and information systems.

One of the major deficiencies of previous decomposition methods has been their inability to consider multicriteria decomposition problems due to its linear programming formulation. Lee and Rho (1979) developed decomposition goal programming algorithms in order to facilitate multicriteria decomposition problems. The algorithms are also effective in providing managerial implications involved in the decomposition process which can be useful for analyzing organizational development and information systems.

4. Separable Goal Programming

The modified simplex method is effective in solving linear goal programming problems. For nonlinear problems, however, it is not possible to apply the simplex algorithm. The optimal solution for nonlinear programs can either be any point along a curved boundary hypersurface of the feasible solution space or any point within the feasible solution space.

Presently, there is no general or universal approach for efficiently solving all general classes of nonlinear programming problems. It appears that the most promising approach to solving nonlinear programming problems is the transformation of the original problem into an acceptable linear approximation form that permits the application of the simplex algorithm. The separable programming approach can be adapted to handle multiple objective optimization problems through goal programming.

5. Chance-Constrained Goal Programming

Chance-constrained goal programming is an effective technique for determining solutions that "satisfice" multiple criterial decision problems which involve elements of risk and uncertainty associated with technological coefficients (a_{ij}) and levels of resources or goals (b_i). Three basic chance-constrained goal-programming approaches have been developed. The first and second approaches present separate derivations that assume that only the technological coefficients (a_{ij}) or resource and/or goal levels (b_i) are random variables. The third approach presents a model that considers the combined effect of random a_{ij} and b_i. Using the general chance-constrained goal programming, an equivalent nonlinear deterministic model can be derived for each of the approaches in a format that is amenable to the separable goal-programming model.

Application Areas of Goal Programming in Academic Administration

The crucial issues in the administration of higher education do not end at operational efficiency or financial solvency. Rather, they embody the very mission, function, and nature of each educational institution. In essence, administrative policies are based on the combined or compromised philosophy of many conflicting interest groups that provide inputs into the university, such as the Board of Regents, state legislature, state administrators, taxpayers, faculty, staff, students, alumni, and benefactors.

The present situation in many colleges or universities is one of compromise and tense coexistence among various parties involved. Any effective decision-making model must, therefore, be capable of reflecting the various goals and priorities of the many groups seeking their interests. Academic administrators must demonstrate to the various forces demanding justification for the policies or decisions. Thus, the administrative decision-making process must include explicit consideration of the various conflicting goals of the interest groups. If the demands of certain groups are not met, the decision-making process should be capable of explaining why such a result is obtained.

A. Resource Allocation

Resource allocation problems exist at all levels of academic administration. The rising expenditure of higher education in the inflationary environment has caused lawmakers and the public to develop a more critical view of the operational efficiency of educational institutions. Institutions can no longer request prodigious sums of money from the legislature without clear justification in terms of viable objectives, alternatives, and expected results. The increasing financial pressure has greatly enhanced the anxiety and competitiveness among major components and programs within the institution. Thus, effective resource allocation and reallocation decisions are extremely important in order to secure both internal and external harmony for the institution.

1. At the macrolevel
   a. Among educational systems (e.g., university systems, state college systems, etc.)
   b. Among institutions (e.g., among universities)
   c. Among categories of identified missions (e.g., teaching, research, service, undergraduate vs. graduate education, etc.)
2. At the microlevel
   a. Among major components within an institution (e.g., colleges, research institutes, library, art museums, athletic programs, etc.)
   b. Among departments or programs within a major unit
   c. Among personnel categories (faculty ranks, staff, and students) within the institution, a college, or a department.
3. Resource reallocation
   a. Among educational systems
   b. Among institutions
   c. Among major components within an institution
   d. Among departments within a college
   e. Among personnel or expenditure categories

B. Blending or Mix Problems
In academic administration, it is often impossible to distinguish resource allocation and blending or mix problems. However, a problem can be classified predominantly as one type or the other, or a combination of the two.
1. Student mix
   a. Admission policies
   b. Student counselling with regard to academic majors, course work, and occupational goals
2. Faculty or staff mix
   a. Hiring policy, equal opportunity and affirmative action
   b. Tenure policy and decisions
   c. Promotion policy and salary adjustments

3. Facility mix
   a. Physical plant
   b. Computer
   c. Library
   d. Research facilities and equipment
   e. Service facilities

C. Scheduling Problems
   Scheduling problems can also be integrated into resource allocation or blending problems. Scheduling problems which require the attention of administrators of higher education include:
   1. Scheduling of student output
      a. Undergraduate degrees
      b. Graduate degrees
      c. Student majors (engineering, business, liberal arts, education, etc.)
   2. Scheduling of nonstudent output
      a. Research
      b. Extension and service activities
   3. Scheduling of faculty inputs
      a. Senior faculty
      b. Junior faculty
      c. Instructors and graduate assistants
      d. Research staff
   4. Scheduling of nonfaculty inputs
      a. Buildings
      b. Equipment
      c. Books

D. Transportation, Location, and Allocation Problems
   There are a number of transportation, location, or allocation problems that deal with the supply and demand of various services involving several sources and destination locations.
   1. Facility locations (computer facilities, dormitories, student union, faculty club, bookstores, etc.)
   2. Busing routes on campus
   3. Mail collection and distribution routes
   4. Office equipment and supply allocation

E. Financial Analysis
   Financial analysis models can be formulated to monitor expenditure trends, cash flows, resource requirements for various programs, or the capital budgeting process.

1. Resource requirement analysis for various programs
2. Monthly or quarterly cash flow analysis
3. Expenditure pattern analysis for various programs or time periods
4. Capital budgeting for major capital investment projects

F. Overall Planning Models
   With the recent advances in management science and computer technology, it is possible to formulate an overall planning model for the entire operation of an institution or for a planning horizon emcompassing several time periods.
   1. A system-wide planning model
   2. A university-wide planning model
   3. A college-wide planning model
   4. A program-based planning model
   5. A long-range planning model

G. Predictive Models
   Academic administrators can be assisted by a number of prediction models.
   1. Student enrollment and flows
   2. Faculty and staff manpower requirements and flows
   3. Facilities and equipment requirements
   4. Library acquisition requirements
   5. Computing facilities and personnel requirements

An Admission Planning Model for a University

In order to demonstrate the applicability of goal programming to academic administration, an admission planning model for a university is presented in this section. A function performed by the college or university, which is receiving increasing attention, is the formulation of admissions policy for newly entering students. Accordingly, the administrative procedures utilized to implement these policies are a vital concern. For example, empty rooms in university-operated residence halls must be filled, junior and community college transfers must be accommodated, a balanced mix of male-female and freshmen-through-senior students must be achieved, and specific long-range admissions quotas must be met. Thus, the admissions officer has numerous factors to weigh and consider before making a final decision regarding the composition of admissions.

The admissions office must not only admit students in such a manner as to achieve an efficient utilization of university resources, but must also be able to demonstrate, to the various forces demanding a justification of its actions, a rational basis for the selection process.

In this section a university admissions planning model will be presented (for a more complete model, see Lee, 1972). The model is designed to determine the basic composition of the total group of new students to be admitted into a university. Although it does not specify which individual students should be offered admission, it does consider the institutional and societal objectives and the applicants available. It then yields the quantity in each of the various categories that should be admitted.

In order to formulate the goal-programming model for admission planning, data were obtained from a land-grant university. The university has a student body of approximately 11,000. For the goal programming model formulation, the following variables, priority structure of goals, and constraints were specified:

A. The model
Variables
The following variables were included in the model:
x_1 = number of in-state [1] freshman [2] men.
x_2 = number of in-state freshman women.
x_3 = number of in-state transfer [3] men.
x_4 = number of in-state transfer women.
x_5 = number of in-state readmitted [4] men.
x_6 = number of in-state readmitted women.
y_1 = number of out-of-state [5] freshman men.
y_2 = number of out-of-state freshman women.
y_3 = number of out-of-state transfer men.
y_4 = number of out-of-state transfer women.
y_5 = number of out-of-state readmitted men.
y_6 = number of out-of-state readmitted women.

Priority Structure of Goals
The admissions officer of the university under study established the following priority structure (P_1 = highest priority):
P_1 = at least 80 percent of the total number of students admitted must meet the state residency requirement.
P_2 = avoid lowering university admission standards.
P_3 = meet minimum percentages for student categories.
P_4 = achieve residence hall occupancy at least 98.5 percent of capacity.
P_5 = achieve full utilization of the physical plant.
P_6 = limit admission of women students to the desired level (1,000).
P_7 = avoid overutilization of physical plant.
P_8 = limit the residence hall occupancy to 103 percent of capacity.
P_9 = limit the admission of transfer students to the desired level (600).

Model Constraints
1. State Residency Constraint
The university administration has a long-standing policy which requires that at least 80 percent of entering students be in-state students. Stated in algebraic terms, the constraint is:

$$\sum_{i=1}^{6} x_i \leq 0.8 \sum_{i=1}^{6} (x_i + y_i).$$

Adding deviational variables and rearranging the terms yields the following:

$$\sum_{i=1}^{6} x_i - 4 \sum_{i=1}^{6} y_i + d_1^- - d_1^+ = 0.$$

2. Admission Standards Constraint
The director of admissions has a very reliable estimate of the numbers of applicants who will meet the university's minimum standards for admission. These numbers of acceptable applicants for admission give rise to the following algebraic constraints:

$$
\begin{array}{ll}
x_1 \leq 2{,}400 & y_1 \leq 1{,}500 \\
x_2 \leq 1{,}000 & y_2 \leq 500 \\
x_3 \leq 400 & y_3 \leq 300 \\
x_4 \leq 225 & y_4 \leq 75 \\
x_5 \leq 250 & y_5 \leq 50 \\
x_6 \leq 50 & y_6 \leq 20.
\end{array}
$$

Adding the deviational variables, the following equations result:

$$
\begin{array}{ll}
x_1 + d_2^- - d_2^+ = 2{,}400 & y_1 + d_8^- - d_8^+ = 1{,}500 \\
x_2 + d_3^- - d_3^+ = 1{,}000 & y_2 + d_9^- - d_9^+ = 500 \\
x_3 + d_4^- - d_4^+ = 400 & y_3 + d_{10}^- - d_{10}^+ = 300 \\
x_4 + d_5^- - d_5^+ = 225 & y_4 + d_{11}^- - d_{11}^+ = 75 \\
x_5 + d_6^- - d_6^+ = 250 & y_5 + d_{12}^- - d_{12}^+ = 50 \\
x_6 + d_7^- - d_7^+ = 50 & y_6 + d_{13}^- - d_{13}^+ = 20.
\end{array}
$$

3. Physical Plant Constraint
The university has projected that between 3,000 and 4,500 new students must be admitted if the current level of operation is to be maintained. This results in the following constraint inequalities:

$$3{,}000 \leq \sum_{i=1}^{6} (x_i + y_i) \leq 4{,}500,$$

which reduces to the following equations, with the addition of deviational variables:

$$\sum_{i=1}^{6} (x_i + y_i) + d_{14}^- - d_{14}^+ = 4,500$$

$$\sum_{i=1}^{6} (x_i + y_i) + d_{15}^- - d_{15}^+ = 3,000.$$

4. Student Mix Constraint

The university receives many more applications for admission from women than it can possibly accept. The constraint involving the admission of women is stated as follows:

$$x_2 + x_4 + x_6 + y_2 + y_4 + y_6 \leq 1,000.$$

Adding the deviational variables, the constraint becomes:

$$x_2 + x_4 + x_6 + y_2 + y_4 + y_6 + d_{16}^- - d_{16}^+ = 1,000.$$

The constraint for transfer admission is as follows:

$$x_3 + x_4 + y_3 + y_4 \leq 600.$$

Adding the deviational variables, the following equation is formed:

$$x_3 + x_4 + y_3 + y_4 + d_{17}^- - d_{17}^+ = 600.$$

5. Residence Hall Capacity Constraint

In order to achieve the needed level for the coming year, the university must admit 3,500 new students (1,110 females and 2,400 males). The actual numbers of students can exceed these estimates by 3 percent or be 1.5 percent lower without causing serious overcrowding or revenue loss.

The following percentages of students choose to live in the university residence halls:

	Men	Women
Freshman	100%	100%
Transfers	60	90
Readmitted	30	60

Considering the above conditions, the following constraints are developed:

$$x_1 + 0.6x_3 + 0.3x_5 + y_1 + 0.6y_3 + 0.3y_5 \leq 2,472$$

$$x_1 + 0.6x_3 + 0.3x_5 + y_1 + 0.6y_3 + 0.3y_5 \geq 2,364$$

$x_2 + 0.9x_4 + 0.6x_6 + y_2 + 0.9y_4 + 0.6y_6 \leqslant 1,133$

$x_2 + 0.9x_4 + 0.6x_6 + y_2 + 0.9y_4 + 0.6y_6 \geqslant 1,083,$

which, with the addition of deviational variables, yields:

$x_1 + 0.6x_3 + 0.3x_5 + y_1 + 0.6y_3 + 0.3y_5 + d_{18}^- - d_{18}^+ = 2,472$

$x_1 + 0.6x_3 + 0.3x_5 + y_1 + 0.6y_3 + 0.3y_5 + d_{19}^- - d_{19}^+ = 2,364$

$x_2 + 0.9x_4 + 0.6x_6 + y_2 + 0.9y_4 + 0.6y_6 + d_{20}^- - d_{20}^+ = 1,133$

$x_2 + 0.9x_4 + 0.6x_6 + y_2 + 0.9y_4 + 0.6y_6 + d_{21}^- - d_{21}^+ = 1,083.$

6. Minimum Percentages for Student Categories

The minimum desired percentages of the total new students for each student category are presented below:

State Residence
In-State Students	80%
Out-of-State Students	20%

Male-Female Ratio
Male Students	70%
Female Students	30%

Academic Standing
Freshmen Students	80%
Transfer Students	15%
Readmitted Students	5%

By using the above percentages, a minimum percentage can be derived for each student category as below.

Variable	Percentage of Total New Students	Variable	Percentage of Total New Students
x_1	44.8%	y_1	11.2%
x_2	19.2	y_2	4.8
x_3	8.4	y_3	2.1
x_4	3.6	y_4	0.9
x_5	2.8	y_5	0.7
x_6	1.2	y_6	0.3

With the assigned percentages, the following constraints can be formulated and be incorporated in the model.

$x_1 - 0.448T + d_{22}^- - d_{22}^+ = 0 \qquad y_1 - 0.112T + d_{28}^- - d_{28}^+ = 0$

$x_2 - 0.192T + d_{23}^- - d_{23}^+ = 0 \qquad y_2 - 0.048T + d_{29}^- - d_{29}^+ = 0$

$$x_3 - 0.084T + d_{24}^- - d_{24}^+ = 0 \qquad y_3 - 0.012T + d_{30}^- - d_{30}^+ = 0$$

$$x_4 - 0.036T + d_{25}^- - d_{25}^+ = 0 \qquad y_4 - 0.009T + d_{31}^- - d_{31}^+ = 0$$

$$x_5 - 0.028T + d_{26}^- - d_{26}^+ = 0 \qquad y_5 - 0.007T + d_{32}^- - d_{32}^+ = 0$$

$$x_6 - 0.012T + d_{27}^- - d_{27}^+ = 0 \qquad y_6 - 0.003T + d_{33}^- - d_{33}^+ = 0$$

where, $T = \sum_{i=1}^{6} (x_i + y_i)$.

The Objective Function

$$\text{Min } Z = P_1 d_1^- + P_2 \sum_{i=2}^{13} d_i^+ + P_3 \sum_{i=22}^{33} d_i^- + 3P_4 d_{19}^- + 2P_4 d_{21}^- +$$

$$P_5 d_{15}^- + P_6 d_{16}^+ + P_7 d_{14}^+ + 2P_8 d_{18}^+ + 3P_8 d_{20}^+ + P_9 d_{17}^+.$$

In the above objective function, differential weights are assigned at the P_4 and P_8 levels. The fourth goal was to achieve residence hall occupancy of at least 98.5 percent of capacity for men and women students. The admissions director feels that meeting the residence hall capacity for men's dormitories is more important because of a larger number of students involved. Therefore, the weight of 3 was assigned to the meeting of residence hall capacity of at least 98.5 percent for men and the weight of 2 for meeting that of women. Goal eight was concerned with limiting the residence hall occupancy to 103 percent of capacity. Since women students tend to object more to the crowded dormitory facilities than do men, the admissions director assigned a greater weight (3) for women than for men (2). The admissions model was solved by using modified simple program.

B. *Results and Discussion*

The results of the computer solution are as follows:

Variables

$x_1 = 1,665 \qquad y_1 = 462$

$x_2 = 739 \qquad y_2 = 165$

$x_3 = 287 \qquad y_3 = 44$

$x_4 = 129 \qquad y_4 = 33$

$x_5 = 101 \qquad y_5 = 26$

$x_6 = 44 \qquad y_6 = 11$

Goal Attainment

P_1: State Residence Requirement	Achieved
P_2: Admission Standards	Achieved

P_3: Minimum Percentages for Student Categories	Achieved
P_4: Minimum Residence Hall Occupancy	Achieved
P_5: Minimum Physical Plant Utilization	Achieved
P_6: Maximum Admission of Women	Not Achieved
P_7: Maximum Physical Plant Utilization	Achieved
P_8: Maximum Residence Hall Occupancy	Achieved
P_9: Maximum Admission of Transfers	Achieved

The results of the model indicate that all goals are completely achieved except the sixth goal. The university decided to limit the admission of female students to 1,000 for the coming academic year. However, the solution derived 1,121 new female students in order to satisfy the higher order (P_3) goal for minimum percentages of various student categories. However, in view of the increasing number of new incoming students and the desired 70–30 ratio between the male and female students, it should be clear that the 1,000 female student goal is indeed unrealistic. As a matter of fact, 1,121 female students admitted is exactly 30 percent of the 3,706 total new students. One of the most important advantages of goal programming is the result of the model provides the decision maker an opportunity to review the soundness of his goal structure.

Summary

Virtually all models developed for administrative decision making have neglected the unique organizational environment, bureaucratic decision process, individual administrators' management style, and the multiple conflicting nature of organizational objectives. In reality, however, these are crucial factors that greatly influence administrative decisions. In this chapter, the goal programming approach is presented as a tool for administration by objectives. Goal programming appears to be the most appropriate technique, not only because of its explicit consideration of the existing decision environment but also because of the fact that it most closely resembles the actual administrative decision process in public organizations.

Developing and solving the goal programming model reveals those goals that cannot be achieved under the desired policy and, hence, where trade-offs must be made among conflicting objectives. Furthermore, the model solution allows the administrator to critically review the priority structure in view of the system constraints and trade-offs among conflicting objectives.

Goal programming can serve as an effective tool for administration by objectives. However, it is neither a substitute nor the ultimate panacea for administrative decision making. In order to use goal programming, an administrator must be capable of defining, quantifying, and ordering objectives.

The technique simply provides the best satisficing solution under the given constraints, aspiration levels, and priority structure of goals. Although there have been many important developments in goal programming, as presented in this chapter, there are future research needs concerning the identification, formulation, and ranking of multiple objectives.

References

Arthur, J. L., and Ravindran, A. "An Efficient Goal Programming Algorithm Using Constraint Partitioning and Variable Elimination." *Management Science* 24, no. 8 (1978): 867–68.

Charnes, A., and Cooper, W. W., *Management Models and Industrial Applications of Linear Programming*. 2 vols. New York: Wiley, 1961.

Charnes, A.; Cooper, W. W., and Ferguson, R. O. "Optimal Estimation of Executive Compensation by Linear Programming." *Management Science* 1, no. 2 (1955): 138–51.

Charnes, A.; Cooper, W. W.; and Niehaus, R. J. "A Goal Programming Model for Manpower Planning." *Management Science Research Report*. no. 115 (August 1968) Carnegie-Mellon University.

Charnes, A.; Cooper, W. W.; Harrald, K. Karwan; and Wallace, W. A. *A Goal Interval Programming Model for Resource Allocation in a Marine Environmental Protection Program*. School of Management Research Report. Renssalear Polytechnic Institute, September 1975.

Charnes, A., et al. "Note on the Application of a Goal Programming Model for Media Planning." *Management Science* 14, no. 8 (1968): 431–36.

Ignizio, J. P. *Goal Programming and Extensions*. Lexington, Massachusetts: Lexington Books, 1976.

Ijiri, Y. *Management Goals and Accounting for Control*. Chicago: Rand McNally, 1965.

Jaaskelainen, V. "A Goal Programming Model of Aggregate Production Planning." *Swedish Journal of Economics*, no. 2 (1969): 14–29.

Lee, S. M. "Decision Analysis Through Goal Programming." *Decision Sciences* 2, no. 2 (1971): 172–80.

Lee, S. M. *Goal Programming for Decision Analysis*. Philadelphia: Auerbach, 1972.

Lee, S. M. "Goal Programming for Decision Analysis with Multiple Objectives." *Sloan Management Review* 14, no. 2 (1973): 11–24.

Lee, S. M. *Goal Programming Methods for Multiple Objective Integer Programs*. Atlanta: American Institute of Industrial Engineers, 1979.

Lee, S. M., and Clayton, E. R. "A Goal Programming Model for Academic Resource Allocation." *Management Science* 17, no. 8 (1972): 395–408.

Lee, S. M., and Lerro, A. J. "Optimizing the Portfolio Selection for Mutual Funds." *Journal of Marketing* 38, no. 1 (1974): 1,087–1,101.

Lee, S. M., and Moore, L. J. "Optimizing Transportation Problems with Multiple Objectives." *AIIE Transactions* 4, no. 4 (1973): 333–38.

Lee, S. M., and Moore, L. J. "Optimizing University Admissions Planning." *Decision Sciences* 5, no. 3 (July 1974): 405–515.

Lee, S. M., and Moore, L. J. "A Practical Approach to Production Scheduling." *Production Inventory Management* 15, no. 1 (1974): 79–92.

Lee, S. M., and Morris, R. "Integer Goal Programming Methods." In *Multiple Criteria Decision Making*, ed. M. Starr and M. Zeleny. TIMS Studies in the Management Sciences, Vol. 6. Amsterdam: North-Holland, 1977. pp. 273–89.

Lee, S. M., and Nicely, R. "Goal Programming for Marketing Decisions: A Case Study." *Journal of Marketing* 38, no. 1 (1974): 24–32.

Lee, S. M., and Rho, B. H. "The Binary Search Decomposition in a Decentralized Organization." *Theory and Decision* 11 (1979): 353–62.

Part Three

Application of the Goal Programming Methodology

This part of the book describes, in detail, a generalized goal programming model for academic administration. Chapter 5 includes an explanation of the formulation of a model to be used for the analysis of budgets, departmental structures, and resource allocations in academic departments. Four tests are then performed on the model, including: (1) the initial formulation of the model—using the existing departmental data for a social science department from a large midwestern state university; (2) the simulation of various priority arrangements in an attempt to replicate current departmental budgets and organizational structures for the three departments being studied; (3) the application of tests I and II to other departments for the purpose of resource allocation comparisons; (4) change of a parameter (average class size) and examination of the impact of the change on departmental resource needs. An analysis of these tests of the model show that it is very effective in providing valuable information regarding departmental budgets and structures.

Chapter 6 explains some possible extensions of the model described in Chapter 5. More specifically, resource allocation comparisons are developed for the three social science departments studied and are then formulated into a schedule of fixed, variable, and semivariable costs. These data are then used in a more traditional microeconomic framework to provide for the development of an approximate production possibilities frontier.

Chapter 7 discusses the development of a decision-support system for use in connection with the goal programming models. Decision-support systems focus on the decision process rather than on the decision itself. In this approach, the decision makers' perceptions about the solution to a particular problem may actually be viewed as more important than the solution itself. Thus, a decision-support system is actually a "feedback" model which can help academic administrators find improvement in their solutions to problems. The chapter also provides an example of a specific application of a decision-support system to an academic administrative resource allocation problem.

Chapter 5

A Generalized Goal-Programming Model for Academic Administration

The general resource planning model of a college developed by Sang M. Lee (1972) demonstrated the application potential of goal programming to complex decision problems in university management. The use of goal programming as the solution procedure for the model allowed for the inclusion of multiple, competitive, and often conflicting goals and for experimentation with various goal structures or objectives within a college or university. In this regard, the model goes further than other existing operational models in encompassing system outputs, unique institutional values, and bureaucratic decision structures. The model was primarily designed to assist academic decision makers in achieving a good allocation of resources with the adjective *good* conditioned by the value systems of the decision makers.

The model adopted in this book and its application differ from Lee's original formulation in three ways. First, constraints and goals have been added to allow for a comparison of the model's "optimal" solution with actual structural data from the departments being analyzed. These constraints (identified later as numbers six through sixteen) define the number of instructional staff members currently employed in each category and the number of tenured professorial staff members, again by category. These constraints and resulting goals are necessary for the model to be used later as an analytical, rather than a descriptive or prescriptive type of tool for academic planning.

Second, constraints have also been added to consider the difference between undergraduate and graduate student activities, undergraduate advising and graduate supervisory responsibilities, departmental operating budgets, and a professional development fund.

Of added importance is the use of the model and, particularly, goal programming, as a *diagnostic* technique to examine existing departmental budgets and structures. This analysis is accomplished by testing various priority arrangements in the objective function until the model provides a "fit" for the actual data for the departments being studied. By itself, this process of fitting the objective function to the existing data provides considerable insight into the "revealed preferences" of previous resource allocation decisions. In essence, these simulations of various priority arrangements allow for the identification of the current state of the model's variables. This feature is a unique application of decision analysis in higher education.

Once a workable and relevant priority structure is found for the goals of the model, further simulations can be used for the purpose of resource allocation comparisons both within and between academic departments. These simulations, later defined as tests III and IV, provide a basis for examining educational productivity under the traditional framework of microeconomics.

The Model Formulation

In the model, the following variables and constraints are defined for each department.

Variables for each department:

x_1 = the number of graduate research assistants (GRA)
x_2 = the number of graduate teaching assistants (GTA)
x_3 = the number of instructors (Inst.)
x_4 = the number of assistant professors
x_5 = the number of associate professors
x_6 = the number of professors
x_7 = the number of technical/professional support staff (TPS)
x_8 = the number of secretarial support staff (SS)
x_9 = total payroll budget for the fiscal year
x_{10} = departmental operating budget based on student credit hours
x_{11} = departmental operating budget based on student credit hours and number of faculty
x_{12} = faculty development fund

Constants for each department:

a_1 = the number of GRA presently budgeted
a_2 = the number of GTA presently budgeted
a_3 = the number of Inst. presently budgeted

a_4 = the number of assistant professors presently budgeted
a_5 = the number of associate professors presently budgeted
a_6 = the number of professors presently budgeted
a_7 = the number of TPS presently budgeted
a_8 = the number of SS presently budgeted

b_1 = the number of assistant professors with tenure
b_2 = the number of associate professors with tenure
b_3 = the number of professors with tenure

c_1 = estimated number of undergraduate student credit hours (USCH)
c_2 = estimated number of graduate student credit hours (GSCH)
c_3 = number of undergraduate students enrolled
c_4 = number of graduate students enrolled in Masters programs
c_5 = number of graduate students enrolled in terminal degree programs
    (Ph.D., Ed.D., M.F.A., etc.)
c_6 = desired average undergraduate class size
c_7 = desired average graduate class size
c_8 = operating budget needed per SCH (in dollars)
c_9 = operating budged needed per FTE faculty (in dollars)
c_{10} = base operating budget (in dollars)

d_1 = desired GRA/faculty ratio
d_2 = desired TPS/faculty ratio
d_3 = desired SS/faculty ratio

e_1 = desired maximum ratio of GTA/total academic staff
e_2 = desired maximum ratio of Inst./total academic staff
e_3 = desired maximum ratio of assistant professors/total academic staff
e_4 = desired maximum ratio of associate professors/total academic staff
e_5 = desired maximum ratio of professors/total academic staff

f_1 = average current salary for GRA
f_2 = average current salary for GTA
f_3 = average current salary for Inst.
f_4 = average current salary for assistant professors
f_5 = average current salary for associate professors
f_6 = average current salary for professors
f_7 = average current salary for TPS
f_8 = average current salary for SS

g_1 = desired percentage increase in salary for GRA
g_2 = desired percentage increase in salary for GTA
g_3 = desired percentage increase in salary for Inst.

g_4 = desired percentage increase in salary for assistant professors
g_5 = desired percentage increase in salary for associate professors
g_6 = desired percentage increase in salary for professors
g_7 = desired percentage increase in salary for TPS
g_8 = desired percentage increase in salary for SS

The maximum teaching, advising, and supervisory loads are defined as in table 5.1:

Table 5.1
Teaching, Advising, and Supervisory Loads
for the Department of History

Variable	Teaching Load		Advising Load	Thesis Supervision	
	Undergraduate	Graduate	Undergraduate	M.A.	Doctoral
X_1	—	—	—	—	—
X_2	s_1	—	—	—	—
X_3	s_2	—	—	—	—
X_4	s_3	s_3'	h_3	j_3	j_3'
X_5	s_4	s_4'	h_4	j_4	j_4'
X_6	s_5	s_5'	h_5	j_5	j_5'
X_7	—	—	—	—	—
X_8	—	—	—	—	—

Constraints for Each Department

The constraints used in the model are formulated under eleven categories:

A. Undergraduate Instruction

To furnish an adequate instructional setting for both undergraduate and graduate levels, and to achieve an equitable instructional work-load assignment among academic staff, the college or departmental administrator must consider three factors: the student/teacher ratio, the average class size, and the teaching work-load distribution.

The AAUP "Statement of Faculty Workload" pointed out factors that should be regarded by administrators in setting up the institutional faculty teaching load policies (*AAUP Bulletin*, March 1970, p. 30). The two most important principles that contribute to work-load equity are: (a) that the scope and difficulty of the course should not be overlooked—graduate courses are more demanding than introductory courses; and (b) that class size should be considered—teaching difficulty increases as the number of students in the class increases, especially if courses are generally comparable.

A constraint is needed to ensure an appropriate number of instructional staff members for the estimated undergraduate student credit hours anticipated in each department. This equation is based on three factors: (a) the desired average undergraduate class size, (b) the estimated total number of undergraduate student credit hours, and (c) the proposed faculty workload as set forth in table 5.1. The general constraint is:

$$(1) \quad \sum_{i=1}^{5} s_i x_i + d_1^- - d_1^+ = \frac{c_1}{c_6}$$

B. Graduate Instruction

This constraint is similar to (1) and is to ensure an appropriate number of instructional staff members for the estimated graduate student credit hours anticipated in each department. It must be recognized, however, that graduate courses are less amenable to aggregation in terms of average class size. Using the data from table 5.1 again, this equation is:

$$(2) \quad \sum_{i=3}^{5} s_i' x_i + d_2^- - d_2^+ = \frac{c_2}{c_7}$$

C. Undergraduate Advising

It is necessary to include a constraint setting forth the staffing requirements for undergraduate advising. This constraint is based on the advising load described in table 5.1 and is similar to a desired faculty/student ratio frequently found in models of higher education. The equation is set equal to the number of undergraduate majors in the given department:

$$(3) \quad \sum_{i=4}^{6} h_i x_i + d_3^- - d_3^+ = c_3$$

D. Graduate Student Supervision

It is desirable to make sure that sufficient senior staff are available to supervise masters and doctoral student research and independent study. Again, the constraints follow the workload parameters outlined in table 5.1 and are set equal to the expected numbers of M.A. and doctoral students, respectively:

$$(4) \quad \sum_{i=4}^{6} j_i x_i + d_4^- - d_4^+ = c_4$$

$$(5) \quad \sum_{i=4}^{6} j_i' x_i + d_5^- - d_5^+ = c_5$$

E. Presently Budgeted Faculty and Staff

In order to use the model as an analytical tool, some base must exist against which the computed data can be compared. Since the desire is to be able to simulate the effect of different policy decisions on existing departmental budgets, it is necessary to include in the model constraints giving the presently budgeted faculty and staff by category. Equations 6 through 13 specify these data by giving the existing distribution of staff:

(6) $x_1 + d_6^- - d_6^+ = a_1$ Graduate Research Assistants

(7) $x_2 + d_7^- - d_7^+ = a_2$ Graduate Teaching Assistants

(8) $x_3 + d_8^- - d_8^+ = a_3$ Instructors

(9) $x_4 + d_9^- - d_9^+ = a_4$ Assistant Professors

(10) $x_5 + d_{10}^- - d_{10}^+ = a_5$ Associate Professors

(11) $x_6 + d_{11}^- - d_{11}^+ = a_6$ Professors

(12) $x_7 + d_{12}^- - d_{12}^+ = a_7$ Technical/Professional Staff

(13) $x_8 + d_{12}^- - d_{12}^+ = a_8$ Support Staff

F. Tenured Faculty

It is also necessary to know the number of tenured faculty members, by rank, that are presently budgeted in each department. These constraints are needed in the same manner as are those in category E (above). Equations 14 through 16 specify the number of tenured faculty in each rank:

(14) $x_4 + d_{14}^- - d_{14}^+ = b_1$ Assistant professors with tenure

(15) $x_5 + d_{15}^- - d_{15}^+ = b_2$ Associate professors with tenure

(16) $x_6 + d_{16}^- - d_{16}^+ = b_3$ Professors with tenure

G. Graduate Research Assistants and Support Staff

The number of graduate research assistants and clerical support staff needed by a particular department is determined by a simple ratio. The importance of each of these categories can be handled in the objective function by the assignment of priorities to the deviations. For graduate research assistants, technical and professional staff, and clerical staff, the respective constraints are:

(17) $\sum_{i=4}^{6} x_i - d_3 x_1 + d_{17}^- - d_{17}^+ = 0$ Graduate research assistants

(18) $\sum_{i=4}^{6} x_i - d_4 x_7 + d_{18}^- - d_{18}^+ = 0$ Technical/professional staff

(19) $\displaystyle\sum_{i=4}^{6} x_i - d_5 x_8 + d_{19}^- - d_{19}^+ = 0$ Support staff

H. Budget Constraints

Calculation of the salary costs for the departmental budget is based on average salaries and is specified as follows:

(20) $\displaystyle\sum_{i=1}^{8} f_i x_i - x_9 + d_{20}^- - d_{20}^+ = 0$

A separate facet of the projected budget for a department is the desired annual salary increases. Given limited resources, it is essential that the costs of such increases be considered by the planning model. The generalized total budget constraint, including the salary increase factors, is:

(21) $\displaystyle\sum_{i=1}^{8} g_i x_i + x_9 + d_{21}^- - d_{21}^+ = 0$

I. Distribution of Academic Staff

It is necessary to impose some constraints on the distribution of the academic faculty. If such constraints were not included, the solution would call for the least-expensive type of faculty in terms of teaching load and salary expense, e.g., graduate teaching assistants, instructors, and assistant professors. To provide for an appropriate distribution of such staff members, the following constraints are included:

(22) $\displaystyle\sum_{i=3}^{6} e_1 x_i - x_2 + d_{22}^- - d_{22}^+ = 0$ Graduate teaching assistants

(23) $\displaystyle\sum_{i=4}^{6} e_2 x_i - x_3 + d_{23}^- - d_{23}^+ = 0$ Instructors

(24) $\displaystyle\sum_{i=3}^{6} e_3 x_i - x_4 + d_{24}^- - d_{24}^+ = 0$ Assistant professors

(25) $\displaystyle\sum_{i=3}^{6} e_4 x_i - x_5 + d_{25}^- - d_{25}^+ = 0$ Associate professors

(26) $\displaystyle\sum_{i=3}^{6} e_5 x_i - x_6 + d_{26}^- - d_{26}^+ = 0$ Professors

J. Operating Budget

Associated with increased (or decreased) academic staff and student enrollments, is the need for adjustments in departmental operating budgets. Included in this category are expenses for such things as telephones, photocopying, computer allocations, office supplies, travel expenses, equipment, and the like. Consideration of these factors in this model is based on the following two equations involving projected student-credit-hour production and full-time equivalent staff members:

$$(27) \quad (1/c_8)x_{10} + d_{27}^- - d_{27}^+ = c_1 + c_2$$

$$(28) \quad x_{11} - (\sum_{i=3}^{6} c_9x_i + X_{10}) + d_{28}^- - d_{28}^+ = c_{10}$$

K. Professional Development

Provision should be made to allow released time for professional development for each senior faculty member in order to enhance instructional and research productivity. Activities in this area include such things as sabbatical leaves, research initiation, lecture visits to other universities, duties in a professional organization, travel, summer-release time, visiting scholars, and public service projects. The following constraint budgets the establishment of a professional development fund which will cover only salary expenses but which will allow each associate professor and professor a one-semester leave with pay every seven years:

$$(29) \quad \sum_{i=5}^{6} f_ix_i - 14x_{12} + d_{29}^- - d_{29}^+ = 0$$

Objective Function

The objective function can be formulated with numerous different priority arrangements so long as at least one of the deviational variables (either positive or negative) for each constraint is included. The goal is to minimize the absolute value of the deviations, either positive or negative, from the set goals given certain "preemptive" priority factors. In the final model form, nine priority levels are used.

Testing and Evaluating the Model

In order to be useful, the model formulated in this chapter, like other planning models, must be capable of being tested against "real-time" data. To qualify for application in an actual situation, we should (1) validate the model's representativeness for the operations or budget of a particular department or college, and (2) experiment with the model for the purposes of demonstrating its applicability and of evaluating its performance under different conditions. However, it should not be expected that the model will provide an exact replica of the real world because all models are simplifications.

In addressing the question of model applicability, four experimental tests were performed on the model. These tests were based on actual data from the departments of History, Political Science, and Sociology at a large midwestern state university. The tests were:

I. Of the initial formulation of the model—using existing departmental data.

II. To simulate various priority arrangements in an attempt to replicate current departmental budgets and organizational structures.

III. To apply tests I and II to two other departments for the purpose of resource allocation comparisons.

IV. To change a decision rule (average class size) and examine the impact of the change on departmental resource needs.

Test I

In test I the initial formulation of the model with actual data from the Department of History was undertaken. For this first formulation of the model, the data listed below were used.

Constants for the Department of History:

a_1 = 0.00 FTE	c_6 = 30 students	f_1 = $ 3,871
a_2 = 16.00 FTE	c_7 = 7 students	f_2 = $ 3,871
a_3 = 1.00 FTE	c_8 = $.75	f_3 = $10,000
a_4 = 9.00 FTE	c_9 = $75.00	f_4 = $13,409
a_5 = 2.00 FTE	c_{10} = $2,000	f_5 = $15,706
a_6 = 12.00 FTE		f_6 = $21,907
a_7 = 0.00 FTE	d_1 = 10:1	f_7 = $10,000
a_8 = 2.00 FTE	d_2 = 10:1	f_8 = $ 7,608
	d_3 = 1:8	
b_1 = 0.00 FTE	d_4 = 1:8	g_1 = 5%
b_2 = 1.00 FTE	d_5 = 1:8	g_2 = 5%
b_3 = 11.00 FTE		g_3 = 5%
	e_1 = .15/1.0	g_4 = 10%
c_1 = 7,649 SCH	e_2 = .05/1.0	g_5 = 10%
c_2 = 366 SCH	e_3 = .40/1.0	g_6 = 10%
c_3 = 197 MAJ	e_4 = .09/1.0	g_7 = 10%
c_4 = 25 M.A.	e_5 = .50/1.0	g_8 = 10%
c_5 = 20 Ph.D.		

The maximum teaching, advising, and supervisory loads for the Department of History under this formulation are given in table 5.2. Accordingly, for the Department of History the formulation of the twenty-nine constraints is:

$$6X_2 + 9X_3 + 6X_4 + 6X_5 +$$
$$6X_6 \qquad\qquad + d_1^- - d_1^+ = 255 \quad (1)$$
$$3X_4 + 3X_5 + 3X_6 \qquad + d_2^- - d_2^+ = 52 \quad (2)$$
$$20X_4 + 15X_5 + 10X_6 \qquad + d_3^- - d_3^+ = 197 \quad (3)$$
$$20X_4 + 15X_5 + 10X_6 \qquad + d_4^- - d_5^+ = 25 \quad (4)$$
$$4X_5 + 5X_6 \qquad\qquad + d_5^- - d_5^+ = 20 \quad (5)$$
$$X_1 \qquad\qquad + d_6^- - d_6^+ = 0 \quad (6)$$
$$X_2 \qquad\qquad + d_7^- - d_7^+ = 16 \quad (7)$$
$$X_3 \qquad\qquad + d_8^- - d_8^+ = 1 \quad (8)$$
$$X_4 \qquad\qquad + d_9^- - d_9^+ = 9 \quad (9)$$
$$X_5 \qquad\qquad + d_{10}^- - d_{10}^+ = 2 \quad (10)$$
$$X_6 \qquad\qquad + d_{11}^- - d_{11}^+ = 12 \quad (11)$$
$$X_7 \qquad\qquad + d_{12}^- - d_{12}^+ = 0 \quad (12)$$
$$X_8 \qquad\qquad + d_{13}^- - d_{13}^+ = 2 \quad (13)$$
$$X_4 \qquad\qquad + d_{14}^- - d_{14}^+ = 0 \quad (14)$$
$$X_5 \qquad\qquad + d_{15}^- - d_{15}^+ = 1 \quad (15)$$
$$X_6 \qquad\qquad + d_{16}^- - d_{16}^+ = 11 \quad (16)$$
$$-8X_1 + X_4 + X_5 + X_6 + d_{17}^- - d_{17}^+ = 0 \quad (17)$$
$$X_4 + X_5 + X_6 - 8X_7 + d_{18}^- - d_{18}^+ = 0 \quad (18)$$
$$X_4 + X_5 + X_6 - 8X_8 + d_{19}^- - d_{19}^+ = 0 \quad (19)$$
$$3{,}871X_1 + 3{,}871X_2 + 10{,}000X_3 + 13{,}409X_4 +$$
$$15{,}706X_5 + 21{,}907X_6 + 10{,}000X_7 + 7{,}608X_8 - X_9 + d_{20}^- - d_{20}^+ = 0 \quad (20)$$
$$193X_1 + 193X_2 + 500X_3 + 1{,}341X_4 +$$
$$1{,}571X_5 + 2{,}191X_6 + 1{,}000X_7 + 761X_8 + X_9 + d_{21}^- - d_{21}^+ = 0 \quad (21)$$
$$- X_2 + .15X_3 + .15X_4 + .15X_5 +$$
$$.15X_6 \qquad\qquad + d_{22}^- - d_{22}^+ = 0 \quad (22)$$
$$- X_3 + .05X_4 + .05X_5 + .05X_6 + d_{23}^- - d_{23}^+ = 0 \quad (23)$$
$$.40X_3 - .60X_4 + .40X_5 + .40X_6 + d_{24}^- - d_{24}^+ = 0 \quad (24)$$
$$.09X_3 + .09X_4 - .91X_5 + .09X_6 + d_{25}^- - d_{25}^+ = 0 \quad (25)$$
$$.50X_3 + .50X_4 + .50X_5 - .50X_6 + d_{26}^- - d_{26}^+ = 0 \quad (26)$$
$$1.33X_{10} \qquad\qquad + d_{27}^- - d_{27}^+ = 8{,}015 \quad (27)$$
$$- 5X_3 - 5X_4 - 5X_5 - 5X_6$$
$$- X_{10} + X_{11} \qquad + d_{28}^- - d_{28}^+ = 2{,}000 \quad (28)$$
$$15{,}706X_5 + 21{,}907X_6 - 14X_{12} + d_{29}^- - d_{29}^+ = 0 \quad (29)$$

Test II

In actuality test II consisted of two parts. The first problem was to develop an objective function that would work in the model and provide intelligible results. Part two involved numerous rearrangements of the objective function until a priority setting was found that would give a reasonable replication of the existing structure and budget of the Department of History.

Table 5.2
Teaching, Advising, and Supervisory Loads
for the Department of History

Variable	Teaching Load		Advising Load	Thesis Supervision	
	Undergraduate	Graduate	Undergraduate	M.A.	Ph.D.
X_1	—	—	—	—	—
X_2	6	—	—	—	—
X_3	9	—	—	—	—
X_4	6	3	20	3	—
X_5	6	3	15	4	—
X_6	3	3	10	5	5
X_7	—	—	—	—	—
X_8	—	—	—	—	—

Although the final sets of objective functions are all that are given here, a great deal of trial and error work was done before arriving at these final formulations. Because there are twenty-nine separate constraints, each with a positive and a negative deviational variable, there are 2^{58} possible combinations of priority settings for the objective function! However, the number of actual combinations of priority settings that can be considered is usually quite small because the importance of the goals should not be random.

The testing of various priority arrangements was simplified somewhat conceptually by considering five broad classes of concern: (1) the desire to make certain that sufficient academic staff were available to provide the estimated number of undergraduate and graduate student credit hours, (2) the desire to maintain an appropriate distribution of academic staff according to rank, (3) the desire not to "violate" existing tenure commitments, (4) the desire to budget for adequate support staff and operating funds on the departmental level, and for a professional development fund on the college level, and (5) the desire to minimize the entire budget of each department.

As might be expected, the entire model is quite sensitive to the priorities assigned to the budgetary equations (numbers twenty and twenty-one). Only when the total budget equation is given the lowest priority (nine in this formulation) are all other decision variables present in the final solution set.

It was also necessary to assign a relatively high priority to minimizing the number of graduate teaching assistants, instructors, and assistant professors called for by the model because of their low cost and high student-credit-hour productivity.

Objective Function

As mentioned earlier, the priority structure set for the model determines the sequence in which the model seeks to satisfy the constraints. The priorities are preemptive and do not signify weights; e.g., it cannot be said that priority one is "twice as important" as priority two. The priorities are simply related in sequential order of importance with priority one defined as being of the highest importance.

The goals and priorities of the objective function as formulated for the Department of History may be restated as follows:

Goal 1: From a functional point of view, it was most desirable to make certain that sufficient academic staff be available to provide for the estimated number of undergraduate student credit hours. But it was also desired that no excess academic staff be called for by the model. Therefore, both the positive and negative deviational variables were set at priority one. In the goal-programming solution procedure, the inclusion of both deviational variables at a high priority will assure the exact achievement of the goal.

Similarly, in order to guarantee sufficient staff to provide for the estimated number of graduate student credit hours, the negative deviational variable for constraint number two was also included in goal one.

Goal 2: In institutions of higher education, it is essential to maintain contractual commitments to those members of the academic staff who have been awarded tenure (except in cases of financial exigency). Accordingly, goal two was devoted to assuring that budgeted positions were included for each tenured staff member in the assistant, associate, and professor categories. Here, the desire for this goal was to achieve a solution set including at least the number of tenured positions, by rank; therefore, only the negative deviational variables were included in the objective function for constraints fourteen, fifteen, and sixteen.

Goal 3: After considerable experimentation with priority settings, it became apparent that it was also essential to give high priority to the constraints involving the existing number of graduate teaching assistants (GTAs) and instructors. Even with the budget constraint set at the lowest possible priority, the model would call for most of the undergraduate instruction to be done by these two categories of low-cost but "equally productive" (in terms of student credit hour production) members of the academic staff. It is clearly recognized throughout higher education that some "appropriate" distribution of staff should be maintained and that this distribution should include some percentage of senior-level professors. The purpose of the third priority goal, therefore, was to minimize the number of GTAs and instructors called for by the model. Both the negative and positive variables were to be minimized to zero for constraints seven and eight.

Constraints numbers six and twelve, representing the existing number of budgeted positions for graduate research assistants and technical/professional staff members were also assigned to priority level three with both the positive and negative deviational variables included. As the Department of History does not now employ any graduate research assistants or technical/professional staff, the need to include these constraints at this relatively high priority level represents a strong preference for not budgeting funds for these "support" positions (see goal level five).

Goal 4: The model also attempts to ensure an appropriate distribution of academic staff by the inclusion of constraints specifying a desired percentage for the number of staff in each category (constraints numbers twenty-two, twenty-three, twenty-four, twenty-five, and twenty-six). In the first formulation of the model, these percentages were set to provide an "ideal" distribution; that is, without regard to the existing distribution of staff, the percentages were set, rather arbitrarily, at 10 percent for GTAs, 5 percent for instructors, 20 percent for assistant professors, 30 percent for associate professors, and 35 percent for professors. However, the solution set provided under these percentages did not relate well to the actual numbers of staff in these categories. The constraints were therefore reformulated using percentages for each category that were based on the existing distribution of staff in each department. The Department of History at the time had 16.00 GTAs, 1.00 instructor, 9.00 assistant professors, 2.00 associate professors, and 12.00 professors; accordingly the percentages were set at 15 percent, 5 percent, 40 percent, 9 percent, and 50 percent respectively.

Since the desire was to achieve a solution set which met these percentage constraints as closely as possible, both the negative and the positive deviational variables for these constraints were included. The achievement of the percentage distributions for all five categories was set at priority four.

Goal 5: In the Department of History (as well as for the other two social science departments modeled later), it is important to provide adequate support staff in terms of secretarial and clerical assistance. These services include such things as typing examinations, research papers, and grant proposals, photocopying, collating, recordkeeping, and so forth, which are essential support services. Goal five includes the positive deviational variable for constraint number nineteen and thus calls for the model to provide at least one secretarial position for every eight full-time equivalent academic staff members.

It should be noted that other types of support services are also needed by academic departments. These services are generally of the "technician" or "research assistant" type and vary in nature depending on the discipline or department. For instance, social science departments often need computer programmers or audiovisual coordinators; the physical sciences often need electronics technicians, instrumentation specialists, or laboratory assistants; and the arts frequently need slide librarians, to name just a few. In addition, professional managers have also proven to be beneficial for assisting the directors of larger departments or as supervisors of shops or production facilities.

As mentioned earlier (goal three) the Department of History does not now employ any graduate research assistants or technical/professional staff members; but it does desire to do so should funding become available. Thus a lower-level request for these positions was included in priority five based on a ratio of 1:8 to the number of academic staff. This request was represented by the inclusion of only the positive deviational variables for constraints numbers seventeen and eighteen.

Goal 6: It is important that sufficient faculty resources be provided to allow for undergraduate advising and for graduate student supervision. Accordingly, positive deviational variables were included at priority six for constraints numbers three, four, and five.

Goal 7: It was necessary to include at a relatively low-priority level the constraints specifying the existing number of staff members in each category. These constraints (numbers nine, ten, eleven, and thirteen) are included primarily for the purpose that they be available in the output format for comparison purposes. In each case, the negative deviational variables were used.

Goal 8: The model provides for budgeting for salary increases or salary adjustments for all employees. For the Department of History, it was decided that funds should be provided for increases of 5 percent for GTAs, GRAs, and instructors, and 10 percent for all other staff members. Since these were the minimum desired raises, only the positive deviational variable was included in the objective function. As it was necessary to include this constraint in a goal class higher than that for the budget constraint, goal eight was given to funding these salary increases.

Goal 9: This last goal was reserved for the constraints for the determination of the operating budget, the professional development fund, and the overall budget.

The two constraints (numbers twenty-seven and twenty-eight) specifying the desired funding level for the departmental operating budget were included with both the negative and positive deviational variables present in order to allow for the exact achievement of this subgoal.

Similarly, both deviational variables for the professional development fund (constraint number twenty-nine) were included at priority nine. It should be noted that while this part of the budget is calculated by the model on a departmental basis (because of the necessity of using the FTE salary calculations), in most actual situations such a fund would probably be aggregated on a college-wide or campus-wide basis.

Finally, the total budget constraint (number twenty) was also assigned to priority level nine. Early runs of the model were made with the minimization of the deviations for this constraint set at various other higher priorities. In each instance, any goal(s) below the priority level of the total budget constraint were excluded from the solution set. Thus the only acceptable priority level for this constraint became that associated with the last, or lowest priority, in this case, goal nine.

Based on approximately thirty simulations, the objective function given below was found to provide a reasonably good "fit" for the organizational structure and budget in the Department of History.

$$\text{Minimize } Z = P_1 d_i^+ + P_1 d_i^- + P_1 d_2^- + P_2 \sum_{i=14}^{16} d_i^- + P_3 \sum_{i=6}^{8} d_i^- + P_3 \sum_{i=6}^{8} d_i^+ + P_3 d_{12}^-$$

(USCH)	(GSCH)	(Ten)	(#GTA, I, GRA)	(#TPS)

$$+P_3 d_{12}^+ + P_4 \sum_{i=22}^{26} d_i^- + P_4 \sum_{i=23}^{24} d_i^+ + P_5 \sum_{i=17}^{19} d_i^+ + P_6 \sum_{i=3}^{5} d_i^- + P_7 \sum_{i=9}^{11} d_i^-$$

(#TPS)	(% Dist)	(Dist)	(R/GRA, TPS, SS)	(#U,MA, PhD)	(#ASST, ASSOC)

$$+P_7 d_{13}^- + P_8 d_{21}^+ + P_9 \sum_{i=27}^{29} d^+ + P_9 \sum_{i=27}^{29} d^- + P_9 d_{20}^+$$

(Prof, SS) (Sal Incr) (Oper Bud, Prof Dev)   (T. Bud)

Tables 5.3 and 5.4 provide easy-reference summaries of the goals and priorities of this formulation of the model.

Results of Test II

After numerous "runs" of the model with different priority arrangements, the above set of goals was felt to be a good representation of the decision-making and goal-setting tasks that the college and departments studied had used in

Table 5.3
Summary of Goals and Priorities by Row Level
Department of History Formulation

Row	Desc.	Goal (RHS)	Prty.	Neg. Dev. Weight	Pos. Dev. Weight
1	USCH	255.0	1	1.0	1.0
2	GSCH	52.0	1	1.0	——
3	U-majors	197.0	6	1.0	——
4	#M.A.	25.0	6	2.0	——
5	#Ph.D.	20.0	6	3.0	——
6	#GRA	0.0	3	1.0	1.0
7	#GTA	16.0	3	1.0	1.0
8	#Inst.	1.0	3	1.0	1.0
9	#Asst.	9.0	7	1.0	——
10	#Assoc.	2.0	7	1.0	——
11	#Prof.	12.0	7	1.0	——
12	#TPS	0.0	3	1.0	1.0
13	#SS	2.0	7	1.0	——
14	#Asst/Ten.	0.0	2	1.0	——
15	#Assoc/Ten.	1.0	2	1.0	——
16	#Prof/Ten.	11.0	2	3.0	——
17	Ratio/GRA	0.0	5	——	4.0
18	Ratio/TPS	0.0	5	——	5.0
19	Ratio/SS	0.0	5	——	1.0
20	T. Budget	0.0	9	——	1.0
21	Sal. Incr.	0.0	8	——	1.0
22	% GTA	0.0	4	1.0	1.0
23	% Inst.	0.0	4	1.0	1.0
24	% Asst.	0.0	4	1.0	1.0
25	% Assoc.	0.0	4	1.0	——
26	% Prof.	0.0	4	1.0	——
27	$/SCH	8,015.0	9	1.0	1.0
28	Oper. Bud.	2,000.0	9	1.0	1.0
29	Prof. Dev.	0.0	9	1.0	1.0

the development of each academic unit under the prevailing circumstances. The model was believed to be a good, objective description of a real-world situation.

The purpose of test II was to replicate current departmental budgets and organizational structures through the simulation of various priority arrangements in the objective function. One evaluation of this test can be made by examining table 5.5, which illustrates the output of the model for the Depart-

Table 5.4
Summary of Goals and Priorities by Priority Level
Department of History Formulation

Prty.	Desc.	Row No.	Goal (RHS)	Neg. Dev. Weight	Pos. Dev. Weight
1	USCH	1	255.0	1.0	1.0
1	GSCH	2	52.0	1.0	——
2	#Asst/Ten.	14	0.0	1.0	——
2	#Assoc/Ten.	15	1.0	1.0	——
2	#Prof/Ten.	16	11.0	3.0	——
3	#GTA	7	16.0	1.0	1.0
3	#Inst.	8	1.0	1.0	1.0
3	#GRA	6	0.0	1.0	1.0
3	#TPS	12	0.0	1.0	1.0
4	% GTA	22	0.0	1.0	1.0
4	% Inst.	23	0.0	1.0	1.0
4	% Asst.	24	0.0	1.0	1.0
4	% Assoc.	25	0.0	1.0	——
4	% Prof.	26	0.0	1.0	——
5	Ratio/GRA	17	0.0	——	1.0
5	Ratio/TPS	18	0.0	——	1.0
5	Ratio/SS	19	0.0	——	1.0
6	U-majors	3	197.0	1.0	——
6	#M.A.	4	25.0	2.0	——
6	#Ph.D.	5	20.0	3.0	——
7	#Asst.	9	9.0	1.0	——
7	#Assoc.	10	2.0	1.0	——
7	#Prof.	11	12.0	1.0	——
7	#SS	13	2.0	1.0	——
8	Sal. Incr.	21	0.0	——	1.0
9	#SCH	27	8,015.0	1.0	1.0
9	Oper. Bud.	28	2,000.0	1.0	1.0
9	Prof. Dev.	29	0.0	1.0	1.0
9	T. Budget	20	0.0	——	1.0

ment of History formulation. This "slack analysis" section of the output describes the initial goal amount available (the RHS) and also the values of the negative and positive deviational variables for each of the twenty-nine constraints.

First, it should be noted that the model, as formulated, did not contain integer-solution requirements for the output variables. Accordingly, the solution sets include fractional portions of positions. While academic departments

Table 5.5
Slack Analysis
Output from History Department Formulation

Row	Available	Pos. Dev.	Neg. Dev.
1	255.0	0.00	0.00
2	52.0	23.00	0.00
3	197.0	168.70	0.00
4	25.0	340.70	0.00
5	20.0	50.66	0.00
6	0.0	0.00	0.00
7	16.0	0.00	0.00
8	1.0	0.00	0.00
9	9.0	1.40	0.00
10	2.0	0.34	0.00
11	12.0	0.26	0.00
12	0.0	0.00	0.00
13	2.0	1.13	0.00
14	0.0	10.40	0.00
15	1.0	1.34	0.00
16	11.0	1.26	0.00
17	0.0	24.99	0.00
18	0.0	24.99	0.00
19	0.0	0.00	0.00
20	0.0	540,496.74	0.00
21	0.0	50,450.35	0.00
22	0.0	0.00	12.10
23	0.0	0.25	0.00
24	0.0	0.00	0.00
25	0.0	0.00	0.00
26	0.0	0.74	0.00
27	8,015.0	0.00	0.00
28	2,000.0	0.00	0.00
29	0.0	0.00	0.00

normally recruit new staff members (or reduce existing positions) on the basis of 1.00 FTE budgeted lines, it is reasonable to examine departmental budgets on the basis of fractional positions. For instance, any fractional part of a line could be added to (or deleted from) the GTA budget.

Slack Analysis

Constraints 1–5: The first constraint (for sufficient USCH production), which was also assigned the highest possible priority, was achieved exactly. That is, the model's final solution set includes sufficient academic staff to provide for teaching 7,649 undergraduate student-credit hours, based on an average class size of 30 students, and a faculty workload of six undergraduate and three graduate credit hours for all faculty ranks. Since the achievement of this goal was assigned priority one, it was met exactly and thus resulted in no positive or negative deviation from the goal.

Constraint number two (GSCH production), for which the negative deviational variable was also assigned to priority one, shows positive deviation of 23.0. In other words, the academic staff called for to meet the USCH requirement of priority one is sufficient to allow for the production of 525 GSCH, some 161 GSCH more than the target number of 364 set in the original formulation for the Department of History. This is calculated as follows: the goal of 52, plus positive-deviation of 23, equals 75; 75 times the average graduate-level class size of seven, equals 525 GSCH.

Similarly, constraints numbers three, four, and five also show positive values for the positive deviational variables. These results mean that sufficient staff will be available to meet the undergraduate advising and the graduate student supervisory requirements, as specified in the workload assignments of table 5.2. The relatively large positive deviation values for these constraints may suggest the need to review the policies for advising and supervisory workloads.

Constraints 6–13: Equations six through thirteen allowed for a comparison of the number of staff called for by the model with those currently budgeted in the departments. For the Department of History, the solution set contained no GRAs; since the department does not have any at present, this goal was achieved exactly with both the positive and negative deviational values being zero. The department has 16.0 GTAs, the solution set includes exactly 16.0 GTAs, so again both deviational variables are zero. The same is true for the number of instructors (1.0 based on constraint number eight).

At the assistant-professor level, the model provided for 10.40 staff members; as the department currently has 9.0 faculty members in this category, the slack analysis shows positive deviation of 1.40. At the associate-professor level, the model calls for 2.34 staff members versus the department's 2.00, resulting in a positive-deviation value of .34. For the professor category, the goal-programming solution is for 12.26 as compared with 12.00 currently budgeted in the department, for a positive-deviation value of .26.

Equations twelve and thirteen relate to the currently budgeted numbers of technical/professional staff (TPS) and support staff (SS). The Department of History has no TPS, the same as that called for by the model, so the deviational variables are again both zero. History has 2.00 secretaries budgeted as support staff, a goal which the model overachieved by 1.13 FTE. (The latter positive deviation can be attributed to equation number nineteen, assigned to priority five).

Deviational variables for constraints nine through eleven and thirteen were all assigned to priority-level seven, so it may seem somewhat surprising to find the values so close to zero for most of them. However, keep in mind that the goal of test II was to find a priority arrangement that would replicate current departmental budgets. Also, recall that for each of these constraints, other higher-priority goals were actually in "control" of the numbers of staff selected for each category.

Constraints 14–16: Deviations from these three constraints were all included in priority two and were only subordinated to the goal of having sufficient staff to meet the SCH projections. In addition, the goal of desiring to maintain tenure commitments is complementary to the goals of limiting the amount of teaching done by GTAs and Instructors (Goal 3).

The model's solution set includes 10.40 FTE assistant professors, and since the Department of History has no tenured assistant professors, these 10.40 positions all are shown as a positive deviation from the goal of constraint number fourteen. At the associate-professor level, the model calls for 2.34 FTE positions. This is 1.34 FTE positions more than the one tenured associate-professor position in the Department of History. In the professor rank, the department has 11.00 FTE positions with tenure; the model's solution includes 12.26 FTE professors, or positive deviation of 1.26 FTE for constraint sixteen.

Constraints 17–19: Constraints seventeen and eighteen strive for funding GRAs and TPS based on ratios of 1:8 to the total number of academic staff members. Since both of these requirements were assigned to the relatively low-level priority of five, and since neither position is essential for the teaching program being emphasized in this formulation of the model, neither has a value in the final solution set. Based on the construction of equations seventeen and eighteen, each of these results appears as a 24.99 positive deviation from the goals (e.g., the academic staff outnumbers the GRAs and the TPS by 25 to 0).

Deviations from constraint number nineteen were also assigned to priority level five. This goal was met exactly as both deviational variables have values of zero.

Constraints 20–21: The total budget constraint (number twenty) was set up so as to reflect the value of the personal-services budget as the positive deviation from the goal of a zero budget. (The goal for the budget could be set at any positive value with the d^+ or the d^- values then being the amount by which the projected budget was over- or underexpended.) Accordingly, for the present Department of History formulation, the total personal services budget, excluding the desired salary increases from equation number twenty-one, is $540,497 as shown in the positive-deviation column of table 5.5.

Constraint number twenty-one, providing for salary increases for all staff members, is set up in the same way as equation number twenty. The cost of providing the desired raises is $50,450.

Constraints 22–26: These equations require the model to provide for a distribution of the teaching staff based on percentages which relate to the existing departmental distribution. Each constraint will be separately analyzed.

The solution set for this run provides for 16.0 GTAs. Constraint number twenty-two requires that the number of GTAs be no more than 15 percent of the total instructional staff. Since the solution set has a total of 26 staff in all other instructional categories, constraint number twenty-two has a negative-deviational value of 12.1 (calculated as: 15 percent times 26, equals 3.9; 16.0 minus 3.9, equals 12.1).

The solution set includes a 1.0 instructor position. Since 5 percent of the 25.0 total assistant, associate, and professor categories is 1.25, equation number twenty-three has positive deviation of .25.

The model calls for 10.40 assistant professors; 40 percent of the total number of instructors, assistants, associates, and professors is 10.40, so constraint number twenty-four has no positive or negative deviation.

At the associate-professor level, the solution set includes 2.34 positions. With 9 percent of the total number of instructors, assistants, associates, and professors being 2.34 positions, constraint number twenty-five has neither positive nor negative deviation.

The solution set calls for 12.26 professors; 50 percent of the total number of instructors, assistants, associates, and professors is 12.26 positions, thus constraint number twenty-six also has been met very closely.

Constraints 27–28: As stated earlier, the desired operating budget computed by the model is based on two factors: total student credit hours and total FTE instructional staff. Constraints numbers twenty-seven and twenty-eight calculate the operating budget based on these factors. For the Department of History, the operating budget of $9,976 is based on $.75 per student credit hour, a $2,000 base budget, and $5.00 per FTE instructional position called for in the model's solution. Constraints twenty-seven and twenty-eight were met completely.

Constraint 29: The professional development fund is given by the value of variable X_{12}. For this formulation of the model for the Department of History, the value of this variable is $21,809. With both of the deviational variables for this constraint being zero, the goal of providing a semester's leave with pay every seven years for each senior-level faculty member has been attained.

Table 5.6
Variable Analysis
Department of History Formulation

Variable	Description	Value
X_1	Graduate Research Assistants	0.00 FTE
X_2	Graduate Teaching Assistants	16.00 FTE
X_3	Instructors	1.00 FTE
X_4	Assistant Professors	10.40 FTE
X_5	Associate Professors	2.34 FTE
X_6	Professors	12.26 FTE
X_7	Technical/Professioanal Staff	0.00 FTE
X_8	Support Staff	3.13 FTE
X_9	Total Budget (goal)	0.00
X_{10}	Operating Budget (based on SCH)	$6,026
X_{11}	Operating Budget (based on SCH & FTE)	$9,976
X_{12}	Professional Development Fund	$21,809

Variable Analysis

The computer output section entitled "Analysis of Decision Variables" gives the model's solution set for this formulation for the Department of History. These values are summarized in table 5.6.

Comparisons with Departmental Structures and Budgets

In order to more easily compare the model's solution set with the current budget and organizational structure of the Department of History, table 5.7 has been developed. This table is based on a faculty workload of six undergraduate and three graduate credit hours for all three faculty ranks. GTAs would teach six undergraduate credit hours and instructors would teach nine hours at the undergraduate level. As stated before, this particular formulation is based on a desired average undergraduate class size of 30 students and an average graduate class size of 7 students.

Column (1) in table 5.7 gives the existing distribution of staff members currently budgeted in the department by category. Column (2) indicates the number of tenured faculty positions, again by category. Column (3) gives the goal programming (GP) distribution as provided by the model, and column (4) displays the difference between the existing distribution and the GP distribution.

Table 5.7
Comparative Analysis for First Formuation

Department: History
Workload: 6 & 3, 6 & 3, 6 & 3
SCH: Undergraduate   7,649
    Graduate   366

    Total   8,015
Average Class Size:
    Undergraduate   30 students
    Graduate   7 students

Category	(1) Existing Staff Distribution	(2) Number With Tenure	(3) G.P. Distribution	(4) Difference (Col 3 − Col 1)
GRA	0		0	0
GTA	16.00		16.00	0
Instructor	1.00		1.00	0
Asst. Prof.	9.00		10.40	1.40
Assoc. Prof.	2.00	1.00	2.34	.34
Full Prof.	12.00	11.00	12.26	.26
Subtotal	40.00	12.00	42.00	2.00
Tech. Staff	0		0	0
Support Staff	2.00		3.12	1.12
Total	42.00	12.00	45.12	3.12
Total Salaries	$492,120		$540,497	$48,377
Operating Budget	$10,000		$9,976	−24
Leave Fund	0		$24,584	$24,584
Salary Costs/SCH:	61.40		67.43	6.03

Data are also provided for comparing the department's total salary budget, operating budget, and instructional salary costs per SCH, with the budgets called for by the model's solution set.

An examination of table 5.7 reveals a very close "fit" for the model when compared with actual data from the budget of the Department of History. The 2.00 FTE additional teaching staff required to meet the desired average undergraduate class size of 30 students represents only a 5 percent addition to the present staff of 40. Of added importance is that the tenure constraints were not violated. Similarly, the GP distribution of staff aligns nicely with the existing distribution of academic staff. The solution set does call for a sizable increase (1.12 FTE) in the secretarial support staff, but this can be attributed to the desired 1:8 ratio of constraint number nineteen. The total salaries budget

Table 5.8
Evaluation of the Objective Function
Department of History Formulation

Priority Level (Goal)	Evaluation
1	0.00
2	0.00
3	0.00
4	12.35
5	50.00
6	0.00
7	0.00
8	$50,450
9	$540,497

under the GP distribution is $48,377 greater than the existing salaries budget of $492,120 but this additional amount is caused by the higher total FTE count under the model's solution.

Indications of the closeness of the model's fit can also be seen by an evaluation of the model's objective function. This portion of the computer output is reproduced in table 5.8.

Note that goals numbers one, two, three, six, and seven have been exactly attained. The 12.35 deviation from goal number four represents the model's failure to meet exactly the percentage distribution requirements for the GTAs and instructors. Constraint number twenty-two (percent GTAs) resulted in negative deviation of 12.10, and constraint number twenty-three (percent instructors) resulted in positive deviation of .25, for total deviation for goal four of 12.35.

The 50.00 total deviation for goal number five is created by the model's failure to meet the ratios for the desired numbers of GRAs and TPS (positive deviation of 25.00 each for constraints seventeen and eighteen). The desired ratio for the number of support staff, which was also included in goal five, had no deviation and did not contribute to the total deviation from this goal.

The deviation for goal number eight represents the funding required to provide the stipulated percentage salary increases. Because constraint number twenty-one was unrealistically set equal to zero, the deviation from this goal does not actually represent the unattainment of a goal.

The $540,497 deviation for goal number nine is the value for the total salaries budget. Again, this goal deviation was by design because the budget goal was also set unrealistically at a value of zero.

Conclusions for Test II

Both the comparison of the model's solution set with the real departmental data and the evaluation of the objective function show that the model itself and the objective function as formulated for the Department of History will provide an excellent replication of the current departmental budget and organizational structure.

Test III

The purpose of test III was to apply tests I and II to two other departments for the purpose of resource allocation comparisons. This process actually involved two steps: (1) to see if the generalized model would also provide good replications of the two other departmental budgets and structures, and (2) to examine the solution sets for resource allocation comparison purposes. The two other departments studied were Political Science and Sociology.

The Political Science Department Formulation

The following constants were used for the first formulation for the Department of Political Science:

a_1 = 0.00 FTE	c_6 = 30 students	e_1 = .15/1.0	g_1 = 5%
a_2 = 6.00 FTE	c_7 = 7 students	e_2 = .05/1.0	g_2 = 5%
a_3 = 1.00 FTE	c_8 = $.75	e_3 = .20/1.0	g_3 = 5%
a_4 = 2.50 FTE	c_9 = $75.00	e_4 = .30/1.0	g_4 = 10%
a_5 = 9.58 FTE	c_{10} = $2,000	e_5 = .35/1.0	g_5 = 10%
a_6 = 5.00 FTE			g_6 = 10%
a_7 = 0.00 FTE	d_1 = 10:1	f_1 = $ 3,939	g_7 = 10%
a_8 = 2.00 FTE	d_2 = 10:1	f_2 = $ 3,939	g_8 = 10%
	d_3 = 8:1	f_3 = $10,000	
b_1 = 0.00 FTE	d_4 = 8:1	f_4 = $14,069	
b_2 = 9.33 FTE	d_5 = 8:1	f_5 = $16,843	
b_3 = 5.00 FTE		f_6 = $19,202	
		f_7 = $10,000	
c_1 = 6,072 SCH		f_8 = $ 7,250	
c_2 = 235 SCH			
c_3 = 197			
c_4 = 25			
c_5 = 20			

The maximum teaching, advising, and supervisory loads for the Department of Political Science under this formulation are the same as those given in table 5.2, the first formulation for the Department of History. Accordingly, the twenty-nine constraints for the Political Science formulation are as follows:

$$6X_2 + 9X_3 + 6X_4 + 6X_5 + 6X_6 + d_1^- - d_1^+ = 202 \quad (1)$$

$$3X_4 + 3X_5 + 3X_6 + d_2^- - d_2^+ = 34 \quad (2)$$

$$20X_4 + 15X_5 + 10X_6 + d_3^- - d_3^+ = 197 \quad (3)$$

$$3X_4 + 4X_5 + 5X_6 + d_4^- - d_4^+ = 25 \quad (4)$$

$$4X_5 + 5X_6 + d_5^- - d_5^+ = 20 \quad (5)$$

$$X_1 + d_6^- - d_6^+ = 0 \quad (6)$$

$$X_2 + d_7^- - d_7^+ = 6.00 \quad (7)$$

$$X_3 + d_8^- - d_8^+ = 1.00 \quad (8)$$

$$X_4 + d_9^- - d_9^+ = 2.50 \quad (9)$$

$$X_5 + d_{10}^- - d_{10}^+ = 9.58 \quad (10)$$

$$X_6 + d_{11}^- - d_{11}^+ = 5.00 \quad (11)$$

$$X_7 + d_{12}^- - d_{12}^+ = 0.00 \quad (12)$$

$$X_8 + d_{13}^- - d_{13}^+ = 2.00 \quad (13)$$

$$X_4 + d_{14}^- - d_{14}^+ = 0.00 \quad (14)$$

$$X_5 + d_{15}^- - d_{15}^+ = 9.33 \quad (15)$$

$$X_6 + d_{16}^- - d_{16}^+ = 5.00 \quad (16)$$

$$-8X_1 + X_4 + X_5 + X_6 + d_{17}^- - d_{17}^+ = 0 \quad (17)$$

$$X_4 + X_5 + X_6 - 8X_7 + d_{18}^- - d_{18}^+ = 0 \quad (18)$$

$$X_4 + X_5 + X_6 - 8X_8 + d_{19}^- - d_{19}^+ = 0 \quad (19)$$

$$3{,}939X_1 + 3{,}939X_2 + 10{,}000X_3 + 14{,}069X_4 + 16{,}843X_5 + 19{,}202X_6 + 10{,}000X_7 + 7{,}250X_8 - X_9 + d_{20}^- - d_{20}^+ = 0 \quad (20)$$

$$197X_1 + 197X_2 + 500X_3 + 1{,}407X_4 + 1{,}684X_5 + 1{,}920X_6 + 1{,}000X_7 + 725X_8 + X_9 + d_{21}^- - d_{21}^+ = 0 \quad (21)$$

$$- X_2 + .15X_3 + .15X_4 + .15X_5 + .15X_6 + d_{22}^- - d_{22}^+ = 0 \quad (22)$$

$$- X_3 + .05X_4 + .05X_5 + .05X_6 + d_{23}^- - d_{23}^+ = 0 \quad (23)$$

$$20X_3 - .80X_4 + .20X_5 + .20X_6 + d_{24}^- - d_{24}^+ = 0 \quad (24)$$

$$.30X_3 + .30X_4 - .70X_5 + .30X_6 + d_{25}^- - d_{25}^+ = 0 \quad (25)$$

$$.35X_3 + .35X_4 + .35X_5 - .65X_6 + d_{26}^- - d_{26}^+ = 0 \quad (26)$$

$$1.33X_{10} + d_{27}^- - d_{27}^+ = 6{,}307 \quad (27)$$

$$- 5X_3 - 5X_4 - 5X_5 - 5X_6 - X_{10} + X_{11} + d_{28}^- - d_{28}^+ = 2{,}000 \quad (28)$$

$$16{,}843X_5 + 19{,}202X_6 - 14X_{12} + d_{29}^- - d_{29}^+ = 0 \quad (29)$$

In order to allow for accurate comparisons with the output from the history department formulation in order to validate test II for the political science department formulation, the objective function from the history formulation (for reference see page 145) was used without modification for this run of the model. Thus all goals and priorities for this second run of the model remain exactly as they were for the first run for tests I and II for the Department of History.

Results of Political Science Department Formulation

Table 5.9 displays the slack-analysis section of the computer output for this run of the model. This analysis of the deviational variables will again be used to analyze the details of the model's goal attainments.

Slack Analysis

Constraint 1: The goal of providing staff for sufficient USCH production was met exactly with zero values for both deviational variables.

Constraint 2: This constraint, for sufficient GSCH production, was over-achieved by some 312 SCH (positive deviation of 44.5 times the average graduate class size of 7).

Constraints 3–5: Relatively large positive-deviation values for these three equations indicate that the advising and supervisory responsibilities can easily be met.

Constraints 6–13: Constraints numbers six, seven, and eight all show zero values for both deviational variables, indicating that the solution set called for exactly the same numbers of GRA, GTA, and instructors as are presently budgeted in the political science department.

The deviations for constraints numbers nine, ten, and eleven indicate that 4.83 additional assistant professors, .25 less associate professors, and 4.51 additional professors should be hired in order to meet the USCH requirements based on the stated average class sizes.

The 1.27 positive deviation for constraint number thirteen shows that this solution set calls for a total of 3.27 support staff positions, or 1.27 positions more than the 2.00 presently budgeted for this department.

Constraints 14–16: These are the "tenure" constraints; numbers fourteen and seventeen show positive deviation values, and constraint number fifteen is exactly achieved, meaning that all tenure commitments have been met under this solution.

Constraints 17–19: Again, the goals of providing GRAs and TPS members based on the 1:8 ratio have not been attained. As with the history department formulation, constraints seventeen and eighteen were included in priority five and were not provided for in the final output.

Constraint number nineteen, which provides for secretarial support staff based on the same ratio (1:8), was met exactly.

Constraints 20–21: The positive deviation from constraint number twenty gives the total salary budget for this distribution of staff as $500,174. It should again be noted that constraint number twenty was set equal to zero (the RHS). Any other budget goal could have been set as the RHS value with the

Table 5.9
Slack Analysis
Output from Political Science Department
Formulation

Row	Available	Pos. Dev.	Neg. Dev.
1	202.0	0.00	0.00
2	34.0	44.50	0.00
3	107.0	184.60	0.00
4	25.0	81.85	0.00
5	20.0	64.86	0.00
6	0.0	0.00	0.00
7	6.0	0.00	0.00
8	1.0	0.00	0.00
9	2.5	4.83	0.00
10	9.5	0.00	.25
11	5.0	4.50	0.00
12	0.0	0.00	0.00
13	2.0	1.27	0.00
14	0.0	7.33	0.00
15	9.3	0.00	0.00
16	5.0	4.50	0.00
17	0.0	26.17	0.00
18	0.0	26.17	0.00
19	0.0	0.0	0.00
20	0.0	500,174.15	0.00
21	0.0	48,332.05	0.00
22	0.0	0.00	1.93
23	0.0	0.31	0.00
24	0.0	0.00	1.90
25	0.0	0.00	1.18
26	0.0	0.00	0.00
27	6,307.0	0.00	0.00
28	2,000.0	0.00	0.00
29	0.0	0.00	0.00

deviations for equation number twenty then showing how much more (d^+) or less d^-) funding would be needed in order to provide the personnel called for by the model.

The positive deviation from the goal of constraint number twenty-one, $48,332, gives the cost of the desired salary increases. This constraint functions in the same manner as constraint number twenty.

Constraints 22–26: The negative deviation of 1.93 for constraint number twenty-two indicates that the model "violated" the requirement that GTAs comprise no more than 15 percent of the academic staff. This deviational value, however, is less than the negative-deviational value of the same constraint for the history formulation.

Constraint number twenty-three shows a small amount of positive deviation (.31) indicating that 1.00 FTE Instructor included in the solution set is somewhat less than 5 percent of the total number of academic staff.

Constraint number twenty-four shows a negative deviation of 1.89 meaning that the 7.33 FTE assistant professors called for in the solution set is greater than 20 percent of the full-time instructional staff.

The negative deviational value of 1.18 for constraint number twenty-five provides that the number of associate professors in the solution set (9.33) represents a little more than 30 percent of the full-time instructional staff.

For constraint number twenty-six the slack analysis shows no deviation, meaning that the 9.51 professors meet the 35 percent goal exactly.

Constraints 27–28: Both of these equations have no deviation, again indicating exact achievement of the desired goals for the amount of the operating budget.

Constraint 29: This constraint, for the provision of a leave fund, also has zero deviation which assures sufficient funding for the stipulated one-semester leaves for one-seventh of the senior-level staff.

Comparisons with Departmental Structures and Budgets

Table 5.10 provides for a summary comparison of the model's solution set with the current budget and structure of the Department of Political Science. The table is in the same format as table 5.7 which showed a similar comparison for the Department of History (see page 153).

The actual "fit" of the model to the existing data for the Department of Political Science can be seen as acceptable, although not as good as for the Department of History. Notice that the number of GTAs and instructors have been kept to a minimum, that the distribution of the other academic positions is reasonable, that the tenure commitments have not been violated, that the operating budget level is quite close, and that the support staff increase is consistent with that called for in the earlier part of the model.

The closeness of the model's fit can also be seen by an evaluation of the model's objective function. This portion of the computer output is reproduced as table 5.11. Note that goals numbers one, two, three, six, and seven have been exactly attained. The deviations for goals eight and nine are purposeful because they give the salary increase and total budget figures, respectively. The deviation from goal number four represents the model's failure to exactly maintain the percentage distribution for GTAs and instructors. The 52.33

Table 5.10

Comparative Analysis for First Formuation

Department: Political Science
Workload: 6 & 3, 6 & 3, 6 & 3
SCH: Undergraduate   6,072
     Graduate   235

     Total   6,307
Average Class Size:
     Undergraduate 30 students
     Graduate   7 students

Category	(1) Existing Staff Distribution	(2) Number With Tenure	(3) G.P. Distribution	(4) Difference (Col 3 − Col 1)
GRA	0		0	0
GTA	6.00		6.00	0
Instructor	.50		1.00	.50
Asst. Prof.	2.50		7.33	4.83
Assoc.Prof.	9.58	9.33	9.33	.25
Full Prof.	5.00	5.00	9.50	4.50
Subtotal	23.58	14.33	33.16	9.58
Tech. Staff	0	0	0	0
Support Staff	2.00	0	3.27	1.27
Total	25.58	14.33	36.43	10.85
Total Salaries	$348,096		$500,174	$152,078
Operating Budget	$7,795		$8,780	$985
Leave Fund	0		$24,266	$24,266
Salary Costs/SCH:	$55.19		$80.14	$24.95

total deviation for goal number five represents the deviation for the constraints for the desired numbers of GRAs and GTAs. As the political science department does not have budgeted positions in either of these categories, this deviation was not unexpected.

On a resource-comparison basis, however, there is a somewhat larger discrepancy between the two departmental solution sets. Keeping in mind that both formulations were based on a desired average undergraduate class size of 30 students, it is interesting to note that the history formulation called for a 5 percent increase (2.00 FTE) in academic staff and a 9.8 percent increase ($48,377) in the total salary budget. For the political science department, the respective increases are 41 percent (9.58 FTE) and 44 percent ($152,078).

These budgeting and staffing inconsistencies could be the result of numerous factors. Examples would include such things as differences in departmen-

Table 5.11
Evaluation of the Objective Function
Department of Political Science Formulation

Priority Level (goal)	Evaluation
1	0.00
2	0.00
3	0.00
4	5.31
5	52.33
6	0.00
7	.25
8	$48,332
9	$500,174

tal leadership styles or managerial philosophies, differences in departmental goals and program emphases, differing faculty strengths and weaknesses, student demand and competition, and so forth.

More will be said about the resource-allocation comparisons later in this chapter. At this point, it is felt that the model has successfully demonstrated its applicability to a second department.

The Sociology Department Formulation

The following constants were used for the first formulation for the Department of Sociology:

a_1 = 0.00 FTE	c_1 = 6,582 SCH	e_1 = .15:1.0	g_1 = 5%
a_2 = 17.00 FTE	c_2 = 252 SCH	e_2 = .05:1.0	g_2 = 5%
a_3 = 0.00 FTE	c_3 = 197	e_3 = .16:1.0	g_3 = 5%
a_4 = 2.60 FTE	c_4 = 39	e_4 = .26:1.0	g_4 = 10%
a_5 = 4.00 FTE	c_5 = 13	e_5 = .58:1.0	g_5 = 10%
a_6 = 9.00 FTE	c_6 = 30 students		g_6 = 10%
a_7 = 0.00 FTE	c_7 = 7 students	f_1 = $ 3,733	g_7 = 10%
a_8 = 2.50 FTE	c_8 = $.75	f_2 = $ 3,733	g_8 = 10%
	c_9 = $75.00	f_3 = $10,000	
b_1 = 0.00 FTE	c_{10} = $2,000	f_4 = $13,789	
b_2 = 3.00 FTE		f_5 = $16,278	
b_3 = 9.00 FTE	d_1 = 10:1	f_6 = $22,232	
	d_2 = 10:1	f_7 = $10,000	
	d_3 = 8:1	f_8 = $ 7,953	
	d_4 = 8:1		
	d_5 = 8:1		

The maximum teaching, advising, and supervisory loads for the Department of Sociology under this formulation are the same as those given in table 5.2 for the first formulation for the Department of History. Based on the constants given above and the workloads from table 5.2, the twenty-nine constraints for the sociology department formulation are as follows:

$$6X_2 + 9X_3 + 6X_4 + 6X_5 + 6X_6 + d_1^- - d_1^+ = 219 \quad (1)$$
$$3X_4 + 3X_5 + 3X_6 + d_2^- - d_2^+ = 36 \quad (2)$$
$$20X_4 + 15X_5 + 10X_6 + d_3^- - d_3^+ = 197 \quad (3)$$
$$20X_4 + 15X_5 + 10X_6 + d_4^- - d_4^+ = 39 \quad (4)$$
$$4X_5 + 5X_6 + d_5^- - d_5^+ = 13 \quad (5)$$
$$X_1 + d_6^- - d_6^+ = 0 \quad (6)$$
$$X_2 + d_7^- - d_7^+ = 17.00 \quad (7)$$
$$X_3 + d_8^- - d_8^+ = 0.00 \quad (8)$$
$$X_4 + d_9^- - d_9^+ = 2.60 \quad (9)$$
$$X_5 + d_{10}^- - d_{10}^+ = 4.00 \quad (10)$$
$$X_6 + d_{11}^- - d_{11}^+ = 9.00 \quad (11)$$
$$X_7 + d_{12}^- - d_{12}^+ = 0 \quad (12)$$
$$X_8 + d_{13}^- - d_{13}^+ = 2.50 \quad (13)$$
$$X_4 + d_{14}^- - d_{14}^+ = 0.00 \quad (14)$$
$$X_5 + d_{15}^- - d_{15}^+ = 3.00 \quad (15)$$
$$X_6 + d_{16}^- - d_{16}^+ = 9.00 \quad (16)$$
$$-8X_1 + X_4 + X_5 + X_6 + d_{17}^- - d_{17}^+ = 0 \quad (17)$$
$$X_4 + X_5 + X_6 - 8X_7 + d_{18}^- - d_{18}^+ = 0 \quad (18)$$
$$X_4 + X_5 + X_6 - 8X_8 + d_{1\,9}^- - d_{1\,9}^+ = 0 \quad (19)$$
$$3{,}733X_1 + 3{,}733X_2 + 10{,}000X_3 + 13{,}789X_4 +$$
$$16{,}278X_5 + 22{,}232X_6 + 10{,}000X_7 + 7{,}953X_8 - X_9 + d_{20}^- - d_{20}^+ = 0 \quad (20)$$
$$187X_1 + 187X_2 + 500X_3 + 1{,}379X_4 +$$
$$1{,}629X_5 + 2{,}223X_6 + 1{,}000X_7 + 795X_8 + X_9 + d_{21}^- - d_{21}^+ = 0 \quad (21)$$
$$- X_2 + .15X_3 + .15X_4 + .15X_5 + .15X_6 + d_{22}^- - d_{22}^+ = 0 \quad (22)$$
$$- X_3 + .05X_4 + .05X_5 + .05X_6 + d_{23}^- - d_{23}^+ = 0 \quad (23)$$
$$.16X_3 - .84X_4 + .16X_5 + .16X_6 + d_{24}^- - d_{24}^+ = 0 \quad (24)$$
$$.26X_3 + .26X_4 - .74X_5 + .26X_6 + d_{25}^- - d_{25}^+ = 0 \quad (25)$$
$$.58X_3 + .58X_4 + .58X_5 - .42X_6 + d_{26}^- - d_{26}^+ = 0 \quad (26)$$
$$1.33X_{10} + d_{27}^- - d_{27}^+ = 6{,}834 \quad (27)$$
$$-75X_3 - 75X_4 - 75X_5 - 75X_6 -$$
$$X_{10} + X_{11} + d_{28}^- - d_{28}^+ = 2{,}000 \quad (28)$$
$$16{,}278X_5 + 22{,}230X_6 - 14X_{12} + d_{29}^- - d_{29}^+ = \quad (29)$$

Again, in order to allow for accurate comparisons with the output from the history and the political science formulations, and in order to validate test II for the sociology department formulation, the objective function from the history formulation (for reference see page 145) was again used, without modification. Accordingly, all goals and priorities for this third formulation remain exactly the same as for the other two departments under tests I and II.

Table 5.12
Slack Analysis
Output from Sociology Department Formulation

Row	Available	Pos. Dev.	Neg. Dev.
1	219.0	0.00	0.00
2	36.0	22.50	0.00
3	197.0	54.55	0.00
4	25.0	212.55	0.00
5	20.0	63.83	0.00
6	0.0	0.00	0.00
7	17.0	0.00	0.00
8	0.0	0.00	0.00
9	2.6	0.52	0.00
10	4.0	1.07	0.00
11	9.0	2.31	0.00
12	0.0	0.00	0.00
13	2.5	0.00	0.00
14	0.0	3.12	0.00
15	3.0	2.07	0.00
16	9.0	2.31	0.00
17	0.0	19.50	0.00
18	0.0	19.50	0.00
19	0.0	0.00	.50
20	0.0	460,338.45	0.00
21	0.0	42,870.12	0.00
22	0.0	0.00	14.08
23	0.0	0.97	0.00
24	0.0	0.00	0.00
25	0.0	0.00	0.00
26	0.0	0.00	0.00
27	6,834.0	0.00	0.00
28	2,000.0	0.00	0.00
29	0.0	0.00	0.00

Results of the Sociology Department Formulation.

Table 5.12 shows the slack analysis section of the computer output for this run of the model. This analysis of the deviational variables will again be used to briefly analyze the details of the model's goal attainments.

Slack Analysis

Constraint 1: As in the other two runs of the model, this priority-one goal of providing for sufficient USCH production was met exactly.

Constraint 2: This constraint, for sufficient GSCH production, was again overachieved, this time by 158 GSCH (positive deviation of 22.50 times the average graduate class size of 7).

Constraints 3–5: For this department, we also see relatively large positive-deviational values for these constraints, indicating that the advising and graduate student supervisory assignments can easily be met.

Constraints 6–13: Constraints numbers six, seven, eight, and twelve all show zero deviation, meaning the model provided for exactly the same number of GRAs, GTAs, instructors and TPS as presently budgeted in the department.

The positive deviation for equations nine, ten, and eleven show that .52 additional assistant professors, 1.07 additional associate professors and 2.31 additional professors would need to be hired in order to meet the SCH requirements based on the stated average class sizes. The zero deviation for equation number thirteen indicates that the model's solution set calls for exactly the same number of support staff as are presently budgeted.

Constraints 14–16: As in the other two formulations, these three "tenure" constraints all show positive deviation, meaning that all tenure commitments have been met under this solution.

Constraints 17–19: Once again the low-priority requests to include GRAs and TPS members at a ratio of 1:8 to the number of academic staff have not been attained.

Constraint number nineteen, however, does provide for meeting the 1:8 ratio for the secretarial support staff almost exactly.

Constraints 20–21: The positive deviation for constraint number twenty gives the total salary budget as $460,338; the same variable for constraint number twenty-one gives the cost of the desired percentage salary increases as $42,870.

Constraints 22–26: The 14.08 value for the d^- variable for constraint number twenty-two indicates that the model did not meet the requirement that GTAs comprise no more than 15 percent of the academic staff. The d^+ value of .97 for the equation number twenty-three means that on a percentage basis it would have been acceptable for the solution set for this formulation to have included approximately a 1.00 FTE instructor, although other constraints eliminated this choice.

Constraints numbers twenty-four, twenty-five, and twenty-six, giving the percentage distributions for the assistant, associate and professor categories, were met exactly and show neither positive nor negative deviational values.

Constraints 27–28: Both of these equations have no deviation, indicating exact achievement of the goals for the funding level for the departmental operating budget.

Table 5.13

Comparative Analysis of First Formuation

Department: Sociology
Workload: 6 & 3, 6 & 3, 6 & 3
SCH: Undergraduate   6,582
     Graduate   252

     Total   6,834
Average Class Size:
     Undergraduate 30 students
     Graduate   7 students

Category	(1) Existing Staff Distribution	(2) Number With Tenure	(3) G.P. Distribution	(4) Difference (Col 3 − Col 1)
GRA	0		0	0
GTA	17.00		17.00	0
Instructor	0		0	0
Asst. Prof.	2.60	0	3.12	.52
Assoc. Prof.	4.00	3.00	5.07	1.07
Full Prof.	9.00	9.00	11.31	2.31
Subtotal	32.60	12.00	36.50	3.90
Tech. Staff	0	0	0	0
Support Staff	2.50	0	2.50	0
Total	35.10	12.00	38.94	3.90
Total Salaries	$384,771		$460,338	$75,567
Operating Budget	$7,859		$8,601	$742
Leave Fund	0		$23,854	$23,854
Salary Costs/SCH:	$56.30		$67.36	$11.06

Constraint 29: The zero deviation for this equation assures a sufficient budget for the leave fund so that the stipulated one-semester leaves for one-seventh of the senior-level staff can again be provided.

Comparisons with Departmental Structures and Budgets

Table 5.13 uses the same format as tables 5.7 and 5.10 to show a summary comparison of the model's solution set with the actual data from the Department of Sociology's budget. A review of this table shows that the model has again provided a solution set very closely approximating the actual data for the budget in the Department of Sociology. It can be seen that the number of GTAs and instructors used has been kept to a minimum, that the distribution

Table 5.14
Evaluation of the Objective Function
Department of Sociology Formulation

Priority Level (goal)	Evaluation
1	0.00
2	0.00
3	0.00
4	15.05
5	39.00
6	0.00
7	0.00
8	$42,870
9	$460,338

of the other academic staff is reasonable, that the tenure commitments have not been violated, that the number of support staff equates with the existing number, and that the operating budget is at an acceptable level.

Table 5.14 displays the evaluation of the objective function as produced in the output section of the model. The closeness of the model's fit for the sociology department can be seen by noting that goals numbers one, two, three, six, and seven have been totally attained. As mentioned previously, the deviations from goals eight and nine are by design; the deviation for goal four again represents the failure to exactly meet the percentage distribution requirements for GTAs and instructors; the deviation for goal five relates to the desired ratio of GRA and TPS members, neither of which is currently included in the sociology department's budget.

Again, it should be noted that many organizational and environmental elements, such as different departmental emphases or priorities, different management styles, and the like, could account for the existing differences between departmental budgets and structures.

Resource Allocation Comparisons

Resource comparisons for the three departments now modeled are shown in table 5.15. It is clear from these data that three departments have very different resource support levels. The discrepancies between the amounts of additional resources needed by the different departments to allow them to meet the goals of an average undergraduate class size of 30 students and an average graduate class size of 7 students is considerable. The reasons for these differing support levels could be numerous. They could also be, and probably are, educationally sound. It is not the purpose of this model to attempt to draw conclusions about the meaning of these differing support levels; rather the desire is to be able to provide for improved insights into existing academic resource allocations and funding patterns.

The purpose of test III was to see if the generalized model could be used to replicate departmental budgets and organizational structures for two additional departments and to examine the solution sets for resource comparison purposes. The above analysis has successfully demonstrated these capabilities.

Test IV

The purpose of test IV is to evaluate further the performance of the model under varying conditions. This analysis of the effects of parameter changes is called *sensitivity analysis*. Because there usually exists some degree of uncertainty in real-world problems regarding the parameters of the model— i.e., priority factors, coefficients of the choice variables, available resources, and goal constraints—sensitivity analysis is an important part of the goal-programming solution.

After examining the different amounts of increased resources needed to meet the goals of the 30-student average undergraduate and the 7-student average graduate class sizes of the model's first formulation, it was decided that it would be useful to change this decision rule (class size) and examine the impact of the change on departmental resource needs. All three of the departments included in tests I, II, and III were used in test IV in order to study further their resource-allocation patterns.

In essence, test IV is an example of *heuristic programming*—it is an attempt to incorporate into the theoretical structure of the model the selective, rule-of-thumb processes that humans employ in solving complex problems.

Specifically, test IV consisted of parametrically varying the average undergraduate class size (constant c_6) by sequences of five, between the levels of twenty and fifty. This change resulted in a different RHS value for constraint number one. For instance, for the Department of History, changing the desired average undergraduate class to 35 students would result in a RHS value of 218 (7,649 SCH ÷ 35). Table 5.16 gives the RHS values used for each department at the specified class-size level.

The following section provides a discussion of the model's staffing patterns and goal achievements, by department, under this sensitivity analysis.

Table 5.15

Budget Comparisons

Additional resources required to meet the goals of an average undergraduate class size of 30 and an average graduate class size of 7.

	Δ FTE	Δ Total Budget	% Chg. FTE	% Chg. Total Budget
History	2.00	$48,377	5%	9.8%
Political Science	9.58	$152,078	44%	45.2%
Sociology	3.90	$75,567	12%	19.5%

The Department of History

The computer outputs for each of the model's simulations for all three departments are given in the Appendix. Perhaps the most pertinent section of this output is the evaluation of the objective function which gives the analysis of the goal achievements. These evaluations for the Department of History simulation have been summarized by undergraduate class-size level in table 5.17.

Notice that goals one, two, and six have been exactly met at all class sizes. These goals relate to the ability to produce sufficient undergraduate and graduate student credit hours, providing positions to allow for the maintenance of tenure commitments, and providing for the undergraduate advising and the graduate supervisory needs, respectively.

Table 5.16

RHS Values for Constraint #1

Under Varying Average Undergraduate Class Sizes

	Class Size						
	20	25	30	35	40	45	50
History	382	306	255	218	191	170	153
Political Science	304	243	202	173	152	135	121
Sociology	329	263	219	188	165	146	132

Table 5.17
Evaluation of the Objective Function
(Goal Achievements)
History Department

Undergraduate Class Size

Goal #	20	25	30	35	40	45	50
1	0	0	0	0	0	0	0
2	0	0	0	0	0	0	0
3	0	0	0	0	2.50	6.00	8.83
4	10.23	11.50	12.35	15.27	16.70	13.20	10.37
5	92.33	67.00	50.00	37.67	34.67	34.67	34.67
6	0	0	0	0	0	0	0
7	0	0	0	4.17	5.67	5.67	5.67
8	$ 90,462	$ 66,518	$ 50,450	$ 40,215	$ 36,888	$ 36,212	$ 35,665
9	$940,562	$701,153	$540,497	$438,158	$397,923	$384,374	$373,406

Goal three is met at all class size levels except the 40-, the 45-, and the 50-student levels. In each of these cases, the solution set called for fewer GTAs and instructors than were actually currently budgeted in the Department of History, thus the deviations from goal three.

Goal four refers to the percentage distribution of the instructional staff, by rank. The reason this goal is the least underachieved at each end of the class-size range can be attributed mostly to the 15 percent ratio for GTAs. At the lower class sizes, sufficient additional full-time instructional staff members are called for to allow the 16.00 FTE GTAs currently budgeted in the Department of History to more closely approximate the desired 15 percent distribution. At the higher class sizes, the model reduces the number of GTAs needed (in favor of keeping tenure commitments) and, thus, again brings the percentage distribution of GTAs more closely in line with the desired 15 percent ratio.

The entire underachievement for goal five can be attributed to the constraints for the ratios of GRAs and TPS. This result was "forced" onto goal five by a higher-priority goal and thus is not surprising. The range of the underachievement for this goal is directly proportional to the total number of academic staff called for by the model at the seven various class-size levels.

The underachievement of goal seven at the class sizes of 35, 40, 45, and 50 shows the aggregate potential reduction in full-time permanent staff that could be accomplished at these class-size levels. Note that after reaching the 40-student class size, no further reduction in full-time staff is possible without violating tenure commitments or other priority constraints of the model. Of course, reductions in the numbers of GTAs and instructors are still possible in this range.

Goal eight's underachievement represents the total cost of the desired salary increases. These amounts are a function of the total number of staff members, and the resulting personal-services budget given in priority nine.

The underachievement of goal nine gives the total personal-services budget which, of course, decreases as class size is increased and faculty and staff requirements lowered accordingly. These figures are perhaps the most important ones on this table. The relationships of the total FTE requirements and corresponding personal-services budgets for the Department of History at the various class sizes have been summarized on a comparative basis in table 5.18. Particular notice should be made of the decreasing rate of the decreases in the total salaries budget as class size is increased. More will be said about this relationship and its implications later in this book.

To provide for an easier comparison of the model's solution sets at the selected class sizes with the current budget and organizational structures of the Department of History, tables 5.19 through 5.25 have been developed.

Table 5.18

Summary of FTE and Personal-Services Budgets
Department of History

	Average Undergraduate Class Size						
	20	25	30	35	40	45	50
(A) Total FTE	63.16	50.50	42.00	35.83	31.83	28.33	25.50
(B) Total Personal-Services Budget	$940,562	$701,153	$540,497	$438,158	$397,923	$384,374	$373,406
(C) Increase/Decrease in FTE from current level	26.93	12.69	3.12	-3.82	-8.17	-11.50	-14.50
(D) Increase/Decrease in Personal-Services Budget from current level	$448,142	$209,033	$48,377	-$53,960	-$94,197	-$107,746	-$118,714
(E) % Chg. represented by (C)	64%	30%	7%	-9%	-19%	-27%	-35%
(F) % Chg. represented by (D)	+91%	+42%	+10%	-11%	-19%	-22%	-24%
(G) Salary Costs/SCH:	$117	$87	$67	$55	$50	$48	$47

Table 5.19

Comparative Analysis

Department: History
Workload: 6 & 3, 6 & 3, 6 & 3
SCH: Undergraduate 7,649
    Graduate 366

    Total 8,015
Average Class Size:
    Undergraduate 20 students
    Graduate 7 students

Category	(1) Existing Staff Distribution	(2) Number With Tenure	(3) G.P. Distribution	(4) Difference (Col 3 − Col 1)
GRA	0		0	0
GTA	16.00		16.00	0
Instructor	1.00		1.00	0
Asst. Prof.	9.00		18.87	9.87
Assoc. Prof.	2.00	1.00	4.24	2.24
Full Prof.	12.00	11.00	23.05	11.05
Subtotal	40.00	12.00	63.16	23.16
Tech. Staff	0		0	0
Support Staff	2.00		5.77	3.77
Total	42.00	12.00	68.93	26.93
Total Salaries	$492,120		$940,562	$448,142
Operating Budget	$10,000		$11,563	$1,563
Leave Fund	0		$40,838	$40,838
Salary Costs/SCH:	$61.40		$117.35	$55.95

Table 5.20
Comparative Analysis

Department: History
Workload: 6 & 3, 6 & 3, 6 & 3
SCH: Undergraduate   7,649
    Graduate   366

    Total   8,015
Average Class Size:
    Undergraduate   25 students
    Graduate   7 students

Category	(1) Existing Staff Distribution	(2) Number With Tenure	(3) G.P. Distribution	(4) Difference (Col 3 − Col 1)
GRA	0		0	0
GTA	16.00		16.00	0
Instructor	1.00		1.00	0
Asst. Prof.	9.00		13.80	4.80
Assoc. Prof.	2.00	1.00	3.10	1.10
Full Prof.	12.00	11.00	16.60	4.60
Subtotal	40.00	12.00	50.50	10.50
Tech. Staff	0		0	0
Support Staff	2.00		4.19	2.19
Total	42.00	12.00	54.69	12.69
Total Salaries	$492,120		$701,153	$209,033
Operating Budget	$10,000		$10,614	$614
Leave Fund	0		$29,451	$29,451
Salary Costs/SCH:	$61.40		$87.48	$26.08

Table 5.21

Comparative Analysis

Department: History
Workload: 6 & 3, 6 & 3, 6 & 3
SCH: Undergraduate 7,649
     Graduate 366

    Total 8,015
Average Class Size:
    Undergraduate 30 students
    Graduate 7 students

Category	(1) Existing Staff Distribution	(2) Number With Tenure	(3) G.P. Distribution	(4) Difference (Col 3 − Col 1)
GRA	0		0	0
GTA	16.00		16.00	0
Instructor	1.00		1.00	0
Asst. Prof.	9.00		10.40	1.40
Assoc. Prof.	2.00	1.00	2.34	.34
Full Prof.	12.00	11.00	12.26	.26
Subtotal	40.00	12.00	42.00	2.00
Tech. Staff	0		0	0
Support Staff	2.00		3.12	1.12
Total	42.00	12.00	44.12	3.12
Total Salaries	$492,120		$540,497	$48,377
Operating Budget	$10,000		$9,976	−$24
Leave Fund	0		$21,809	$21,809
Salary Costs/SCH:	$61.40		$67.43	$6.03

Table 5.22
Comparative Analysis

Department: History
Workload: 6 & 3, 6 & 3, 6 & 3
SCH: Undergraduate   7,649
    Graduate   366

    Total   8,015
Average Class Size:
    Undergraduate 35 students
    Graduate   7 students

Category	(1) Existing Staff Distribution	(2) Number With Tenure	(3) G.P. Distribution	(4) Difference (Col 3 − Col 1)
GRA	0		0	0
GTA	16.00		16.00	0
Instructor	1.00		1.00	0
Asst. Prof.	9.00		6.83	−2.17
Assoc. Prof.	2.00	1.00	1.00	−1.00
Full Prof.	12.00	11.00	11.00	−1.00
Subtotal	40.00	12.00	35.83	−4.17
Tech. Staff	0		0	0
Support Staff	2.00		2.35	.35
Total	42.00	12.00	38.18	−3.82
Total Salaries	$492,120		$438,158	−$53,962
Operating Budget	$10,000		$9,513	−$487
Leave Fund	0		$18,334	$18,334
Salary Costs/SCH:	$61.40		$54.67	−$6.73

Table 5.23

Comparative Analysis

Department: History
Workload: 6 & 3, 6 & 3, 6 & 3
SCH: Undergraduate   7,649
     Graduate   366
     Total   8,015
Average Class Size:
     Undergraduate   40 students
     Graduate   7 students

Category	(1) Existing Staff Distribution	(2) Number With Tenure	(3) G.P. Distribution	(4) Difference (Col 3 − Col 1)
GRA	0		0	0
GTA	16.00		14.50	−1.50
Instructor	1.00		0	−1.00
Asst. Prof.	9.00		5.33	−3.67
Assoc. Prof.	2.00	1.00	1.00	−1.00
Full Prof.	12.00	11.00	11.00	−1.00
Subtotal	40.00	12.00	31.83	−8.17
Tech. Staff	0		0	0
Support Staff	2.00		2.17	.17
Total	42.00	12.00	34.00	−8.00
Total Salaries	$492,120		$397,923	−$94,197
Operating Budget	$10,000		$9,319	−$681
Leave Fund	0		$18,334	$18,334
Salary Costs/SCH:	$61.40		$50.01	−$11.39

Table 5.24
Comparative Analysis

Department: History
Workload: 6 & 3, 6 & 3, 6 & 3
SCH: Undergraduate   7,649
    Graduate   366
               ——
    Total   8,015
Average Class Size:
    Undergraduate   45 students
    Graduate   7 students

Category	(1) Existing Staff Distribution	(2) Number With Tenure	(3) G.P. Distribution	(4) Difference (Col 3 − Col 1)
GRA	0		0	0
GTA	16.00		11.00	−5.00
Instructor	1.00		0	−1.00
Asst. Prof.	9.00		5.33	−3.67
Assoc. Prof.	2.00	1.00	1.00	−1.00
Full Prof.	12.00	11.00	11.00	−1.00
Subtotal	40.00	12.00	28.33	−11.67
Tech. Staff	0	0	0	0
Support Staff	2.00		2.17	.17
Total	42.00	12.00	30.50	−11.50
Total Salaries	$492,120		$384,374	−$107,746
Operating Budget	$10,000		$9,319	−$681
Leave Fund	0		$18,334	$18,334
Salary Costs/SCH:	$61.40		$48.32	−$13.08

Table 5.25

Comparative Analysis

Department: History
Workload: 6 & 3, 6 & 3, 6 & 3

SCH: Undergraduate	7,649
Graduate	366
Total	8,015

Average Class Size:

Undergraduate	50 students
Graduate	7 students

Category	(1) Existing Staff Distribution	(2) Number With Tenure	(3) G.P. Distribution	(4) Difference (Col 3 – Col 1)
GRA	0		0	0
GTA	16.00		8.17	−7.83
Instructor	1.00		0	−1.00
Asst. Prof.	9.00		5.33	−3.67
Assoc. Prof.	2.00	1.00	1.00	−1.00
Full Prof.	12.00	11.00	11.00	−1.00
Subtotal	40.00	12.00	25.50	−14.50
Tech. Staff	0		0	0
Support Staff	2.00		2.17	.17
Total	42.00	12.00	27.67	−14.33
Total Salaries	$492,120		$373,406	−$118,714
Operating Budget	$10,000		$9,319	−$681
Leave Fund	0		$18,336	$18,336
Salary Costs/SCH:	$61.40		$46.95	−$14.45

The Department of Political Science

The analysis of goal achievements for the Department of Political Science has been summarized by class-size level in table 5.26. Notice that again both goals one and two have been exactly met at all class sizes, assuring the availability of sufficient staff to meet the USCH and the GSCH requirements.

Goal three is met at all class-size levels except 50, where the model called for 1.00 less instructor and .16 less GTAs than are currently budgeted in the political science department.

Goals four and five are underachieved at all levels. Goal four relates to the percentage distribution of faculty by rank. For this department, much of this slack is attributable to the six budgeted GTAs, which are more than 15 percent of the total number of academic staff, and to the proportionally large (56 percent) number of associate professors with tenure.

The underachievement for goal five represents the model's failure to provide budgeted positions for GRAs and TPS members. Again, this deviation was "forced" onto goal five by a higher-priority goal and thus is not surprising.

Goal six is underachieved only at the 50-student class-size level. A review of the slack analysis section shows that at this level, the Department of Political Science, under the model's solution set would not be able to meet the undergraduate advising standards originally defined in table 5.2.

The underachievement of goal seven shows the aggregate potential reduction in full-time permanent staff that could be accomplished at the 40-, 45-, and 50-student class sizes. Note that the reductions are not appreciable until the 45-student level is reached, where the value becomes 2.08. By comparison, for the Department of History, the model called for a reduction of 4.17 staff members beginning at the 35-student class size level (see table 5.17).

Goal eight's underachievement gives the total cost of the desired salary increases. Again, these amounts are a function of the total number and the distribution of staff members.

The underachievement of goal nine is the value of the total personal-services budget. An analysis of the relationships of the total FTE requirements and corresponding personal-services budgets by class-size level, compared with existing departmental figures for these categories, is given in table 5.27. Tables 5.28 through 5.34 have also been developed to allow an easy comparison of the model's solution sets at the selected class sizes with current budgets and structures in the Department of Political Science.

Table 5.26
Evaluation of the Objective Function
(Goal Achievements)
Political Science Department

Goal #	Undergraduate Class Size						
	20	25	30	35	40	45	50
1	0	0	0	0	0	0	0
2	0	0	0	0	0	0	0
3	0	0	0	0	0	0	1.16
4	7.35	5.64	5.31	5.35	7.23	10.91	12.30
5	86.00	65.67	52.33	42.67	35.67	30.00	28.66
6	0	0	0	0	0	0	7.05
7	0	0	.25	.25	.25	2.08	2.75
8	$77,636	$59,740	$48,332	$40,082	$33,539	$29,386	$27,912
9	$793,234	$614,261	$500,174	$417,673	$352,239	$310,716	$290,646

Table 5.27
Summary of FTE and Personal-Services Budgets
Department of Political Science

		Average Undergraduate Class Size					
	20	25	30	35	40	45	50
(A) Total FTE	50.00	39.83	33.17	28.34	24.83	22.60	20.16
(B) Total Personal-Services Budget	$793,234	$614,261	$500,174	$417,673	$352,230	$310,716	$290,646
(C) Increase/Decrease in FTE from current level	+23.92	+13.75	+7.09	+2.26	-1.25	-3.48	-5.92
(D) Increase/Decrease in Personal-Services Budget from current level	$445,138	$266,165	$152,078	$69,577	$4,134	-$37,380	-$57,450
(E) % Chg. represented by (C)	+92%	+53%	+27%	+9%	-5%	-13%	-23%
(F) % Chg. represented by (D)	+127%	+77%	+45%	+20%	+1%	-11%	-17%
(G) Salary Costs/SCH:	$126	$97	$80	$66	$56	$49	$46

Table 5.28

Comparative Analysis

Department: Political Science
Workload: 6 & 3, 6 & 3, 6 & 3
SCH: Undergraduate 6,072
    Graduate 235

    Total 6,307
Average Class Size:
    Undergraduate 20 students
    Graduate 7 students

Category	(1) Existing Staff Distribution	(2) Number With Tenure	(3) G.P. Distribution	(4) Difference (Col 3 − Col 1)
GRA	0		0	0
GTA	6.00		6.00	0
Instructor	1.00		1.00	0
Asst. Prof.	2.50		14.40	11.90
Assoc. Prof.	9.58	9.33	13.20	3.62
Full Prof.	5.00	5.00	15.40	10.40
Subtotal	24.08	14.33	50.00	25.92
Tech. Staff	0	0	0	0
Support Staff	2.00	0	5.38	3.38
Total	26.08	14.33	28.38	29.30
Total Salaries	$348,096		$793,235	$445,139
Operating Budget	$7,795		$10,042	$2,247
Leave Fund	0		$37,003	$37,003
Salary Costs/SCH:	$55.19		$125.77	$70.58

Table 5.29
Comparative Analysis

Department: Political Science
Workload: 6 & 3, 6 & 3, 6 & 3
SCH: Undergraduate 6,072
    Graduate   235

    Total   6,307
Average Class Size:
    Undergraduate   25 students
    Graduate   7 students

Category	(1) Existing Staff Distribution	(2) Number With Tenure	(3) G.P. Distribution	(4) Difference (Col 3 − Col 1)
GRA	0		0	0
GTA	6.00		6.00	0
Instructor	1.00		1.00	0
Asst. Prof.	2.50		10.84	8.34
Assoc. Prof.	9.58	9.33	10.15	.57
Full Prof.	5.00	5.00	11.84	6.84
Subtotal	24.08	14.33	39.83	15.75
Tech. Staff	0	0	0	0
Support Staff	2.00	0	4.10	2.10
Total	26.08	14.33	33.78	17.85
Total Salaries	$348,096		$614,261	$266,165
Operating Budget	$7,795		$9,280	$1,485
Leave Fund	0		$28,453	$28,453
Salary Costs/SCH:	$55.19		$97.39	$42.20

Table 5.30

Comparative Analysis

Department: Political Science
Workload: 6 & 3, 6 & 3, 6 & 3
SCH: Undergraduate 6,072
    Graduate   235

    Total   6,307
Average Class Size:
    Undergraduate 30 students
    Graduate   7 students

Category	(1) Existing Staff Distribution	(2) Number With Tenure	(3) G.P. Distribution	(4) Difference (Col 3 − Col 1)
GRA	0		0	0
GTA	6.00		6.00	0
Instructor	.50		1.00	.50
Asst. Prof.	2.50		7.33	4.83
Assoc. Prof.	9.58	9.33	9.33	−.25
Full Prof.	5.00	5.00	9.51	4.51
Subtotal	23.58	14.33	33.17	9.09
Tech. Staff	0	0	0	0
Support Staff	2.00	0	3.27	1.27
Total	26.08	14.33	36.44	10.36
Total Salaries	$348,096		$500,174	$152,078
Operating Budget	$7,795		$8,780	$985
Leave Fund	0		$24,266	$24,266
Salary Costs/SCH:	$55.19		$80.14	$24.95

Table 5.31

Comparative Analysis

Department: Political Science
Workload: 6 & 3, 6 & 3, 6 & 3
SCH: Undergraduate 6,072
    Graduate 235

    Total 6,307
Average Class Size:
    Undergraduate 35 students
    Graduate 7 students

Category	(1) Existing Staff Distribution	(2) Number With Tenure	(3) G.P. Distribution	(4) Difference (Col 3 − Col 1)
GRA	0		0	0
GTA	6.00		6.00	0
Instructor	1.00		1.00	0
Asst. Prof.	2.50		4.47	1.97
Assoc. Prof.	9.58	9.33	9.33	−.25
Full Prof.	5.00	5.00	7.54	2.54
Subtotal	24.08	14.33	28.34	4.26
Tech. Staff	0	0	0	0
Support Staff	2.00	0	2.67	.67
Total	26.08	14.33	31.01	4.93
Total Salaries	$348,096		$417,673	$69,577
Operating Budget	$7,795		$8,417	$622
Leave Fund	0		$21,562	$21,562
Salary Costs/SCH:	$55.19		$66.22	$11.03

Table 5.32
Comparative Analysis

Department: Political Science
Workload: 6 & 3, 6 & 3, 6 & 3
SCH: Undergraduate 6,072
      Graduate 235

      Total 6,307
Average Class Size:
      Undergraduate 40 students
      Graduate 7 students

Category	(1) Existing Staff Distribution	(2) Number With Tenure	(3) G.P. Distribution	(4) Difference (Col 3 − Col 1)
GRA	0		0	0
GTA	6.00		6.00	0
Instructor	1.00		1.00	0
Asst. Prof.	2.50		3.50	1.00
Assoc. Prof.	9.58	9.33	9.33	−.25
Full Prof.	5.00	5.00	5.00	0
Subtotal	24.08	14.33	24.83	.75
Tech. Staff	0	0	0	0
Support Staff	2.00	0	2.23	.23
Total	26.08	14.33	27.06	.98
Total Salaries	$348,096		$352,239	$4,143
Operating Budget	$7,795		$8,154	$359
Leave Fund	0		$18,083	$18,083
Salary Costs/SCH:	$55.19		$55.85	.66

Table 5.33
Comparative Analysis

Department: Political Science
Workload: 6 & 3, 6 & 3, 6 & 3
SCH: Undergraduate   6,072
    Graduate   235

    Total   6,307
Average Class Size:
    Undergraduate   45 students
    Graduate   7 students

Category	(1) Existing Staff Distribution	(2) Number With Tenure	(3) G.P. Distribution	(4) Difference (Col 3 − Col 1)
GRA	0		0	0
GTA	6.00		6.00	0
Instructor	1.00		1.00	1.00
Asst. Prof.	2.50		.67	−1.83
Assoc. Prof.	9.58	9.33	9.33	−.25
Full Prof.	5.00	5.00	5.00	0
Subtotal	24.08	14.33	22.00	−1.08
Tech. Staff	0	0	0	0
Support Staff	2.00	0	2.00	0
Total	26.08	14.33	24.00	−1.08
Total Salaries	$348,096		$310,716	−$37,380
Operating Budget	$7,795		$7,942	$147
Leave Fund	0		$18,083	$18,083
Salary Costs/SCH:	$55.19		$49.26	−$5.92

Table 5.34

Comparative Analysis

Department: Political Science
Workload: 6 & 3, 6 & 3, 6 & 3
SCH: Undergraduate   6,072
      Graduate   235

      Total   6,307
Average Class Size:
      Undergraduate   50 students
      Graduate   7 students

Category	(1) Existing Staff Distribution	(2) Number With Tenure	(3) G.P. Distribution	(4) Difference (Col 3 − Col 1)
GRA	0		0	0
GTA	6.00		5.84	−.16
Instructor	1.00		0	−1.00
Asst. Prof.	2.50		0	−2.50
Assoc. Prof.	9.58	9.33	9.33	−.25
Full Prof.	5.00	5.00	5.00	0
Subtotal	24.08	14.33	20.17	−3.91
Tech. Staff	0	0	0	0
Support Staff	2.00	0	2.00	0
Total	26.08	14.33	22.17	−3.91
Total Salaries	$348,096		$290,646	−$57,450
Operating Budget	$7,795		$7,817	$22
Leave Fund	0		$18,082	$18,082
Salary Costs/SCH:	$55.19		$46.08	−$9.11

The Department of Sociology

The analysis of goal achievements for the Department of Sociology has been summarized by class-size level in table 5.35. As with both the history and political science departments, both goals one and two have been exactly met at all class sizes. Goal three for the sociology department formulation is underachieved at the 40-, the 45-, and 50-student class sizes. In each case, this underachievement represents the reduction in the existing number of GTAs that is called for by the model's solution set.

Goals four and five are again underachieved at all levels. As with the other two departments modeled, the percentage distribution requirements of goal four have been violated mostly in the GTA category. For instance, for the Department of Sociology at the 50-student class size, the model calls for 12.00 FTE full-time teaching staff members and 10.00 GTAs. The 10.00 value for GTAs violates the 15 percent distribution requirement by 8.20. This 8.20 negative deviation for constraint number twenty-two accounts for most of the total 12.76 deviation for goal four. The underachievement of goal five is again totally attributable to the absence of budgeted positions for GRAs and TPS members in the solution set.

The underachievement for goal six starts at the 35-student class size, which is much lower than for the other two departments. This indicates that the Department of Sociology would not be able to meet the undergraduate advising standards defined in table 5.2, and that this difficulty is actually quite severe for this department.

Goal seven again shows the aggregate potential full-time staff reduction that would be possible at the various average class sizes. Comparatively speaking, the sociology department is more overstaffed at the higher class-size levels than is the political science department, but is less overstaffed than is the history department at these same levels.

Goal eight's underachievement gives the total cost of the desired salary increases and goal nine's deviations show the required total personal-services budgets at each level. Tables 5.36 through 5.43 provide comparative analyses of the solution sets with existing departmental data.

Table 5.35
Evaluation of the Objective Function
(Goal Achievements)
Sociology Department

Goal #	Undergraduate Class Size						
	20	25	30	35	40	45	50
1	0	0	0	0	0	0	0
2	0	0	0	0	0	0	0
3	0	0	0	0	1.33	5.33	7.00
4	13.22	14.32	15.05	16.25	18.43	14.43	12.76
5	75.67	53.67	39.00	28.67	24.00	24.00	24.00
6	0	0	0	15.53	62.00	62.00	62.00
7	0	0	0	1.27	3.60	3.60	3.60
8	$80,090	$57,728	$42,870	$33,288	$29,811	$29,063	$28,752
9	$832,507	$608,908	$460,338	$364,539	$327,288	$312,356	$306,135

Table 5.36
Summary of FTE and Personal-Services Budgets
Department of Sociology

	Average Undergraduate Class Size						
	20	25	30	35	40	45	50
(A) Total FTE	54.83	43.83	36.50	31.33	27.67	23.67	22.00
(B) Total Personal-Services Budget	$832,507	$608,908	$460,338	$364,539	$327,288	$312,356	$306,135
(C) Increase/Decrease in FTE from current level	+19.73	+8.73	+1.40	−3.77	−7.43	−11.43	−13.10
(D) Increase/Decrease in Personal-Services Budget from current level	$447,736	$224,137	$75,568	−$20,232	−$57,483	−$72,419	−$78,636
(E) % Chg. represented by (C)	+56%	+25%	+4%	−11%	−21%	−33%	−37%
(F) % Chg. represented by (D)	+116%	+58%	+20%	−5%	−15%	−19%	−20%
(G) Salary Costs/SCH:	$122	$89	$67	$53	$48	$46	$45

Table 5.37

Comparative Analysis

Department: Sociology
Workload: 6 & 3, 6 & 3, 6 & 3
SCH: Undergraduate   6,582
　　　Graduate　　　　　252
　　　─────────────────────
　　　Total　　　　　　6,834
Average Class Size:
　　　Undergraduate　20 students
　　　Graduate　　　　7 students

Category	(1) Existing Staff Distribution	(2) Number With Tenure	(3) G.P. Distribution	(4) Difference (Col 3 − Col 1)
GRA	0		0	0
GTA	17.00		17.00	0
Instructor	0		0	0
Asst. Prof.	2.60	0	6.05	3.45
Assoc. Prof.	4.00	3.00	9.84	5.84
Full Prof.	9.00	9.00	21.94	12.94
Subtotal	32.60	12.00	54.83	22.23
Tech. Staff	0	0	0	0
Support Staff	2.50	0	4.73	2.23
Total	35.10	12.00	59.56	24.46
Total Salaries	$384,771		$832,507	$447,736
Operating Budget	$7,859		$9,976	$2,117
Leave Fund	0		$46,280	$46,283
Salary Costs/SCH:	$56.30		$21.82	$65.52

Table 5.38
Comparative Analysis

Department: Sociology
Workload: 6 & 3, 6 & 3, 6 & 3
SCH: Undergraduate   6,582
 Graduate   252

 Total   6,834
Average Class Size:
 Undergraduate 25 students
 Graduate   7 students

Category	(1) Existing Staff Distribution	(2) Number With Tenure	(3) G.P. Distribution	(4) Difference (Col 3 − Col 1)
GRA	0		0	0
GTA	17.00		17.00	0
Instructor	0		0	0
Asst. Prof.	2.60		4.29	1.69
Assoc. Prof.	4.00	3.00	6.98	2.98
Full Prof.	9.00	9.00	15.56	6.56
Subtotal	32.60	12.00	48.83	11.23
Tech. Staff	0	0	0	0
Support Staff	2.50	0	3.35	.85
Total	35.10	12.00	47.18	12.08
Total Salaries	$384,771		$608,908	$224,137
Operating Budget	$7,859		$9,150	$1,292
Leave Fund	0		$32,824	$32,826
Salary Costs/SCH:	$56.30		$89.11	$32.81

Table 5.39

Comparative Analysis

Department: Sociology
Workload: 6 & 3, 6 & 3, 6 & 3
SCH: Undergraduate 6,582
      Graduate   252

      Total 6,834
Average Class Size:
    Undergraduate 30 students
    Graduate   7 students

Category	(1) Existing Staff Distribution	(2) Number With Tenure	(3) G.P. Distribution	(4) Difference (Col 3 − Col 1)
GRA	0		0	0
GTA	17.00		17.00	0
Instructor	0		0	0
Asst. Prof.	2.60	0	3.12	.52
Assoc. Prof.	4.00	3.00	5.07	1.07
Full Prof.	9.00	9.00	11.31	2.31
Subtotal	32.60	12.00	36.50	3.90
Tech. Staff	0	0	0	0
Support Staff	2.50	0	2.50	0
Total	35.10	12.00	39.00	3.90
Total Salaries	$384,771		$460,338	$75,568
Operating Budget	$7,859		$8,601	$742
Leave Fund	0		$23,854	$23,855
Salary Costs/SCH:	$56.30		$67.36	$11.06

Table 5.40
Comparative Analysis

Department: Sociology
Workload: 6 & 3, 6 & 3, 6 & 3
SCH: Undergraduate 6,582
      Graduate   252

      Total   6,834
Average Class Size:
    Undergraduate 35 students
    Graduate   7 students

Category	(1) Existing Staff Distribution	(2) Number With Tenure	(3) G.P. Distribution	(4) Difference (Col 3 − Col 1)
GRA	0		0	0
GTA	17.00		17.00	0
Instructor	0		0	0
Asst. Prof.	2.60	0	2.29	−.31
Assoc. Prof.	4.00	3.00	3.04	−.96
Full Prof.	9.00	9.00	9.00	0
Subtotal	32.60	12.00	31.33	−1.27
Tech. Staff	0	0	0	0
Support Staff	2.50	0	2.50	0
Total	35.10	12.00	33.83	−1.27
Total Salaries	$384,771		$364,539	−$20,232
Operating Budget	$7,859		$8,213	$354
Leave Fund	0		$17,825	$17,827
Salary Costs/SCH:	$56.30		$53.34	−$2.96

Table 5.41

Comparative Analysis

Department: Sociology
Workload: 6 & 3, 6 & 3, 6 & 3
SCH: Undergraduate   6,582
       Graduate   252

   Total   6,834
Average Class Size:
   Undergraduate   40 students
   Graduate   7 students

Category	(1) Existing Staff Distribution	(2) Number With Tenure	(3) G.P. Distribution	(4) Difference (Col 3 − Col 1)
GRA	0		0	0
GTA	17.00		15.67	−1.33
Instructor	0		0	0
Asst. Prof.	2.60	0	0	−2.60
Assoc. Prof.	4.00	3.00	3.00	−1.00
Full Prof.	9.00	9.00	9.00	0
Subtotal	32.60	12.00	27.67	−4.93
Tech. Staff	0	0	0.	0
Support Staff	2.50	0	2.50	0
Total	35.10	12.00	30.17	−4.93
Total Salaries	$384,771		$327,288	−$57,483
Operating Budget	$7,859		$8,038	$179
Leave Fund	0		$17,779	$17,780
Salary Costs/SCH:	$56.30		$47.89	−$8.41

Table 5.42

Comparative Analysis

Department: Sociology
Workload: 6 & 3, 6 & 3, 6 & 3
SCH: Undergraduate 6,582
    Graduate   252

    Total   6,834
Average Class Size:
    Undergraduate   45 students
    Graduate   7 students

Category	(1) Existing Staff Distribution	(2) Number With Tenure	(3) G.P. Distribution	(4) Difference (Col 3 − Col 1)
GRA	0		0	0
GTA	17.00		11.67	−5.33
Instructor	0		0	0
Asst. Prof.	2.60	0	0	−2.60
Assoc. Prof.	4.00	3.00	3.00	−1.00
Full Prof.	9.00	9.00	9.00	0
Subtotal	32.60	12.00	23.67	−8.93
Tech. Staff	0	0	0	0
Support Staff	2.50	0	2.50	0
Total	35.10	12.00	26.17	−8.93
Total Salaries	$384,771		$312,356	−$72,415
Operating Budget	$7,859		$8,038	$179
Leave Fund	0		$17,779	$17,780
Salary Costs/SCH:	$56.30		$45.71	−$10.59

Table 5.43

Comparative Analysis

Department: Sociology
Workload: 6 & 3, 6 & 3, 6 & 3
SCH: Undergraduate   6,582
    Graduate   252

    Total   6,834
Average Class Size:
    Undergraduate   50 students
    Graduate   7 students

Category	(1) Existing Staff Distribution	(2) Number With Tenure	(3) G.P. Distribution	(4) Difference (Col 3 − Col 1)
GRA	0		0	0
GTA	17.00		10.00	−7.00
Instructor	0		0	0
Asst. Prof.	2.60	0	0	−2.60
Assoc. Prof.	4.00	3.00	3.00	−1.00
Full Prof.	9.00	9.00	9.00	0
Subtotal	32.60	12.00	22.00	−10.60
Tech. Staff	0	0	0	0
Support Staff	2.50	0	2.50	0
Total	35.10	12.00	24.50	−10.60
Total Salaries	$384,771		$306,135	−$78,636
Operating Budget	$7,859		$8,038	$179
Leave Fund	0		$17,779	$17,780
Salary Costs/SCH:	$56.30		$44.80	−$11.50

Conclusion

This chapter introduced a generalized goal-programming model for the analysis of resource-allocation decisions in higher education. The model's applicability was demonstrated by the application of four tests, performed on actual data from three social science departments, in a large, midwestern state-supported university. A key difference between the model described in this chapter and much of the existing research on educational planning and decision making lies in the emphasis placed on examining existing management and budgeting patterns. Most studies have been essentially directed toward developing resource allocation models for planning "independent" or "ideal" educational organizations or systems. The objective of this model is to allow academic administrators to model existing departmental structures with the goal of determining where improvements might be made based both on economic efficiency *and* managerial preferences. It is these characteristics that make the model ideally suited for use with the administration-by-multiple-objectives approach to management.

Chapter 6

Extensions of the Model's Analysis

The purpose of the generalized model developed in Chapter 5 was to allow academic administrators to examine resource-allocation patterns as well as the trade-offs inherent in their planning decisions. One of the subgoals of the model was to provide a model that would be able to replicate current or existing departmental structures and budgets and thus, through sensitivity analysis, be able to help determine the financial advantages or disadvantages of proposed future courses of action. Tests I through IV, as described and analyzed in Chapter 5, show that the model is indeed capable of performing these tasks. The information provided by the sensitivity analysis of test IV can also be used to examine resource-allocation patterns under the traditional type of microeconomic framework. This information can also be seen to be quite useful for future planning purposes.

Resource Allocation Comparisons

Table 6.1 gives a comparative summary of total personnel budgets at the specified class sizes for the three departments being studied. Figure 6.1 gives a graph of the relationships between the changes in total personnel budgets that are possible in each of the three departments as the average undergraduate class size is increased.

Note from table 6.1 and figure 6.1 that the potential dollar and percentage cost reductions that are possible decrease as the average class size is increased. The Department of History, for instance, can be seen reaching a plateau level of "fixed costs" at the 40-student average class size. An increase in class size from 30 students to 35 students would allow an 18.9 percent decrease in this department's budget, and an increase from 35 students to 40

Table 6.1
Comparative Summary of Total Personnel Budgets
at Specified Class Sizes

				Average Undergraduate Class Size			
	20	25	30	35	40	45	50
History	$940,562	$701,153	$540,497	$438,158	$397,923	$384,374	$373,406
Δ Budget		−$239,409	−$160,656	−$102,339	−$40,235	−$13,549	−$10,968
% chg.		−25.5%	−22.9%	−18.9%	− 9.2%	−3.4%	−2.8%
Political Science	$793,234	$614,261	$500,174	$417,673	$352,230	$310,716	$290,646
Δ Budget		−$178,973	−$114,087	−$82,501	−$65,433	−$41,514	−$20,070
% chg.		−22.0%	−18.6%	−16.5%	−15.7%	−11.8%	−6.5%
Sociology	$832,507	$608,908	$460,338	$364,539	$327,288	$312,356	$306,135
Δ Budget		−$223,599	−$148,570	−$95,799	−$37,251	−$14,932	−$6,221
% chg.		−26.9%	−24.4%	−20.8%	−10.2%	−4.6%	−2.0%

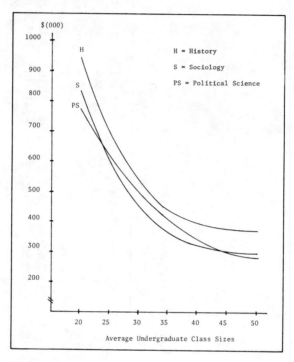

Figure 6.1
Total Personal-Service Budgets

students per class would allow a 9.2 percent decrease in the budget; however, increasing the average undergraduate class size to the 45- and 50-student levels results in only relatively small decreases in salary costs of 3.4 percent and 2.8 percent, respectively. For the Department of Political Science, a similar plateau is not reached until the 50-student average undergraduate class size. For the Department of Sociology, it occurs at the 40-student level.

In terms of absolute dollar amounts, the increase in class size from 40 students to 45 students in the Department of Political Science would allow a salary savings of $41,514, whereas the same change in the Department of History (a much larger department) would only result in a savings of $13,549. Notice that for the Department of Sociology, the increase from the 45-student level to the 50-student level would only allow a budget reduction of $6,221. This same type of analysis could be made for different average graduate class sizes, different teaching loads, different advising responsibilities, and so forth.

The above budgetary relationships, of course, are a function of the priority structures of the model, including the desire not to violate tenure commitments, the desire to maintain as nearly as possible the stated percentage distribution requirements among faculty ranks, the desire to minimize the amount of teaching done by GTAs and instructors, the desire to budget for sufficient support staff, the desire to meet the estimated undergraduate and graduate student credit hour needs, the desire to provide for undergraduate advising and graduate supervisory obligations, the desire to allow for a stipulated salary increase for all staff members, and a desire to minimize the total budget. As test III showed, the priority structure used for the simulations being discussed here provided a good replication of departmental budgets and structures and appears to be consistent with previous resource allocation and budgeting decisions. Different priority arrangements would provide different solution sets, as would any other adjustment in the model's goals or constraints.

It should be noted that an analysis similar to that described above could be made for the class size of graduate courses, for changes in teaching loads, advising loads, desired staff distributions, and so forth. The same type of sensitivity analysis that was used in test IV, to study the impact of changes in average undergraduate class size, could be used to study the impact of changes in any of the model's other constants or right-hand-side (RHS) values.

Within the confines of the "givens" for this formulation of the model, and within the assumed relevant range for the class-size changes, the figures from tables 5.18, 5.27, 5.36 and 6.1 begin to show the development of a schedule of fixed, semivariable, and variable costs in each of the three departments. This type of analysis of cost behavior, although it represents only a beginning and although it is still quite rough, is itself very useful. Lawrence and Service in a recent publication for the American Association of Higher Education, have said, "Each of the generalized planning models (that are currently available) is limited by the fact that so little is known about cost and revenue behavior in higher education. Cost projections are made to a large extent on the basis of average cost information adjusted for changes in price and volume. No thorough analysis has been conducted examining the fixed, variable and semivariable components of cost" (1977, p. 35). These two authors go on to say that the National Association of College and University Business Officers (NACUBO) has developed (but not yet published) a conceptual framework for conducting this type of analysis. They conclude: "If this line of inquiry proves fruitful, the utility of planning models should be substantially enhanced" (ibid., p. 36).

Microeconomic Framework

Although it will provide only a first approximation, it is also possible to use the data from tables 5.18, 5.26, 5.36, and 6.1 to begin the development of production-transformation curves giving the class-size "output" combinations that would be possible for given budget levels for the three departments modeled.

For instance, the data for the Department of History from table 6.1 can be used in a polynomial statistical regression to find the coefficients b_o, b_1, $\ldots$, b_m in the functional relationship of the form $y = b_o + b_1x + b_2x^2 + \ldots + b_mx^m$ between a dependent variable y (in this case total personal-services budget) and a single independent variable x (in this case average undergraduate class size). The IBM Stat Basic program for polynomial regression, when run on the History Department data from table 6.1, gives the following function:

$$y = 31.54 - 1.73x + 35.91x^2 - 2.51x^3$$
(standard error of estimate—$2,741.31).

Once this function is available, total personal-services budgets for any specific class size within the relevant range can be estimated. Similar estimating equations could be found for any other departments modeled.

Consideration can now be given to plotting the "efficient frontier" in a two-department case such as that between the Department of Political Science and the Department of History. Table 6.2 gives the approximate range-sets of class sizes that are possible between the departments of Political Science and History, given a total personal-services budget of approximately $860,000 (note that the budget figure was not an absolute constraint). Figure 6.2 gives a plot of these range-sets, where the y-axis represents decreasing average undergraduate class-sizes for the Department of Political Science and the x-axis represents decreasing average undergraduate class-sizes for the Department of History. Only the relevant-range class sizes (i.e., 30 to 50) from table 6.2 were used in the development of figure 6.2.

Although the cases depicted in figure 6.2 represent discrete consequences, they may be seen as approximating a convex, continuous efficient frontier such as that shown in figure 6.3. This type of efficient frontier, of course, is the easiest to handle analytically and could allow for the application of the more traditional economic decision-making procedures, including the use of preference functions. In addition, although it is more difficult to picture the efficient frontier for the three-department case, it would be possible to handle them mathematically, with similar procedures.

Based on actual data for the first semester of a recent academic year, the overall average undergraduate class size for the Department of Political Sci-

Table 6.2

Approximate Range-Sets of Class-Size Possibilities
for a Given Total Personal-Services Budget of $860,000

Political Science		History		Total Budget
Class Size	Budget	Class Size	Budget	
20	$793.234	—	—	—
25	$614,261	65	$232,826	$847,087
30	$505,432	55	$363,205	$868,637
35	$417,673	35	$445,036	$862,709
40	$352,230	31	$514,674	$866,904
45	$310,716	30	$537,994	$848,710
50	$290,646	29	$563,981	$854,627

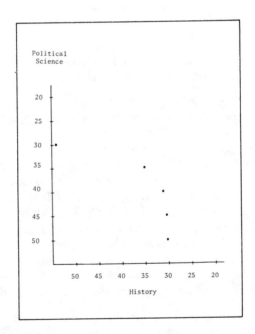

Figure 6.2

Approximate Range-Sets of Class-Size Possibilities
for a Given Total Personal-Services Budget of $860,000

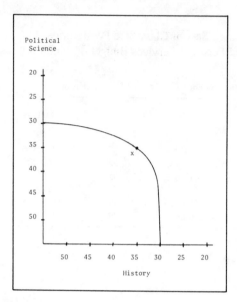

Figure 6.3
Approximate Continuous Function
for Range-Sets of Class-Size Possibilities
for a Given Total Personal-Services Budget of $860,000

ence was 36.35 students; for the Department of History, 35.44 students. This point (x) has also been plotted on figure 6.3, and can be seen as being very close to the "efficient frontier" as developed by the goal-programming model. This fact further validates the model and also indicates the relative efficiency of the departments of Political Science and History so far as teaching loads and average undergraduate class sizes are concerned. The same comparison for the Department of Sociology would not be so good, however. The actual data indicated an average undergraduate class size for that department of 66.48 students for the same semester. Based on their personal-services budget of $384,771, an average undergraduate class size of 35 students should be possible, given the assumptions and workload of the model as formulated in Chapter 5. This department would clearly be operating to the "left" of the efficient frontier.

Summary

The goal programming model, as formulated, could be used to simulate many different policy decisions, or to posit special circumstances, and then to calculate the effects on other decision variables as well as the costs of implementing the new policies or strategies. For example, questions such as the following could easily be examined by the model as formulated:

1. Is the current distribution of resources between academic units equitable so far as faculty workload policies are concerned?
2. Are there departments in an academic unit where existing resources could allow for the expansion of programs, reduced class sizes, different faculty distributions, and so on?
3. In which subunits are the graduate programs alone creating a need for additional faculty beyond those needed for the undergraduate programs?
4. What would it cost to reduce the percentage of SCHs taught by GTAs to one-half the present level? Under this policy, where would the most constrained problems occur?
5. What would be the total cost to the academic unit of expanding the mix of the professional staff to allow, for instance, 20 percent more full professors, 15 percent more associate professors, and no additional assistant professors?
6. What would be the total cost to the academic unit of implementing an across-the-board six-hour teaching load?
7. What are the instructional and advising costs associated with departmental graduate programs?
8. Are departmental resource allocations consistent with the overall institutional objectives and missions?
9. What would it cost the academic unit to reduce the graduate faculty load in all departments to twenty students? Under this policy, where would the most constrained resource problems occur?

Chapter 7

An Interactive Goal Programming Decision-Support System[1]

The model described in detail in Chapter 5 represents a fairly straightforward application of the goal programming technique to a decision problem in academic administration. In that analysis, goal programming was shown to be capable of providing descriptive as well as prescriptive information relating to a resource allocation problem in higher education.

Because of the type of analysis desired in Chapters 5 and 6, the priorities and goal constraints were held constant throughout the "runs" of the model. As described earlier, this allowed for the consistent analysis of resource allocation patterns and departmental structures and thus provided "revealed preferences" regarding previous budgetary decisions.

In real world situations, however, objectives and priorities are not usually constant; they change to reflect new situations and a new awareness of the ramifications of alternative courses of action. In many cases these changes are based on new information, organizational changes, or simply personal preferences. Also, there frequently is disagreement within organizations regarding the appropriate goals, particularly with respect to the best methods for achieving them. As decision makers experience different points of view within the organization, it becomes more important to be able to explore the trade-offs between the various alternatives. Additionally, academic administrators, even within a single institution, often have decidedly different decision-making styles and thus approach the search for solutions to problems in markedly different ways. Furthermore, as discussed in Chapter 4, the bounded rationality of human beings is a very limiting factor in academic planning and decision-

---

1. This chapter is based on a Ph.D. dissertation by Lori Sharp Franz (see bibliography). The authors wish to express special thanks to Dr. Franz for her assistance.

making processes. In order to accommodate these factors and to improve the applicability of the goal-programming model to real-world situations, interactive goal-programming decision-support systems have been developed.

Decision-support systems (DSS) focus on the decision process rather than on the decision itself (Keen, 1977). In so doing, the model is viewed as a methodology supporting the decision makers' problem-solving process in which a solution is only possible in conjunction with inputs and judgments. In this manner, the decision makers' perception about the solution may actually be more important than the solution itself. The decision-support system approach recognizes that the initial statement of the problem often gives little guidance toward the likely solution; this is particularly true in academic institutions where traditional values and policy-making procedures are often in conflict with modern management approaches.

In many colleges and universities, this conflict between traditional policy-making values and the purpose of modern management have clearly thwarted the use of modern management techniques. Michael A. Murry (1976) has summarized the conflict between sophisticated management tools and intangible educational benefits by contrasting the major objectives of each (see table 7.1).

The value of intangible and metaphysical results is protected and cherished in higher education, perhaps more so than in other institutions. But at the same time, almost no other set of institutions is under greater pressure to assess outputs and produce disciplined budgets as is higher education. The development of interactive decision-support systems is aimed specifically at the resolution of these conflicts.

Characteristics of Decision-Support Systems

A decision-support system is actually a feedback system which can be depicted as a "black-box" model (see figure 7.1). In this view, the goal-programming model is seen as the "black-box" whose workings (e.g., the computer algorithm and simplex procedure) may not be thoroughly understood by the decision maker. The model receives input from the organization (or analyst) and delivers output to the decision maker or observer, who then provides additional information to the black-box system. The information from the feedback loop is then used by the model to effect alterations in future system outputs.

In actual practice, of course, the organizational search for preferred alternatives is much more complex than the black-box model infers, and actually necessitates the development of interactive approaches with much higher or-

Table 7.1

Idealized Contrast Between Management Styles

Academic Policy-Making Values	Modern Management Purposes
(1) Academic freedom	(1) Measurement of efficiency and economy
(2) Institutional autonomy	(2) Maximization of efficiency and economy
(3) Long-range social benefits	(3) Production of demonstrable results
(4) Intangible, nonmaterial products	(4) Cost accountability of institutions
(5) Ambiguous, changing objectives	(5) Rational coordination of resources

ders of complexity. Decision-support systems are designed in such a way that careful attention is given to the human, or behavioralist viewpoint. The true goal of a decision-support system is to facilitate interaction between the computer and the decision-maker.

Most academic administrators receive numerous computer-generated reports and statistical summaries but are never really able to perceive (or use) the computer as a personal decision aid. Decision-support systems allow the academic administrator to more constructively use the computer to explore sets of alternative solutions. In order to make the decision-support system as useful as possible, the following criteria must be considered:

1. Provisions should be made for a high degree of flexibility for the decision maker.
2. The information inputs required from the decision maker must be reduced as much as possible to a relatively undemanding form.
3. Input information must be used intelligently to guide the search for improved solutions.
4. Alternative schemes for providing the priority structure must be given in order to deal with cases where a priority determination by the decision maker is not possible.
5. The model should facilitate the decision maker in developing whatever type of solution output is meaningful to him or her.
6. The model should allow the user to revise previous solutions, backtrack, or use any combination of approaches which are meaningful.

To accomplish these tasks, the decision-support system actually consists of two basic subsystems. The first facilitates the decision maker in the deter-

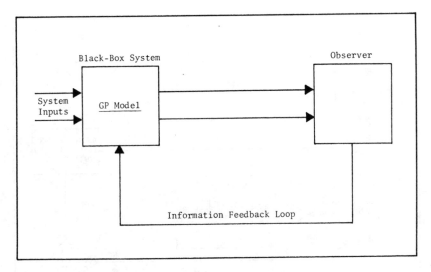

Figure 7.1
Black-Box System as a Feedback Model

mination of the priority structure. The second subsystem provides a mechanism for evaluating the current solution via explicit trade-off analyses and probabilities of goal attainment. The restructuring of priority assignments and revision of goal-attainment levels is then allowed in cases where the decision-maker wishes to explore alternative solutions. The decision maker is not constrained by the model in his or her search. Rather, the decision maker has the freedom to continue the search for alternative solutions until the individual's personal criteria are met.

When an academic administrator begins a session with the model, the initial task is to assign priorities to his goals to whatever extent possible. This can be done either by an explicit ranking or by a "grouping" of priorities. A flow diagram of the logic used in soliciting the decision maker's goal structure is given in figure 7.2. The model is then "run" and an initial solution is obtained. The next step is for the decision maker to restructure the model in an attempt to generate an improved solution. The restructuring is accomplished by revising the current priority structure for the existing goal target levels. The decision-support system then provides three types of feedback information that are beyond the normal or traditional summary of the model's results. The information is designed to help the decision maker determine the next set of priorities and goal weights. The relevant information is provided in three categories:

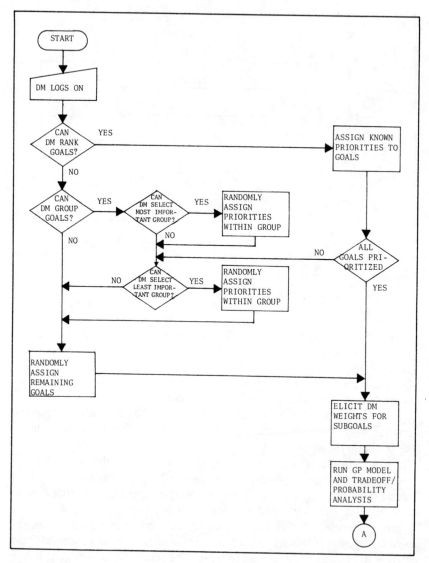

Figure 7.2
Flow Diagram of Prioritization Subsystem

1. A complete enumeration of the trade-offs inherent in restructuring the priorities;
2. A listing of alterations and goal-aspiration levels which would allow achievement of goals not attained in the former formulation; and
3. A determination of the *probability* of achieving any given goal aspiration level based on historical data.

A flow diagram of the solution improvement logic is present in figure 7.3

In the above process, it is important for the decision maker to know the goal achievements that will deteriorate if an attempt is made to satisfy a currently unsatisfied goal. In addition, all other goals that would be affected need to be known. For example, an academic administrator may be faced with the choice of increasing the number of graduate research assistants (priority 4) at the expense of reducing the average undergraduate class size (priority 2). If reprioritization of these goals would lead to the complete achievement of the current priority 4 goal, the move may be attractive to the administrator. However, if the model were to show that current priority 2 achievement would erode, while priority 4 could still not be completely attained, a change might be undesirable. This type of information regarding the trade-offs among goals is found in the final tableau of the simplex solution to the goal programming problem. The information can thus be easily provided to the decision maker through an interactive decision support system.

Example of the Use of a DSS

A decision-support system for the model described in Chapter 5 of this book was recently used to provide information for the budget-planning process at the same institution at which the model was originally formulated. Four individuals, all having direct interest in the programs and budget of the Department of Sociology, were chosen to interact with the model. They were as follows:

DECISION MAKER 1: Assistant Dean of the College of Arts and Sciences. This individual's administrative responsibilities include financial planning and budgeting as well as staffing and class scheduling.

DECISION MAKER 2: Chairman of the Sociology Department. This chairman's administrative duties include the responsibility to allocate the department's resources in a manner which would allow for the best possible combination of activities relating to instruction, advising, and research.

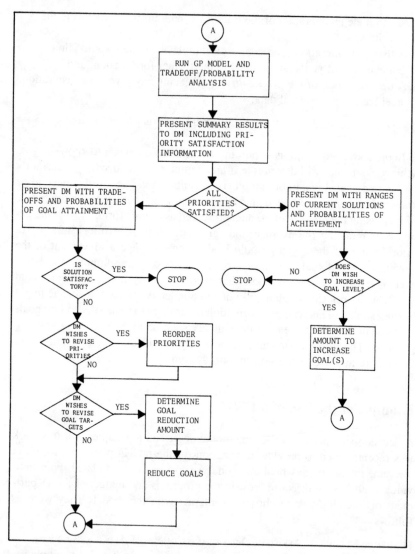

Figure 7.3
Flow Diagram of Solution Improvement Subsystem

DECISION MAKER 3: Assistant Director of Operations Analysis for the University. The operations analysis office is responsible for analyzing the cost and income projections of the various operations of the university and to recommend policies that will lead to the "best" overall uses of the university's resources.

DECISION MAKER 4: Departmental Faculty Member. As usual, this member of the faculty had input into the planning and budgeting decisions through direct access to the chairman and the dean, through campus committees, and through the faculty senate.

A summary of the approaches taken by these four decision makers is provided in table 7.2. While the assistant dean and the operations analyst were able to completely rank all nine of their goals, even initially, the chairman and the faculty member chose to select subgroups of "most important" and "least important" in order to assist them in ranking their goals. All four of the individuals revised their priorities later, however. During the subsequent iterations, all four of the decision makers reordered their priorities and goal levels. Table 7.2 also shows that the faculty member and the operations analyst both used four "runs" of the model in order to obtain an acceptable solution, while the assistant dean required five runs and the chairman seven runs.

Table 7.3 provides a comparison of the final solutions for these four individuals. The results showed that different solutions are acceptable to different individuals. The most notable differences in the final solutions are in the individuals' willingness to use graduate teaching assistants in the classroom, the importance of technical and support staff, and financial considerations relating to salary increases and the establishment of a faculty-development fund. Table 7.4 provides a summary of the goal achievements for the final runs of these four decision makers. It is important to note, however, that the individual decision makers may not consider the final run to be the "best" so far as their preferences are concerned. In some cases, the solution to an earlier run may be preferable, with the goal of the subsequent runs having been for purposes of sensitivity analysis.

Most of the restructuring that was done by these four decision makers was based on the trade-off information provided by the decision-support system. The effect on other goals of attempting to attain underachieved goals was a primary consideration for most of the restructuring efforts. Similarly, the information provided by the decision-support system regarding the probability of achieving a particular set of goals was found to be quite helpful in deciding whether to pursue further improvements in conflicting goals. All four of the decision makers found that being able to see the interaction of their goals was

Table 7.2
Summary of DM Structuring of Academic Resource Allocation Model

Decision Maker	Total Number of Iterations	Initial Prioritization Scheme	1st Restructure	2nd Restructure	3rd Restructure	4th Restructure	5th Restructure	6th Restructure
DM 1	5	Rank	Reorder	Reorder	Reorder	Alter Goal Level		
DM 2	7	Group	Reorder	Alter Goal Level	Alter Goal Level	Alter Technology Coefficient	Alter Goal Level; Change Tech Coefficient Reorder	Alter Goal Level
DM 3	4	Rank	Reorder	Alter Goal Level	Alter Goal Level			
DM 4	5	Group	Reorder With Tie	Reorder	Reorder			

Table 7.3

Comparison of DMs Final Solutions to Academic Resource Problem

Variables	DM 1	DM 2	DM 3	DM 4
Graduate Research Assistants	.92	1.12	1.48	1.37
Graduate Teaching Assistants	2.62	16	2.78	16
Instructors	1.31	0	1.39	0
Assistant Professors	5.26	6	5.56	7.6
Associate Professors	7.85	4	8.34	6.4
Full Professors	9.14	8.00	9.73	8
Technical/Professional Support Staff	5.56	3	5.91	5.5
Secretarial Support Staff	2.78	2.5	2.95	2.75
Total Payroll Budget	$606,180	524,022	645,371	628,214
Operating Budget/SCH and Faculty	$ 7,199	7,173	7,208	7,193
Faculty Development Fund	$ 0	26,970	39,280	31,439
Salary Increases/Faculty	$591.67	481.77	631.11	585.42

Table 7.4

Comparison of DMs Goal Achievement in Final Solutions

Variables Goals	DM 1	DM 2	DM 3	DM 4
A	achieved	——	achieved	achieved
B	achieved	achieved	achieved	achieved
C	——	——	——	——
D	achieved	——	achieved	——
E	achieved	achieved	achieved	achieved
F	achieved	achieved	achieved	achieved
G	——	achieved	——	achieved
H	——	——	——	——
I	——	achieved	achieved	achieved

particularly helpful to them in determining what each of them considered to be the best solution to the resource allocation decision.

Summary

The main purpose of the development of a decision-support system is to provide a tool which can take into account the cognitive limitations of human information processing. The goal of these techniques is to help structure the setting of priorities for institutional and individual goals and to minimize the difficulty of restructuring problems while searching for improved solutions.

As described in Chapters 1 and 2, the planning and budgeting processes in higher education involve a complex matching process that requires the structuring of a broad range of alternatives and the analysis of numerous policy variables, as academic administrators search for improved methods of achieving the goals of the institution. Decision-support systems, such as the one described in this chapter, are clearly capable of providing improved insights into the inherent conflicts in these types of decisions and are ideally suited to the constructive resolutions of questions about the feasibility of proposed courses of action.

References

Blanning, R. W. "The Functions of a Decision-Support System." *Information and Management* 2, no. 3 (1979): 87–93.

Clemson, B. "Beyond Management Information Systems." *Education Administration Quarterly* 14, no. 3 (1978): 13–38.

Franz, L. S. *Elicitation of Decision Maker Preference Structure for Multicriteria Optimization Through Interactive Goal Programming.* Ph.D. dissertation, University of Nebraska-Lincoln, 1980.

Geoffrion, A. M.; Dyer, J. S.; and Feinberg, A. "An Interactive Approach to Multicriteria Optimization." *Management Science* 19, no. 4 (1972): 357–68.

Keen, P. G. W. "The Evolving Concept of Optimality." In *TIMS Studies in the Management Sciences*, ed. M. K. Starr and M. Zeleny. vol. 6 (1977): 31–57.

Massy, W. F. "Reflections on the Application of a Decision Science Model to Higher Education." *Decision Sciences* 9, no. 2 (1978): 362–69.

McCosh, A. M. and Morton, M. Scott. *Management Decision Support Systems.* New York: John Wiley and Sons, 1978.

Murry, Michael A. "Modern Management Applied to Academic Decision." *The Academy of Management Review*, January 1976, pp. 79–88.

Starr, M. K. and Zeleny, M. "MCDM—State and Future of the Arts." In *TIMS Studies in the Management Sciences*, Ed. M. K. Starr and M. Zeleny, vol. 6 (1977): 5–29.

Wehrung, D. A.; Hopkins, D. S. P.; and Massy, W. F. "Interactive Preference Optimization for University Administrators." *Management Science* 24, no. 6 (1978): 599–611.

Wiseman, C. "New Foundations for Planning Models." *Journal of Higher Education* 50, no. 6 (1979): 726–44.

Chapter 8

Meeting the Future Challenges

This chapter is devoted to concluding remarks about the need and importance of systematic planning for multiple objectives in academic institutions. The 1980s appear to be of even more challenge to higher education than the past decade. The difficulties of the past will certainly continue, but many new and more complex problems will provide added challenges for academic administrators. Thus, a systematic planning and decision-making approach based on the goal-programming-imbedded ABO approach would be extremely valuable to academic administration.

Higher education has done a remarkable job of meeting and overcoming the many difficult challenges of the 1960s and 1970s. Today, some fifteen years after the turmoil and campus unrest of the late 1960s, the campuses are, for the most part, quiet. Many observers note the renaissance of the serious student; a recent Harris poll indicates that the public's confidence in higher education has been restored; and, with only a few exceptions, American colleges and universities have accommodated the demands of increased growth and the complexities of double-digit inflation and have still maintained balanced budgets.

In the 1970s, institutions responded quite favorably to the need for improved access for an increasingly diversified student body: they offered more programs and more classes, increased the range of services available, expanded evening and weekend offerings, developed special programs to meet the needs of special population subgroups, and generally instructed students with a wider variety of learning aptitudes than ever before. On balance, the higher-education enterprise met the challenges of unrest, of growth, and of the need for new kinds of services extraordinarily well during the 1970s (Lupton, 1980, p. 19).

The next ten years appear to offer higher education not only a compounding of some of its previous difficulties, but also many new challenges. There is much trepidation among academic administrators about future enrollment patterns, about the future level of state and federal support, about issues of equity and public disclosure, and about the impact of continuing high levels of inflation. There are also difficulties from within the institutions themselves. Among these are moves toward more collective bargaining units for faculty and staff members, lawsuits over tenure votes, academic freedom and the protective rights and privileges of staff members, dramatic shifts in program preferences by both faculty and students, and the increasing difficulty of keeping up with the rapid expansion of both knowledge and technology. The competitiveness of faculty and students is clearly a positive sign, but one which will increase the complexity of the management problems facing administrators. There is little doubt that the greatest challenge for higher education in the 1980s will be to maintain its integrity as well as its quality.

Needed: Better Management Approaches

The uncertainties outlined above as well as throughout other parts of this book place new managerial demands on colleges and universities. The continuing need for economy, for the rational use of scarce resources, for accountability, and for guaranteeing the equitable treatment of individuals and programs will continue to be sources of stress for both the institutions and the individuals who manage them. Such complexity increases the information and specialized skills required to manage institutions of higher education and seems likely to result in additional conflicts between administrators and faculty over policy decisions and governance issues. Earnest L. Boyer, head of the Carnegie Foundation for the Advancement of Teaching, recently announced the reordering of the priorities for the Carnegie Commission's program, and in doing so echoed a growing concern among university administrators: "The lines of decision making have become blurred (in higher education) precisely at a time when tough decisions have to be made. The traditional autonomy of boards of trustees is breaking down. A confused decision-making process is beginning to emerge. As external pressures on the programs and fiscal management of colleges and universities become more intense, the need for fully understanding the constraints and alternatives that lie ahead becomes crucial" (Hudgins, 1980, p. 21).

The need for specialized skills in the area of planning, management, and decision making, and the need for a more thorough theoretical understanding of university budgetary problems suggest that the use of models to assist in the academic-planning process will continue to expand. EDUCOM estimates that only 15 to 20 percent of institutions of higher education are currently using models for some phase of future planning (Linney, May 1980, p. 10). These figures are certain to double or triple during the next few years.

A review of recent literature relating to ways to improve the management of higher education is quite conclusive about the need for the further development of analytical tools to assist academic administrators. For instance, the final report of the Fifty-Sixth American Assembly on the Integrity of Higher Education concluded with thirty-two specific recommendations. Of these thirty-two recommendations, three out of the first five related specifically to the management of institutions and urged: (1) the development of explicitly stated goals; (2) the undertaking of major efforts to provide more accurate and more complete information on planning factors such as finances, investment policies and the percentage of full-time faculty, and (3) that institutions plan and implement, individually and cooperatively, actions to reduce the size and cost of their operations without jeopardizing academic quality and access to higher education (American Assembly, 1979, p. 6).

A similar strategy has recently been outlined by Andrew H. Lupton (1980), senior vice-president of the Academy for Educational Development. Out of the nine recommendations which Mr. Lupton puts forth to help universities as they enter the coming era of uncertainty, three relate specifically to improved management techniques. Lupton recognizes: (1) a need to continue to upgrade planning abilities; (2) the need to develop flexible, accurate, and economical information systems; and (3) the need to develop incentives for better internal management. In Mr. Lupton's words, "The days of making managerial decisions based on intuition are gone. Higher education now has access to more data and information than was thought possible a decade ago. Concurrently, colleges and universities are increasingly asked to provide information to boards, funding agencies, regulatory agencies and other entities. Thus, developing a good information system that meets the institutions' needs is essential" (p. 21).

A third study has been reported by Victor Baldridge and Michael L. Tierney (1979) in their book, *New Approaches to Management*. The conclusions of these authors are based on their study of thirty-four private liberal arts colleges and universities that were recipients of grants from the Exxon Education Foundation to enable them to make improvements in management practices. Their conclusion about improved decision-making aids is truly favorable: Baldridge and Tierney credit MIS and MBO systems with making available to administrators more and better data, with improving problem-solving capabilities, with contributing to better planning, and for facilitating an increase in revenues and reductions of per-student expenditures.

Another recent publication, *The Assessment of College Performance*, by

Richard J. Miller (1979), strikes a balance between the views of system analysts and those of humanists. The humanists hold that the most significant facts about education and its institutions cannot be measured numerically, whereas the systems analysts and cost-effectiveness experts are reluctant to concern themselves with "soft" evidence because it is messy and unquantified. In his book Miller includes suggestions for appraising such things as finances, administrative leadership, buildings, and public relations. He proposes yardsticks for assessing the relevancy of the institution's stated objectives, the effectiveness of the faculty, the relevance of the curriculum, and the effectiveness of the student services.

Carol Frances, in looking at the possibilities of declining enrollments during the 1980s, strongly urges academic administrators to abandon what she considers a "single-minded approach to the management of decline" and instead recommends a model based on "strategic planning and contingency budgeting" (1980, p. 40). Her strategic planning approach (see figure 8.1) is not based on an optimistic forecast of favorable outcomes; rather, it is based on an assessment of what the possible outcomes could be *if* enrollment strategies were effective in attracting students with quality educational programs. It attempts to quantify the enrollment effects that might be expected, given the size of the population group and trends in college-going rates. Her approach provides a *framework* for planning and action, not a basis for complacency. The key is the development of perspectives for alternative future outcomes.

ABO and Goal Programming

Many of the above recommendations could be accommodated by the implementation of an administration-by-objectives management system by an institution of higher education. Further, the use of models, such as the one outlined in this book, will allow administrators to know more about the interactions of the components about which they must make decisions.

Most of the currently available planning models in higher education are "statistically-driven," with the result that more resources are generally given to departments with more students or with improving statistical utilization factors. The goal-programming model developed in this book goes much further than this—it provides the opportunity to interrelate the planning and decision-making process more directly with the goals and objectives of the institution through the systematic structuring of both the constraints and objective functions. While the model in this book was set up specifically to examine policies and resource allocation patterns within departments, the formulation could easily be extended to a larger group of departments, to colleges, or to campuses.

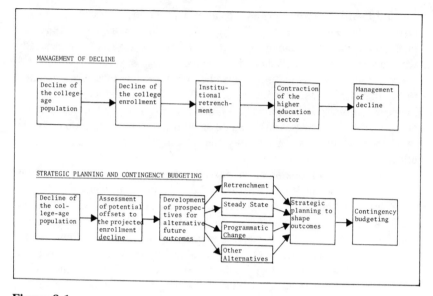

Figure 8.1

Alternative Approaches to Planning for the 1980s
SOURCE: Carol Frances, "Preparing for the 1980s: Apocalyptic vs. Strategic Planning," *Change* 12, no. 5 (July–August 1980).

One of the reasons that many academic administrators have been extremely reluctant to use models in higher education has been the unidimensionality of the objective function (i.e., the inability to accommodate value and quality factors). To a large extent, this reluctance has also extended to the areas of standard costing and resource management.

The idea of standard costing is a rather complex budgeting tool that is well developed and often used in the commercial sector but rarely used, at least by its name, in higher education. Standard cost systems use scientifically determined estimates to calculate what an item should cost. Standard costs are found by applying predetermined sets of policy variables to program cost data; they thus serve as a measuring stick for the determination of efficiency. This management technique has seldom been used in the academic (teaching and research) areas of higher education, mostly because of the assumptions it makes regarding knowledge of the production processes and the standardization of the output "products." However, there are many who do believe that the concept could be extended to academic units, and that universities should operate under a pricing system similar to that which exists in a free market enterprise.

Currently, many colleges and universities do compare their planning and support levels to other peer group institutions. These comparisons often include measures such as weighted student credit hours and relative "manpower" requirements and are used for assigning faculty resources to various subjects, levels, and disciplines. These developments can be seen as tendencies toward costing systems which will eventually require administrators to know more and more about the flexibilities of existing departmental budgets and structures. As these management techniques are studied more closely for their potential applicability to higher education, more attention will also be given to programming models such as the one developed in this book.

Resource management and control are the processes that are intended to monitor expenditures and initiate adjustments in response to changing conditions. Historically, universities have operated with simple financial accounting systems designed mainly to ensure that money is expended for the purposes for which it was granted. In these cases, the control features became important only when expenditures were seriously out of line with original plans. Similarly, accountability obligations are normally met by asking financial officers to publish required reports in prescribed formats. More recently, however, the demand for increased accountability has led administrators to look for better and more thorough ways to inform their constituents about how money and resources are being used.

A heuristic programming methodology, such as the one used in this book, that can take traditional financial information and couple it with a "probing" procedure designed to develop efficiency comparisons, would allow academic administrators to better display the results of their decisions about resource allocations.

Obviously, the model detailed in this book does not encompass all of the important factors that must be considered as trade-offs are made by decision makers in higher education. Further work is needed to allow for the inclusion of the natural values of quality, for the evaluation of research and research efforts, and for many of the other objectives and attributes that constitute important elements of the academic planning, budgeting, and decision-making processes. It is important to note, however, that these types of values, were they available, could easily be incorporated into the model put forth in this book. For instance, the appraisal suggestions developed by Miller (mentioned earlier in this chapter) could be formulated into the goal-programming model quite nicely.

Colleges and universities reflect their planning decisions in a variety of ways—in annual budgets, by adding new programs, by cutting back others, and so on. These decisions and the resultant resource allocations are normally the result of an analysis of alternatives and of a complex array of implicit and explicit value tradeoffs. Administrators usually employ investigative procedures to compare what is achievable with what is desirable; the process proceeds incrementally, where the choice at each step is decided by the decision maker, who must constantly weigh what should be attained with what the institution is able to attain. The purpose of the model described in this book is to help academic administrators systematically structure these types of value trade-offs. By examining the ramifications of these trade-offs, administrators will be able to improve both the effectiveness and efficiency associated with their planning decisions.

References

The American Assembly. *The Integrity of Higher Education*. New York: Columbia University, 1979.

Baldridge, J. Victor, and Tierney, Michael L. *New Approaches to Management*. San Francisco: Jossey-Bass, 1979.

Frances, Carol. "Preparing for the 1980s: Apocalyptic vs. Strategic Planning." *Change* 12, no. 5, (July–August 1980): 19.

Hudgins, Garv, ed. *The Green Sheet*. Washington, D.C.: The National Association of State Universities and Land Grant Colleges, July 31, 1980.

Linney, Thomas J. "Professional Management and Academic Planning: Some Recent Considerations." *AAHE Bulletin* 32, no. 9 (May 1980): 7–10.

Lupton, Andrew H. "Nine Ways Toward Better Management." *Educational Record* 61, no. 3, (Summer, 1980): 19–24.

Miller, Richard J. *The Assessment of College Performance*. San Francisco: Jossey-Bass, 1979.

Appendix

Selected Output Pages for Simplex Solutions to the Goal-Programming Formulations Detailed in Chapter 6

The following pages give three sections of the computer output for the final simplex solution for the models described in Chapter Six. Seven "runs" (one each for average undergraduate class sizes of 20, 25, 30, 35, 40, 45, and 50 students) were completed for each of the three departments modeled (History, Political Science, and Sociology). Within departmental formulations, all other goals and constraints remain unchanged (for details, see Chapter Six). The sections included here are: Analysis of Deviations from Right-hand Side (RHS) Stated Goals; Analysis of Decision Variables; and Analysis of the Objective Function.

Department of History

Average Undergraduate Class Size of 20

ANALYSIS OF DEVIATIONS FROM RHS-STATED GOALS

ROW	RHS-VALUE	D+	D-
1	382.00000	0.0	0.0
2	52.00000	86.50000	0.0
3	197.00000	474.55817	0.0
4	25.00000	646.55817	0.0
5	20.00000	112.25507	0.0
6	0.00001	0.0	0.0
7	16.00000	0.0	0.0
8	1.00000	0.0	0.0
9	9.00000	9.86666	0.0
10	2.00000	2.24499	0.0
11	12.00000	11.05502	0.0
12	0.0	0.0	0.0
13	2.00000	3.77083	0.0
14	0.00001	18.86665	0.0
15	1.00000	3.24499	0.0
16	11.00000	12.05502	0.0
17	0.00001	46.16658	0.0
18	0.00001	46.16658	0.0
19	0.00001	0.0	0.0
20	0.00001	940561.78174	0.0
21	0.00001	90462.23156	0.0
22	0.00001	0.0	8.92501
23	0.00001	1.30832	0.0
24	0.00001	0.0	0.0
25	0.00001	0.0	0.0
26	0.00001	0.52830	0.0
27	8015.00000	0.0	0.0
28	2000.00000	0.0	0.0
29	0.00001	0.0	0.0

ANALYSIS OF DECISION VARIABLES

VARIABLE	AMOUNT
3	1.00000
6	23.05502
8	5.77083
12	40838.44060
4	18.86666
1	0.00001
7	0.00001
2	16.00000
10	6026.31614
11	11563.81614
5	4.24499

ANALYSIS OF THE OBJECTIVE FUNCTION

PRIORITY	NON-ACHIEVEMENT
9	940561.78174
8	90462.23156
7	0.0
6	0.0
5	92.33315
4	10.23333
3	0.0
2	0.0
1	0.0

Department of History

Average Undergraduate Class Size of 25

ANALYSIS OF DEVIATIONS FROM RHS-STATED GOALS

ROW	RHS-VALUE	D+	D-
1	306.00000	0.0	0.0
2	52.00000	48.50000	0.0
3	197.00000	291.52484	0.0
4	25.00000	463.52484	0.0
5	20.00000	75.39507	0.0
6	0.00001	0.0	0.0
7	16.00000	0.0	0.0
8	1.00000	4.79999	0.0
9	9.00000	1.10499	0.0
10	2.00000	4.59502	0.0
11	12.00000	0.0	0.0
12	0.00001	2.18750	0.0
13	2.00000	13.79998	0.0
14	0.00001	2.10499	0.0
15	1.00000	5.59502	0.0
16	11.00000	33.49991	0.0
17	0.00001	33.49991	0.0
18	0.00001	0.0	0.0
19	0.00001	701152.78378	0.0
20	0.00001	66518.11443	0.0
21	0.00001	0.0	10.82501
22	0.00001	0.67499	0.0
23	0.00001	0.0	0.0
24	0.00001	0.0	0.0
25	0.00001	0.65497	0.0
26	0.00001	0.0	0.0
27	8015.00000	0.0	0.0
28	2000.00000	0.0	0.0
29	0.00001	0.0	0.0

ANALYSIS OF DECISION VARIABLES

VARIABLE	AMOUNT
3	1.00000
6	16.59502
8	4.18750
12	29451.00712
4	13.79999
1	0.00001
7	0.00001
2	16.00000
10	6026.31614
11	10613.81614
5	3.10499

ANALYSIS OF THE OBJECTIVE FUNCTION

PRIORITY	NON-ACHIEVEMENT
9	701152.78378
8	66518.11443
7	0.0
6	0.0
5	66.99982
4	11.50000
3	0.0
2	0.0
1	0.0

Department of History

Average Undergraduate Class Size of 30

ANALYSIS OF DEVIATIONS FROM RHS-STATED GOALS

ROW	RHS-VALUE	D+	D-
1	255.00000	0.0	0.0
2	52.00000	23.00000	0.0
3	197.00000	168.69984	0.0
4	25.00000	340.69984	0.0
5	20.00000	50.66006	0.0
6	0.00001	0.0	0.0
7	16.00000	0.0	0.0
8	1.00000	0.0	0.0
9	9.00000	1.39999	0.0
10	2.00000	0.33999	0.0
11	12.00000	0.26002	0.0
12	0.00001	0.0	0.0
13	2.00000	1.12500	0.0
14	0.00001	10.39998	0.0
15	1.00000	1.33999	0.0
16	11.00000	1.26002	0.0
17	0.00001	24.99991	0.0
18	0.00001	24.99991	0.0
19	0.00001	0.0	0.0
20	0.00001	540496.74568	0.0
21	0.00001	50450.35162	0.0
22	0.00001	0.0	12.10001
23	0.00001	0.24999	0.0
24	0.00001	0.0	0.0
25	0.00001	0.0	0.0
26	0.00001	0.73997	0.0
27	8015.00000	0.0	0.0
28	2000.00000	0.0	0.0
29	0.00001	0.0	0.0

ANALYSIS OF DECISION VARIABLES

VARIABLE	AMOUNT
3	1.00000
6	12.26002
8	3.12500
12	21809.43992
4	10.39999
1	0.00001
7	0.00001
2	16.00000
10	6026.31614
11	9976.31614
5	2.33999

ANALYSIS OF THE OBJECTIVE FUNCTION

PRIORITY	NON-ACHIEVEMENT
9	540496.74568
8	50450.35162
7	0.0
6	0.0
5	49.99982
4	12.35000
3	0.0
2	0.0
1	0.0

Department of History

Average Undergraduate Class Size of 35

ANALYSIS OF DEVIATIONS FROM RHS-STATED GOALS

ROW	RHS-VALUE	D+	D-
1	218.00000	0.0	0.0
2	52.00000	4.50000	0.0
3	197.00000	64.66667	0.0
4	25.00000	236.66667	0.0
5	20.00000	39.00000	0.0
6	0.00001	0.0	0.0
7	16.00000	0.0	0.0
8	1.00000	0.0	0.0
9	9.00000	0.0	2.16667
10	2.00000	0.0	1.00000
11	12.00000	0.0	1.00000
12	0.00001	0.0	0.0
13	2.00000	0.35417	0.0
14	0.00001	6.83332	0.0
15	1.00000	0.0	0.0
16	11.00000	0.0	0.0
17	0.00001	18.83324	0.0
18	0.00001	18.83324	0.0
19	0.00001	0.0	0.0
20	0.00001	438157.79586	0.0
21	0.00001	40215.03180	0.0
22	0.00001	0.0	13.02501
23	0.00001	0.0	0.05834
24	0.00001	1.09999	0.0
25	0.00001	0.78499	0.0
26	0.00001	0.0	1.08334
27	8015.00000	0.0	0.0
28	2000.00000	0.0	0.0
29	0.00001	0.0	0.0

ANALYSIS OF DECISION VARIABLES

VARIABLE	AMOUNT
3	1.00000
6	11.00000
8	2.35417
12	18334.50000
4	6.83333
1	0.00001
7	0.00001
2	16.00000
10	6026.31614
11	9513.81614
5	1.00000

ANALYSIS OF THE OBJECTIVE FUNCTION

PRIORITY	NON-ACHIEVEMENT
9	438157.79586
8	40215.03180
7	4.16667
6	0.0
5	37.66649
4	15.26669
3	0.0
2	0.0
1	0.0

Department of History

Average Undergraduate Class Size of 40

ANALYSIS OF DEVIATIONS FROM RHS-STATED GOALS

ROW	RHS-VALUE	D+	D-
1	191.00000	0.0	0.0
2	52.00000	0.0	0.0
3	197.00000	28.53805	0.0
4	25.00000	200.53805	0.0
5	20.00000	39.00000	0.0
6	0.00001	0.0	0.0
7	16.00000	0.0	1.50000
8	1.00000	0.0	1.00000
9	9.00000	0.0	3.66667
10	2.00000	0.0	1.00000
11	12.00000	0.0	1.00000
12	0.00001	0.0	0.0
13	2.00000	0.16667	0.0
14	0.00001	5.33332	0.0
15	1.00000	0.0	0.0
16	11.00000	0.0	0.0
17	0.00001	17.33324	0.0
18	0.00001	17.33324	0.0
19	0.00001	0.0	0.0
20	0.00001	397922.50636	0.0
21	0.00001	36887.71814	0.0
22	0.00001	0.0	11.90001
23	0.00001	0.86666	0.0
24	0.00001	1.59999	0.0
25	0.00001	0.55999	0.0
26	0.00001	0.0	2.33334
27	8015.00000	0.0	0.0
28	2000.00000	0.0	0.0
29	0.00001	256682.99999	0.0

ANALYSIS OF DECISION VARIABLES

VARIABLE	AMOUNT
6	11.00000
8	2.16667
4	5.33333
1	0.00001
7	0.00001
2	14.50000
10	6026.31614
11	9318.65536
5	1.00000

ANALYSIS OF THE OBJECTIVE FUNCTION

PRIORITY	NON-ACHIEVEMENT
9	654605.50635
8	36887.71814
7	5.66667
6	0.0
5	34.66649
4	16.70000
3	2.50000
2	0.0
1	0.0

Appendix **233**

Department of History

Average Undergraduate Class Size of 45

ANALYSIS OF DEVIATIONS FROM RHS-STATED GOALS

ROW	RHS-VALUE	D+	D-
1	170.00000	0.0	0.0
2	52.00000	0.0	0.0
3	197.00000	28.53805	0.0
4	25.00000	200.53805	0.0
5	20.00000	39.00000	0.0
6	0.00001	0.0	0.0
7	16.00000	0.0	5.00000
8	1.00000	0.0	1.00000
9	9.00000	0.0	3.66667
10	2.00000	0.0	1.00000
11	12.00000	0.0	1.00000
12	0.00001	0.0	0.0
13	2.00000	0.16667	0.0
14	0.00001	5.33332	0.0
15	1.00000	0.0	0.0
16	11.00000	0.0	0.0
17	0.00001	17.33324	0.0
18	0.00001	17.33324	0.0
19	0.00001	0.0	0.0
20	0.00001	384374.00636	0.0
21	0.00001	36212.21814	0.0
22	0.00001	0.0	8.40001
23	0.00001	0.86666	0.0
24	0.00001	1.59999	0.0
25	0.00001	0.55999	0.0
26	0.00001	0.0	2.33334
27	8015.00000	0.0	0.0
28	2000.00000	0.0	0.0
29	0.00001	256682.99999	0.0

ANALYSIS OF DECISION VARIABLES

VARIABLE	AMOUNT
6	11.00000
8	2.16667
4	5.33333
1	0.00001
7	0.00001
2	11.00000
10	6026.31614
11	9318.65536
5	1.00000

ANALYSIS OF THE OBJECTIVE FUNCTION

PRIORITY	NON-ACHIEVEMENT
9	641057.00635
8	36212.21814
7	5.66667
6	0.0
5	34.66649
4	13.20000
3	6.00000
2	0.0
1	0.0

Department of History

Average Undergraduate Class Size of 50

ANALYSIS OF DEVIATIONS FROM RHS-STATED GOALS

ROW	RHS-VALUE	D+	D-
1	153.00000	0.0	0.0
2	52.00000	0.0	0.0
3	197.00000	28.53805	0.0
4	25.00000	200.53805	0.0
5	20.00000	39.00000	0.0
6	0.00001	0.0	0.0
7	16.00000	0.0	7.83333
8	1.00000	0.0	1.00000
9	9.00000	0.0	3.66667
10	2.00000	0.0	1.00000
11	12.00000	0.0	1.00000
12	0.00001	0.0	0.0
13	2.00000	0.16667	0.0
14	0.00001	5.33332	0.0
15	1.00000	0.0	0.0
16	11.00000	0.0	0.0
17	0.00001	17.33324	0.0
18	0.00001	17.33324	0.0
19	0.00001	0.0	0.0
20	0.00001	373406.17302	0.0
21	0.00001	35665.38481	0.0
22	0.00001	0.0	5.56668
23	0.00001	0.86666	0.0
24	0.00001	1.59999	0.0
25	0.00001	0.55999	0.0
26	0.00001	0.0	2.33334
27	8015.00000	0.0	0.0
28	2000.00000	0.0	0.0
29	0.00001	256682.99999	0.0

ANALYSIS OF DECISION VARIABLES

VARIABLE	AMOUNT
6	11.00000
8	2.16667
4	5.33333
1	0.00001
7	0.00001
2	8.16667
10	6026.31614
11	9318.65536
5	1.00000

ANALYSIS OF THE OBJECTIVE FUNCTION

PRIORITY	NON-ACHIEVEMENT
9	630089.17301
8	35665.38481
7	5.66667
6	0.0
5	34.66649
4	10.36667
3	8.83333
2	0.0
1	0.0

Department of Political Science

Average Undergraduate Class Size of 20

ANALYSIS OF DEVIATIONS FROM RHS-STATED GOALS

ROW	RHS-VALUE	D+	D-
1	303.00000	0.0	0.0
2	34.00000	95.00000	0.0
3	197.00000	443.00014	0.0
4	25.00000	147.99997	0.0
5	20.00000	109.79992	0.0
6	0.00001	0.0	0.0
7	6.00000	0.0	0.0
8	1.00000	11.90002	0.0
9	2.50000	3.61999	0.0
10	9.58000	10.39999	0.0
11	5.00000	0.0	0.0
12	0.00001	3.37500	0.0
13	2.00000	14.40001	0.0
14	0.00001	3.86999	0.0
15	9.33000	10.39999	0.0
16	5.00000	42.99991	0.0
17	0.00001	42.99991	0.0
18	0.00001	0.0	0.0
19	0.00001	793234.80809	0.0
20	0.00001	77636.47884	0.0
21	0.00001	0.59999	0.0
22	0.00001	1.14999	0.0
23	0.00001	0.0	5.60003
24	0.00001	0.0	0.0
25	0.00001	0.0	0.0
26	0.00001	0.0	0.0
27	6307.00000	0.0	0.0
28	2000.00000	0.0	0.0
29	0.00001	0.0	0.0

ANALYSIS OF DECISION VARIABLES

VARIABLE	AMOUNT
6	15.39999
3	1.00000
8	5.37500
4	14.40002
1	0.00001
7	0.00001
2	6.00000
12	37002.71918
10	4742.10554
11	10042.10554
5	13.19999

ANALYSIS OF THE OBJECTIVE FUNCTION

PRIORITY	NON-ACHIEVEMENT
9	793234.80809
8	77636.37883
7	0.0
6	0.0
5	85.99982
4	7.35001
3	0.0
2	0.0
1	0.0

Department of Political Science

Average Undergraduate Class Size of 25

ANALYSIS OF DEVIATIONS FROM RHS-STATED GOALS

ROW	RHS-VALUE	D+	D-
1	242.00000	0.0	0.0
2	34.00000	64.50000	0.0
3	197.00000	290.50014	0.0
4	25.00000	107.33331	0.0
5	20.00000	79.80825	0.0
6	0.00001	0.0	0.0
7	6.00000	0.0	0.0
8	1.00000	0.0	0.0
9	2.50000	8.34169	0.0
10	9.58000	0.56999	0.0
11	5.00000	6.84166	0.0
12	0.00001	0.0	0.0
13	2.00000	2.10417	0.0
14	0.00001	10.84168	0.0
15	9.33000	0.81999	0.0
16	5.00000	6.84166	0.0
17	0.00001	32.83324	0.0
18	0.00001	32.83324	0.0
19	0.00001	0.0	0.0
20	0.00001	614260.80651	0.0
21	0.00001	59740.34951	0.0
22	0.00001	0.0	0.92501
23	0.00001	0.64166	0.0
24	0.00001	0.0	4.07503
25	0.00001	0.0	0.0
26	0.00001	0.0	0.0
27	6307.00000	0.0	0.0
28	2000.00000	0.0	0.0
29	0.00001	0.0	0.0

ANALYSIS OF DECISION VARIABLES

VARIABLE	AMOUNT
6	11.84166
12	28452.84251
3	1.00000
8	4.10417
4	10.84169
1	0.00001
7	0.00001
2	6.00000
10	4742.10554
11	9279.60554
5	10.14999

ANALYSIS OF THE OBJECTIVE FUNCTION

PRIORITY	NON-ACHIEVEMENT
9	614260.80651
8	59740.34951
7	0.0
6	0.0
5	65.66649
4	5.64170
3	0.0
2	0.0
1	0.0

Department of Political Science

Average Undergraduate Class Size of 30

ANALYSIS OF DEVIATIONS FROM RHS-STATED GOALS

ROW	RHS-VALUE	D+	D-
1	202.00000	0.0	0.0
2	34.00000	44.50000	0.0
3	197.00000	184.60009	0.0
4	25.00000	81.84665	0.0
5	20.00000	64.86162	0.0
6	0.00001	0.0	0.0
7	6.00000	0.0	0.0
8	1.00000	0.0	0.0
9	2.50000	4.82834	0.0
10	9.58000	0.0	0.25000
11	5.00000	4.50832	0.0
12	0.00001	0.0	0.0
13	2.00000	1.27083	0.0
14	0.00001	7.32833	0.0
15	9.33000	0.0	0.0
16	5.00000	4.50832	0.0
17	0.00001	26.16658	0.0
18	0.00001	26.16658	0.0
19	0.00001	500174.15231	0.0
20	0.00001	48332.04542	0.0
21	0.00001	0.0	0.0
22	0.00001	0.0	1.92501
23	0.00001	0.30832	0.0
24	0.00001	0.0	1.89502
25	0.00001	0.0	1.18001
26	0.00001	0.0	0.0
27	6307.00000	0.0	0.0
28	2000.00000	0.0	0.0
29	0.00001	0.0	0.0

ANALYSIS OF DECISION VARIABLES

VARIABLE	AMOUNT
12	24266.00193
3	1.00000
8	3.27083
4	7.32834
1	0.00001
7	0.00001
2	6.00000
6	9.50832
10	4742.10554
11	8779.60554
5	9.33000

ANALYSIS OF THE OBJECTIVE FUNCTION

PRIORITY	NON-ACHIEVEMENT
9	500174.15231
8	48332.04542
7	0.25000
6	0.0
5	52.33315
4	5.30836
3	0.0
2	0.0
1	0.0

Department of Political Science

Average Undergraduate Class Size of 35

ANALYSIS OF DEVIATIONS FROM RHS-STATED GOALS

ROW	RHS-VALUE	D+	D-
1	173.00000	0.0	0.0
2	34.00000	30.00000	0.0
3	197.00000	107.64990	0.0
4	25.00000	63.40335	0.0
5	20.00000	55.00338	0.0
6	0.00001	0.0	0.0
7	6.00000	0.0	0.0
8	1.00000	0.0	0.0
9	2.50000	1.96666	0.0
10	9.58000	0.0	0.25000
11	5.00000	2.53668	0.0
12	0.00001	0.0	0.0
13	2.00000	0.66667	0.0
14	0.00001	4.46665	0.0
15	9.33000	2.53668	0.0
16	5.00000	0.0	0.0
17	0.00001	21.33324	0.0
18	0.00001	21.33324	0.0
19	0.00001	0.0	0.0
20	0.00001	417673.31301	0.0
21	0.00001	40082.06965	0.0
22	0.00001	0.0	2.65001
23	0.00001	0.06666	0.0
24	0.00001	0.0	0.0
25	0.00001	0.0	2.63001
26	0.00001	0.27998	0.0
27	6307.00000	0.0	0.0
28	2000.00000	0.0	0.0
29	0.00001	0.0	0.0

ANALYSIS OF DECISION VARIABLES

VARIABLE	AMOUNT
6	7.53668
12	21561.74718
3	1.00000
8	2.66667
4	4.46666
1	0.00001
7	0.00001
2	6.00000
10	4742.10554
11	8417.10554
5	9.33000

ANALYSIS OF THE OBJECTIVE FUNCTION

PRIORITY	NON-ACHIEVEMENT
9	417673.31301
8	40082.06965
7	0.25000
6	0.0
5	42.66649
4	5.34668
3	0.0
2	0.0
1	0.0

Department of Political Science

Average Undergraduate Class Size of 40

ANALYSIS OF DEVIATIONS FROM RHS-STATED GOALS

ROW	RHS-VALUE	D+	D-
1	152.00000	0.0	0.0
2	34.00000	19.50000	0.0
3	197.00000	63.01667	0.0
4	25.00000	47.83000	0.0
5	20.00000	42.32000	0.0
6	0.00001	0.0	0.0
7	6.00000	0.0	0.0
8	1.00000	1.00333	0.0
9	2.50000	0.0	0.0
10	9.58000	0.00000	0.25000
11	5.00000	0.0	0.0
12	0.00001	0.22917	0.0
13	2.00000	3.50332	0.0
14	0.00001	0.0	0.0
15	9.33000	0.0	0.0
16	5.00000	0.0	0.0
17	0.00001	17.83324	0.0
18	0.00001	17.83324	0.0
19	0.00001	352239.17532	0.0
20	0.00001	33539.06689	0.0
21	0.00001	0.0	0.0
22	0.00001	0.0	3.17501
23	0.00001	0.0	0.10834
24	0.00001	0.26332	0.0
25	0.00001	0.0	3.68001
26	0.00001	1.59166	0.0
27	6307.00000	0.0	0.0
28	2000.00000	0.0	0.0
29	0.00001	0.0	0.0

ANALYSIS OF DECISION VARIABLES

VARIABLE	AMOUNT
6	5.00000
12	18082.51357
3	1.00000
8	2.22917
4	3.50333
1	0.00001
7	0.00001
2	6.00000
10	4742.10554
11	8154.60554
5	9.33000

ANALYSIS OF THE OBJECTIVE FUNCTION

PRIORITY	NON-ACHIEVEMENT
9	352239.17532
8	33539.06689
7	0.25000
6	0.0
5	35.66649
4	7.22669
3	0.0
2	0.0
1	0.0

Department of Political Science

Average Undergraduate Class Size of 45

ANALYSIS OF DEVIATIONS FROM RHS-STATED GOALS

ANALYSIS OF DECISION VARIABLES

ROW	RHS-VALUE	D+	D-
1	135.00000	0.0	0.0
2	34.00000	11.00000	0.0
3	197.00000	6.35000	0.0
4	25.00000	39.33000	0.0
5	20.00000	42.32000	0.0
6	0.00001	0.0	0.0
7	6.00000	0.0	0.0
8	1.00000	0.0	0.0
9	2.50000	0.0	1.83000
10	9.58000	0.0	0.25000
11	5.00000	0.00000	0.0
12	0.00001	0.0	0.0
13	2.00000	0.0	0.0
14	0.00001	0.66999	0.0
15	9.33000	0.0	0.0
16	5.00000	0.0	0.0
17	0.00001	14.99991	0.0
18	0.00001	14.99991	0.0
19	0.00001	0.0	1.00001
20	0.00001	310715.55938	0.0
21	0.00001	29386.42196	0.0
22	0.00001	0.0	3.60001
23	0.00001	0.0	0.25001
24	0.00001	2.52999	0.0
25	0.00001	0.0	4.53001
26	0.00001	0.59999	0.0
27	6307.00000	0.0	0.0
28	2000.00000	0.0	0.0
29	0.00001	0.0	0.0

VARIABLE	AMOUNT
6	5.00000
12	18082.51357
3	1.00000
8	2.00000
4	0.67000
1	0.00001
7	0.00001
2	6.00000
10	4742.10554
11	7942.10554
5	9.33000

ANALYSIS OF THE OBJECTIVE FUNCTION

PRIORITY	NON-ACHIEVEMENT
9	310715.55938
8	29386.42196
7	2.08000
6	0.0
5	29.99982
4	10.91002
3	0.0
2	0.0
1	0.0

Department of Political Science

Average Undergraduate Class Size of 50

ANALYSIS OF DEVIATIONS FROM RHS-STATED GOALS

ROW	RHS-VALUE	D+	D-
1	121.00000	0.0	0.0
2	34.00000	8.99003	0.0
3	197.00000	0.0	7.04980
4	25.00000	37.32003	0.0
5	20.00000	42.32000	0.0
6	0.00001	0.0	0.16334
7	6.00000	0.0	1.00000
8	1.00000	0.0	2.49999
9	2.50000	0.0	0.25000
10	9.58000	0.00000	0.0
11	5.00000	0.0	0.0
12	0.00001	0.0	0.0
13	2.00000	0.0	0.0
14	0.00001	0.0	0.0
15	9.33000	0.0	0.0
16	5.00000	0.0	0.0
17	0.00001	14.32992	0.0
18	0.00001	14.32992	0.0
19	0.00001	0.0	1.67000
20	0.00001	290646.06068	0.0
21	0.00001	27911.56739	0.0
22	0.00001	0.0	3.68717
23	0.00001	0.71649	0.0
24	0.00001	2.86598	0.0
25	0.00001	0.0	5.03101
26	0.00001	0.01549	0.0
27	6307.00000	0.0	0.0
28	2000.00000	0.0	0.0
29	0.00001	0.0	0.0

ANALYSIS OF DECISION VARIABLES

VARIABLE	AMOUNT
12	18082.51357
8	2.00000
4	0.00001
1	0.00001
7	0.00001
2	5.83666
6	5.00000
10	4742.10554
11	7816.85629
5	9.33000

ANALYSIS OF THE OBJECTIVE FUNCTION

PRIORITY	NON-ACHIEVEMENT
9	290646.06068
8	27911.56739
7	2.74999
6	7.04980
5	28.65984
4	12.30064
3	1.16334
2	0.0
1	0.0

Department of Sociology

Average Undergraduate Class Size of 20

ANALYSIS OF DEVIATIONS FROM RHS-STATED GOALS

ROW	RHS-VALUE	D+	D-
1	329.00000	0.0	0.0
2	36.00000	77.49996	0.0
3	197.00000	291.04979	0.0
4	39.00000	449.04979	0.0
5	13.00000	136.06330	0.0
6	0.00001	0.0	0.0
7	17.00000	0.0	0.0
8	0.00001	0.0	0.0
9	2.60000	3.45332	0.0
10	4.00000	5.83668	0.0
11	9.00000	12.94332	0.0
12	0.00001	0.0	0.0
13	2.50000	2.22916	0.0
14	0.00001	6.05331	0.0
15	3.00000	6.83668	0.0
16	9.00000	12.94332	0.0
17	0.00001	37.83323	0.0
18	0.00001	37.83323	0.0
19	0.00001	0.0	0.0
20	0.00001	832506.83464	0.0
21	0.00001	80090.17852	0.0
22	0.00001	0.0	11.32501
23	0.00001	1.89165	0.0
24	0.00001	0.0	0.0
25	0.00001	0.0	0.00002
26	0.00001	0.0	0.0
27	6834.00000	0.0	0.0
28	2000.00000	0.0	0.0
29	0.00001	0.0	0.0

ANALYSIS OF DECISION VARIABLES

VARIABLE	AMOUNT
6	21.94332
3	0.00001
8	4.72916
12	46280.09964
4	6.05332
1	0.00001
7	0.00001
2	17.00000
10	5138.34616
11	9975.84578
5	9.83668

ANALYSIS OF THE OBJECTIVE FUNCTION

PRIORITY	NON-ACHIEVEMENT
9	832506.83464
8	80090.17852
7	0.0
6	0.0
5	75.66646
4	13.21668
3	0.0
2	0.0
1	0.0

Department of Sociology

Average Undergraduate Class Size of 25

ANALYSIS OF DEVIATIONS FROM RHS-STATED GOALS

ROW	RHS-VALUE	D+	D-
1	263.00000	0.0	0.0
2	36.00000	44.49996	0.0
3	197.00000	149.14979	0.0
4	39.00000	307.14979	0.0
5	13.00000	92.72330	0.0
6	0.00001	0.0	0.0
7	17.00000	0.0	0.0
8	0.00001	1.69332	0.0
9	2.60000	2.97668	0.0
10	4.00000	6.56332	0.0
11	9.00000	0.0	0.0
12	0.00001	0.85416	0.0
13	2.50000	4.29331	0.0
14	0.00001	3.97668	0.0
15	3.00000	6.56332	0.0
16	9.00000	26.83323	0.0
17	0.00001	26.83323	0.0
18	0.00001	0.0	0.0
19	0.00001	608907.58145	0.0
20	0.00001	5728.33370	0.0
21	0.00001	0.0	12.97501
22	0.00001	1.34165	0.0
23	0.00001	0.0	0.0
24	0.00001	0.0	0.0
25	0.00001	0.0	0.00002
26	0.00001	0.0	0.0
27	6834.00000	0.0	0.0
28	2000.00000	0.0	0.0
29	0.00001	0.0	0.0

ANALYSIS OF DECISION VARIABLES

VARIABLE	AMOUNT
6	15.56332
3	0.00001
8	3.35416
12	32824.20862
4	4.29332
1	0.00001
7	0.00001
2	17.00000
10	5138.34616
11	9150.84578
5	6.97668

ANALYSIS OF THE OBJECTIVE FUNCTION

PRIORITY	NON-ACHIEVEMENT
9	608907.58145
8	5728.33370
7	0.0
6	0.0
5	53.66646
4	14.31668
3	0.0
2	0.0
1	0.0

Department of Sociology

Average Undergraduate Class Size of 30

ANALYSIS OF DEVIATIONS FROM RHS-STATED GOALS

ROW	RHS-VALUE	D+	D-
1	219.00000	0.0	0.0
2	36.00000	22.49996	0.0
3	197.00000	54.54989	0.0
4	39.00000	212.54989	0.0
5	13.00000	63.82989	0.0
6	0.00001	0.0	0.0
7	17.00000	0.0	0.0
8	0.00001	0.0	0.0
9	2.60000	0.52001	0.0
10	4.00000	1.06999	0.0
11	9.00000	2.30999	0.0
12	0.00001	0.0	0.0
13	2.50000	0.0	0.0
14	0.00001	3.12000	0.0
15	3.00000	2.06999	0.0
16	9.00000	2.30999	0.0
17	0.00001	19.49990	0.0
18	0.00001	19.49990	0.0
19	0.00001	0.0	0.50002
20	0.00001	460338.45023	0.0
21	0.00001	42870.12214	0.0
22	0.00001	0.97498	14.07501
23	0.00001	0.0	0.0
24	0.00001	0.0	0.0
25	0.00001	0.0	0.00002
26	0.00001	0.0	0.0
27	6834.00000	0.0	0.0
28	2000.00000	0.0	0.0
29	0.00001	0.0	0.0

ANALYSIS OF DECISION VARIABLES

VARIABLE	AMOUNT
6	11.30999
3	0.00001
8	2.50000
12	23853.59136
4	3.12001
1	0.00001
7	0.00001
2	17.00000
10	5138.34616
11	8600.84578
5	5.06999

ANALYSIS OF THE OBJECTIVE FUNCTION

PRIORITY	NON-ACHIEVEMENT
9	460338.45023
8	42870.12214
7	0.0
6	0.0
5	38.99979
4	15.05001
3	0.0
2	0.0
1	0.0

Department of Sociology

Average Undergraduate Class Size of 35

ANALYSIS OF DEVIATIONS FROM RHS-STATED GOALS

ROW	RHS-VALUE	D+	D-
1	188.00000	0.0	0.0
2	36.00000	6.99996	0.0
3	197.00000	0.0	15.53361
4	39.00000	142.46639	0.0
5	13.00000	44.15998	0.0
6	0.00001	0.0	0.0
7	17.00000	0.0	0.0
8	0.00001	0.0	0.30668
9	2.60000	0.0	0.96000
10	4.00000	0.0	0.0
11	0.00001	0.00000	0.0
12	0.00001	0.0	0.0
13	2.50000	0.0	0.0
14	0.00001	2.29331	0.0
15	3.00000	0.04000	0.0
16	9.00000	0.0	0.0
17	0.00001	14.33323	0.0
18	0.00001	14.33323	0.0
19	0.00001	0.0	5.66669
20	0.00001	364539.41243	0.0
21	0.00001	33288.16170	0.0
22	0.00001	0.0	14.85001
23	0.00001	0.71665	0.0
24	0.00001	0.0	0.0
25	0.00001	0.68666	0.0
26	0.00001	0.0	0.68668
27	6834.00000	0.0	0.0
28	2000.00000	0.0	0.0
29	0.00001	0.0	0.0

ANALYSIS OF DECISION VARIABLES

VARIABLE	AMOUNT
6	9.00000
3	0.00001
8	2.50000
12	17825.36039
4	2.29332
1	0.00001
7	0.00001
2	17.00000
10	5138.34616
11	8213.34578
5	3.04000

ANALYSIS OF THE OBJECTIVE FUNCTION

PRIORITY	NON-ACHIEVEMENT
9	364539.41243
8	33288.16170
7	1.26668
6	15.53361
5	28.66646
4	16.25334
3	0.0
2	0.0
1	0.0

Department of Sociology

Average Undergraduate Class Size of 40

ANALYSIS OF DEVIATIONS FROM RHS-STATED GOALS

ROW	RHS-VALUE	D+	D-
1	166.00000	0.0	0.0
2	36.00000	0.00003	0.0
3	197.00000	0.0	61.99980
4	39.00000	96.00020	0.0
5	13.00000	44.00000	0.0
6	0.00001	0.0	0.0
7	17.00000	0.0	1.33334
8	0.00001	0.0	0.00001
9	2.60000	0.0	2.59999
10	4.00000	0.00000	1.00000
11	9.00000	0.0	0.0
12	0.00001	0.0	0.0
13	2.50000	0.0	0.0
14	0.00001	0.0	0.0
15	3.00000	0.0	0.0
16	9.00000	0.0	0.0
17	0.00001	11.99992	0.0
18	0.00001	11.99992	0.0
19	0.00001	0.0	8.00000
20	0.00001	327288.40455	0.0
21	0.00001	29811.19045	0.0
22	0.00001	0.0	13.86667
23	0.00001	0.59999	0.0
24	0.00001	1.91998	0.0
25	0.00001	0.11999	0.0
26	0.00001	0.0	2.04000
27	6834.00000	0.0	0.0
28	2000.00000	0.0	0.0
29	0.00001	0.0	0.0

ANALYSIS OF DECISION VARIABLES

VARIABLE	AMOUNT
6	9.00000
8	2.50000
12	17778.85714
4	0.00001
1	0.00001
7	0.00001
2	15.66666
10	5138.34616
11	8038.34691
5	3.00000

ANALYSIS OF THE OBJECTIVE FUNCTION

PRIORITY	NON-ACHIEVEMENT
9	327288.40455
8	29811.19045
7	3.59999
6	61.99980
5	23.99984
4	18.42664
3	1.33335
2	0.0
1	0.0

Department of Sociology

Average Undergraduate Class Size of 45

ANALYSIS OF DEVIATIONS FROM RHS-STATED GOALS

ROW	RHS-VALUE	D+	D-
1	142.00000	0.0	0.0
2	36.00000	0.00003	0.0
3	197.00000	0.0	61.99980
4	39.00000	96.00020	0.0
5	13.00000	44.00000	0.0
6	0.00001	0.0	0.0
7	17.00000	0.0	5.33334
8	0.00001	0.0	0.00001
9	2.60000	0.0	2.59999
10	4.00000	0.0	1.00000
11	9.00000	0.00000	0.0
12	0.00001	0.0	0.0
13	2.50000	0.0	0.0
14	0.00001	0.0	0.0
15	3.00000	0.0	0.0
16	9.00000	0.0	0.0
17	0.00001	11.99992	0.0
18	0.00001	11.99992	0.0
19	0.00001	0.0	8.00000
20	0.00001	312356.40455	0.0
21	0.00001	29063.19045	0.0
22	0.00001	0.0	9.86667
23	0.00001	0.59999	0.0
24	0.00001	1.91998	0.0
25	0.00001	0.11999	0.0
26	0.00001	0.0	2.04000
27	6834.00000	0.0	0.0
28	2000.00000	0.0	0.0
29	0.00001	0.0	0.0

ANALYSIS OF DECISION VARIABLES

VARIABLE	AMOUNT
6	9.00000
8	2.50000
12	17778.85714
4	0.00001
1	0.00001
7	11.66666
2	5138.34616
10	8038.34691
11	3.00000
5	

ANALYSIS OF THE OBJECTIVE FUNCTION

PRIORITY	NON-ACHIEVEMENT
9	312356.40455
8	29063.19045
7	3.59999
6	61.99980
5	23.99984
4	18.42664
3	5.33335
2	0.0
1	0.0

Department of Sociology

Average Undergraduate Class Size of 50

ANALYSIS OF DEVIATIONS FROM RHS-STATED GOALS

ROW	RHS-VALUE	D+	D-
1	132.00000	0.0	0.0
2	36.00000	0.00003	0.0
3	197.00000	0.0	61.99980
4	39.00000	96.00020	0.0
5	13.00000	44.00000	0.0
6	0.00001	0.0	0.0
7	17.00000	0.0	5.33334
8	0.00001	0.0	0.00001
9	2.60000	0.0	2.59999
10	4.00000	0.0	1.00000
11	9.00000	0.00000	0.0
12	0.00001	0.0	0.0
13	2.50000	0.0	0.0
14	0.00001	0.0	0.0
15	3.00000	0.0	0.0
16	9.00000	0.0	0.0
17	0.00001	11.99992	0.0
18	0.00001	11.99992	0.0
19	0.00001	0.0	8.00000
20	0.00001	306134.73788	0.0
21	0.00001	28751.52378	0.0
22	0.00001	0.0	9.86667
23	0.00001	0.59999	0.0
24	0.00001	1.91998	0.0
25	0.00001	0.11999	0.0
26	0.00001	0.0	2.04000
27	6834.00000	0.0	0.0
28	2000.00000	0.0	0.0
29	0.00001	0.0	0.0

ANALYSIS OF DECISION VARIABLES

VARIABLE	AMOUNT
6	9.00000
8	2.50000
12	17778.85714
4	0.00001
1	0.00001
7	0.00001
2	9.99999
10	5138.34616
11	8038.34691
5	3.00000

ANALYSIS OF THE OBJECTIVE FUNCTION

PRIORITY	NON-ACHIEVEMENT
9	306134.73788
8	28751.52378
7	3.59999
6	61.99980
5	23.99984
4	12.75998
3	7.00002
2	0.0
1	0.0

Index